Make Your Own

Electric Guitar and Bass

Dennis Waring and **David Raymond**

with an introduction to playing by

Thomas Randall

Sterling Publishing Co., Inc. New York

A Sterling/Tamos Book

Sterling Publishing Co., Inc.
387 Park Avenue South
New York, NY 10016-8810

Tamos Books Inc.
300 Wales Avenue
Winnipeg, MB Canada R2M 2S9

10 9 8 7 6 5 4 3 2

Distributed in Canada by Sterling Publishing Co., Inc.
c/o Canadian Manda Group, One Atlantic Avenue, Suite 105
Toronto, Ontario, Canada M6K 3E7
Distributed in Great Britain and Europe by Cassell PLC,
Wellington House, 125 Strand, London WC2R OBB, England
Distributed in Australia by Capricorn Link (Australia) Pty Ltd.
P.O. Box 704, Windsor, NSW 2756 Australia

Photography Dennis Waring
Illustrations David Raymond

Printed in China

National Library of Canada Cataloguing-in-Publication Data
Waring, Dennis, 1944–
Make your own electric guitar and bass
"A Sterling/Tamos book".
Includes index.
ISBN 1-895569-70-2
1. Electric guitar–Construction. 2. Bass guitar--Construction.
I. Title.
ML1015.G9W276 2001 787.87'1923 C2001-910635-1

Library of Congress Cataloging-in-Publication Data
Data available

Tamos books Inc. acknowledges the financial support of the Government of Canada through the Book Publishing Development Program (BPIDP) for our publishing activities.

NOTE If you prefer to work in metric measurements, to convert inches to millimeters multiply by 25.4.

The advice and directions given in this book have been carefully checked, prior to printing, by the Authors as well as the Publisher. Nevertheless, no guarantee can be given as to the project outcome due to the possible differences in materials. Authors and Publisher will not be responsible for the results. Anything involving electric wiring is potentially dangerous. Authors and Publisher will not be responsible for the shocks due to faulty connections.

ISBN 1-895569-70-2

About the Authors

DENNIS WARING is an ethnomusicologist, educator, performer, and instrument maker. He teaches education and world music courses, and performs in schools, universities, and other community-based institutions. His books, *Great Folk Instruments To Make and Play*, and *Cool Cardboard Instruments To Make and Play* have delighted students and beginning instrument makers for many years. His other publications include such varied subjects as the Brazilian samba and the American reed organ. He travels throughout the world to learn more about new developments in music and culture studies.

DAVID RAYMOND has been making instruments since 1982 and specializes in building electric guitars and basses. He has performed, produced, and composed music for thirty years.

THOMAS RANDALL is a musician, teacher, and instrument builder. A multi-instrumentalist, Tom plays acoustic, electric, and pedal steel guitars, as well as banjo, mandolin, fiddle, and piano. He is at home with jazz, rock, ol' time, bluegrass, zydeco, blues, and several other types of music. His music contribution to this book is based on many years of teaching guitar to hundreds of students.

Acknowledgments
We would like to thank the following people and organizations for their expertise, advice, and encouragement: Robert and Beverly Raymond, Bob Stern and Bob Smicz of Smicz Amplification, Patrick Hart, Gerald Pavano and Blake Leonard of Melody Music, Dana Walcott of Star Tube, Jimi Bell, Michael Kodas, John Groo, Jeffrey Arnstein, Ralph Gasparello, Ken and Jody Trestman, Matt Syme, Kim Morgan, Karen Zitkus, Susan Grimaldi, The Reverend Horton Heat, Fred Pedemonti, John Warren, Sal D'Alessandro, and The Pigeon.

Contents

Introduction

The guitar is probably the most popular musical instrument in the world. This remarkable device, with its many variant forms, has crossed all geographical boundaries and is now played in an enormous variety of cultural contexts. From African beats to heavy metal, Asian pop to East Indian classical, its ongoing adaptability seems limitless.

In recent decades, the electrification of the guitar, especially in its solid-body form, and the dominance of American popular culture, have transformed musical sensibilities globally. Offering nearly unlimited tonal variety, the electric guitar has become one of the most prominent instruments in jazz, pop, rock, and world music today.

Although much has been written about the electric guitar and its construction, there remains a limited amount of practical material within reach of the amateur woodworker. This book emphasizes accessibility: a clear, methodical step-by-step process resulting in attractive, functional instruments. By using common woodworking tools, easy-to-order materials, and available resources for finding electronic components and other hardware, this volume provides all the necessary information for the aspiring instrument maker and those seeking a better understanding of the instrument.

In addition to instructions for building a standard 6-string solid body model guitar, there are directions for making an electric bass guitar. The guitar section contains detailed discussions of major procedures common to both guitar and bass. Options and references for further development and enhancement are found in the Appendix of this book.

Electric guitars and basses are excellent vehicles for creativity in both building and playing. Every aspect of their design, from the shape to the electronics to the material they are made from, is open to tinkering, customization, or all-out revolution. Solid-body electric instruments represent a unique amalgamation, combining the oldest elements of musical instrument-making knowledge, a "best-of" selection from the history of electronics, stunning visual design, and a capacity to incorporate new ideas. Throughout their short history, these instruments have benefited from the efforts of innovators representing many diverse backgrounds. Electrical engineers, aerospace technicians, fine woodworkers, artists, and even those seeking cheaper means of mass-production have contributed enormously to the advancement of the electric guitar and bass. The result is a unique opportunity for the builder's personal expression on many levels.

One reason for the constant advancement of electric stringed instrument design is the accessibility of the construction process. While technology has made it more difficult for the average person to tune their car or fix household appliances, not to mention build better versions of these items, electric guitars and basses of the highest quality continue to be built by individuals in home workshops. These instruments use relatively simple, traditional, and often old-fashioned technologies to generate sounds that continuously challenge and excite both players and listeners. People seeking to enter this field today have access to resources that were undreamed of a decade ago. A large variety of tools, hardware, electronics, and wood is available from a number of specialty suppliers, and the internet has brought a revolution in access to information, ideas, and experiences of instrument makers all over the world. This unique combination of new and old makes these instruments among the most rewarding pursuits of the creative, technically-inclined individual.

This book outlines the process of building an electric guitar and bass. The instruments are designed to illustrate the fundamentals of electric guitar and bass construction. Step-by-step procedures produce instruments that are straightforward but of high quality. While many of the steps require dauntingly precise operations, they are facilitated by the use of jigs, patterns, and templates that allow the patient, persistent beginner to produce professional results. Our instructions serve as an introduction to the kinds of shop procedures and problem-solving skills used by modern instrument makers.

The two instruments outlined in this book utilize a combination of traditional and modern design features. They are capable of a wide range of musical styles, with versatile yet accessible electronics and construction details that have been chosen to enhance tone and playability. However, the possibilities for designing your own guitar or bass are almost endless, and the reader should feel free to explore as many options as possible to build an instrument that fits personal needs. This book includes advice on available woods, hardware, electronics, and possible design variations. Learning how these factors come together to produce a unique instrument is a fascinating process. You can enrich your own instrument-making experience in the following ways:

1. Read other books and periodicals about instrument making. Go to your library. Send away for further information. Search relevant web sites and chat rooms on the internet.
2. Play as many different instruments as possible to familiarize yourself with their designs and features. Seek out the knowledge and opinions of players, salespeople, repairers, and builders whenever possible. There is a great deal of knowledge available and you will find that people are happy to help when they hear that you are building your own instrument.
3. Research the availability of building materials (wood, tuners, strings, etc.). Begin gathering materials early. Collect relevant catalogues and send away for hard-to-find items. Collecting materials may take some time and effort, but you will discover some good sources and make valuable connections in the process.
4. Gather tools as you require them. There is no need to buy a set of chisels when you may use only one or two of them. Be selective when buying some of the specialty gizmos since they may be useful only to the production builder. When feasible make or improvise your own tools, jigs, and templates.
5. After studying the instructions and thinking through the options, build patiently and consistently, one step at a time.
6. Expect to make some mistakes. They are part of the creative process and often lead to new and better methods.

Guitars Through the Ages

Coupling a stretched string to a volume of enclosed air—the principle of attaching a string to a resonator—undoubtedly dates to prehistory. Over time, musical bows, lyres, harps, zithers, and lutes of all shapes and sizes formed a family tree of chordophones. Members of the lute family of instruments, which includes guitars, feature a neck/body relationship: strings run from the body of the instrument, over a bridge, to the end of the neck. Makers of these early guitar-like instruments utilized gourds, trees, animal skins, plant fibers, and other natural resources. Many ancient civilizations record lute instrument types. From these wellsprings come the Greek bouzouki, Turkish saz, Chinese p'i p'a, Indian sitar, Russian balalaika, Hawaiian ukulele, African ngoni, American banjo, and hundreds of other variant forms.

Lore has it that the guitar, with its familiar hourglass, figure-eight, waisted shape, was introduced to Spain by the Arabs. By the 14th century it had diffused throughout Europe, and by the 17th century had begun to displace the bowl-shaped lute as the plucked stringed instrument of choice. Closely connected with the cittern (a related stringed instrument popular from 1500 to 1800), early guitar forms had various numbers of strings, usually four to six, often doubled. Later, guitars with six single strings came into vogue. Since this arrangement afforded a simpler playing technique than its predecessors, the six-string guitar became the standard. But that was only the beginning.

Because the guitar traveled easily, it accompanied world exploration from Spain throughout the western hemisphere and beyond. By the late 18th and early 19th centuries, it had achieved its classic shape and string arrangement, and was swiftly gaining in popularity. In Europe and elsewhere, classical repertoires were developed specifically for the instrument. With each relocation it continued its evolution of shape and function to suit the expressive needs of different cultures.

In late 19th-century and early 20th-century United States, the guitar caught on as a popular instrument accessible through mail order stores such as Sears, Roebuck Co., and Montgomery Ward. During the American Victorian period, the guitar became an affordable alternative to a piano or reed organ for the parlor. As its availability and popularity increased, it became the instrument of choice for blues and other folk musics. By the turn of the century, pioneering American instrument makers began to feed the growing interest in guitars and popular music. With innovators such as Martin and Gibson (plus scores of lesser-known luthiers), the guitar soon became one of the most played of all instruments. As the 20th century unfolded, the introduction of steel strings and arch-top and metal resonator styles further expanded musical applications. Found in folk, jazz, blues, and dance music of all kinds by the 1930s, the acoustic hollow-body form had reached a high level of maturity. Soon, musicians such as Riley Puckett, the Carter family, Jimmy Rogers, Bob Wills, and later, Hank Williams, Doc Watson, and Merle Travis established the guitar as the quintessential instrument for country music.

From this point on, companies such as Gibson, Rickenbacker, Epiphone, Vivi-Tone, and others experimented with amplifying the hollow-body guitar so it could be heard in the larger and louder bands of the 1920s and 1930s. One of the first players to adopt the early electric guitar was Charlie Christian. At the time, the role of the guitar in large jazz bands was to provide chordal accompaniment as part of the rhythm section, which was the only way it could be heard over the trumpets, trombones, and saxophones. In contrast, Christian used the increased volume of his electric instrument to play flowing single-note solos with a tone that caused a sensation: it had the percussive attack of a guitar but the power of a horn. Electrification had succeeded in making the guitar louder, and such players as Christian responded by creating new roles for the instrument. It wouldn't be the last time.

By the post World War II era, the electric guitar was gaining acceptance with jazz, blues, and country musicians. Meanwhile, several guitar makers and players continued to experiment with alternatives to large, hollow body guitars to allow louder volumes without feedback (that howling sound that occurs when an amplifier sound vibrates a guitar, then re-amplifies the vibrations). The solution was to make the body more solid. Companies such as Rickenbacker, Slingerland, Vivi-Tone, and individuals Paul Bigsby, Les Paul, and others, had built guitars that were, in whole or in part, made of solid pieces of wood. Some were adapted from Hawaiian-style guitars (played on the lap with a slide) that had been both solid and electric for years. Others were designed as Spanish guitars, a term then used for any guitar played upright rather than across the lap. With so many innovators working toward the same end, the actual invention of the solid body electric guitar is impossible to attribute to any one person. It was, however, an idea whose time had come.

While the origin of the solid body electric was the result of the efforts of many, the form of the instrument as we know it today is largely due to one man: Leo Fender. In 1950, the Fender company released the Broadcaster, a solid body Spanish-style guitar which, for the first time, incorporated many of the features that have become industry standards. With a bolt-on maple neck, a body made from a single slab of wood, highly adjustable bridge, and interchangeable parts, the modern electric guitar had arrived. Renamed the Telecaster in 1952, it remains in production to this day, practically unchanged in 50 years and still very popular.

Fender's competition did not think highly of his guitar at first. They failed to see that with its simplified look and bolt-together construction were the very features that made it a powerful and functional instrument whose sound and look would redefine popular music. Within a short time, Fender's success drew almost all of the major instrument manufacturers into the solid body electric guitar market. The Gibson company sought out Les Paul, whose ideas they had dismissed a few years earlier. The result was the Gibson Les Paul guitar, the only solid body model that today matches the Fenders in status as a classic.

Meanwhile, Leo Fender was again plotting revolution. In 1951, he introduced an entirely new concept, the electric bass guitar. The Precision bass, so-called because its frets allowed it to be played in tune more easily than the fretless upright bass, changed everything. It made possible a sound that we take for granted today, but at that time had never been heard before: loud bass. Designed much like the Broadcaster, the Precision produced a deep, percussive sound that brought the bassline forward in the music. It was much easier to play than an upright, and could be picked up quickly by guitar players. Like the Broadcaster, it introduced standards that remain today. It's still available in a form that is remarkably unchanged from the original model.

During the 1950s the electric guitar became increasingly popular in blues, jazz, country, and the latest sensation, rock and roll. Solid body electric guitars and increasingly sophisticated amplification were perfectly suited to this new kind of popular music. It was the electric bass, however, that propelled rock and roll into a new dimension, with its ability to bridge the gap between drums and guitar with a powerful, driving sound. Together the new instruments meant that a small ensemble of musicians could fill a large room with music as never before.

The 1950s saw the birth of many of the instruments that would shape modern music to the present day. Gretsch introduced semi-hollow models such as the White Falcon, Country Gentleman, and Tennessean, whose tones defined the rockabilly sound. Rickenbacker began to produce solid and semi-solid electrics with unique styling and innovative construction features. Danelectro manufactured the Silvertone instruments sold through the Sears, Roebuck catalog, that used inexpensive, non-traditional materials such as masonite and pine to produce unique, colorful tones. The lipstick tube pickups found on Danelectros make an airy, edgy tone that fit into a surprisingly broad range of music, and several manufacturers make popular recreations of these pickups today.

In 1954 Fender introduced the Stratocaster. Developed by Leo Fender and Fred Tavares, it pioneered the use of a highly ergonomic body, an innovative tremelo bridge, and integrated pickguard and electronics. It would prove to be the most popular (and the most imitated) electric guitar of all time.

Gibson graced the decade with a number of remarkable achievements under the leadership of company president Ted McCarty. Among these were the ES-335, a thin, hollow electric guitar with a solid block inside extending from neck to tailpiece. This guitar combined solid body sustain with hollow body richness, making for an extremely versatile instrument. In the middle of the decade Gibson employee Seth Lover invented the Humbucking pickup, solving the problem of noisy single coil pickups and creating a powerful new tone in the process. Toward the end of the decade Gibson brought out its radical Flying V and Explorer guitars. Commercial flops at first, these futuristic designs went on to become classics.

The 1960s were as revolutionary for electric guitars and basses as they were for society. Guitar-based bands dominated popular music, and overdriven tube amplifiers, fuzzboxes, reverberation, and wah-wah pedals created new sonic landscapes. Multi-track recording turned the studio into a musical instrument, and affordable televisions and transistor radios changed the way music and musicians reached their audiences.

In the early part of the decade, guitar companies focused on producing ever-increasing numbers to supply a growing demand, as musicians found previously unimagined ways to use the innovative instruments pioneered in the previous decade. Electric guitars had become big business, and the efforts of the early pioneers had blossomed beyond anyone's wildest expectations. By the end of the 60s, however, the industry looked very different.

In 1965 Leo Fender sold the Fender Company to CBS, resulting in what many consider a dark age in the company's history. Quality control slipped and innovation was replaced with marketing, geared toward the confusing cultural climate of the times. Notable products of this era include the paisley Telecaster and the Wildwood series, which used wood with colorful stripes made by injecting dye into the roots of trees. Throughout the late 1960s, the dominance of the large American guitar companies was undercut by the growth of inexpensive foreign imports, resulting in a general decline in both profits and quality control. Simultaneously, though, something was happening that would breathe new life into the electric guitar and bass.

As the 1960s turned into the 1970s, several individuals and small companies were experimenting with new techniques in electric stringed instrument construction. One of the most important of these was Alembic. Based in the center of the San Francisco psychedelic scene, they produced instruments with high-quality active electronics, neck-through-body construction with exotic hardwoods, and hand-machined brass hardware. As the decade progressed, they were joined by the likes of Carl Thompson, Bernardo Chavez Rico (of B. C. Rich), Veillette-Citron, Stuart Spector, Dean Zelinsky (of Dean Guitars), Wal basses of England, and Paul Hamer and Jol Dantzig (of Hamer), among others, in establishing a tradition of small manufacturers producing innovative, high-quality instruments.

Leo Fender participated in this trend with his work at the Music Man Company, which employed many original Fender workers. The popular Stingray Bass is favored for its modern, aggressive tone and classic feel. Fender later went on to found the G & L Company with his old partner George Fullerton, producing guitars and basses that combined classic Fender features with continuing innovation and a high standard of quality.

Meanwhile, other designers experimented with non-traditional materials to improve tone and stability. Travis Bean built aluminum-necked guitars, while Geoff Gould used his experience in the aerospace industry to produce necks made entirely of carbon fiber, founding Modulus Graphite. These necks were used by companies such as Alembic, Zon, Music Man, and others.

Another welcome development of the 1970s was the growth of the after-market parts industry. As players became more involved in modifying, and even building(!) their own instruments, companies such as Schecter, Mighty Mite, and Boogie Bodies began to offer replacement parts for hot-rodding guitars and basses. DiMarzio produced the Super Distortion humbucker, a high-output pickup that became very popular with rock musicians, and helped start the replacement pickup industry, which today gives players an enormous range of choices in pickup design.

The 1980s saw further growth in innovation by small companies and the availability of resources for home instrument builders. In 1981, Ned Steinberger made a radical design statement with his headless, nearly bodiless, all-graphite bass. With a very consistent response between notes and a tone that can be described as extremely neutral, it was the ultimate statement in minimalism. Not surprisingly, its look made a great impact on another new phenomenon at the time, MTV. Steinberger made several other notable achievements during the 1980s, including the Trans-Trem, a tremelo bridge that keeps whole chords in tune as their pitch is modulated, and can be stopped in place at different positions to transpose the entire instrument.

The other big tremelo advance of the 1980s was the Floyd Rose system. By locking the strings at both bridge and nut, it was capable of remarkable tuning stability through brutal bending, from strings slack against the neck to a major-third up. It was put to great use by the heavy-metal bands of the era, most notably Edward Van Halen. It is difficult to understate the influence of Van Halen on the 1980s, not only on playing styles but also because he built his own guitar, combining a Fender-style body with a Gibson humbucker, and almost non-existent electronics (one volume knob, labeled "tone"). Suddenly everyone was slapping together guitars from parts, discussing the benefits of one pickup over another, and generally showing a great interest in the individual bits that go into a guitar or bass. The Schecter catalog had pages full of Fender-style parts made of all kinds of exotic woods, as well as parts to finish the rest of the instrument. Seymour Duncan and DiMarzio offered wide selections of aftermarket pickups, and instrument-building supply companies such as Stewart-MacDonalds and Luthiers Mercantile made an increasingly wide range of parts and materials available to builders.

The 1980s saw a great deal of sonic exploration on both guitar and bass. While many players pursued virtuosic speed, others found ways of creating highly textural sonic landscapes through creative use of effects, technique, and the recording process. Guitar synthesizers, long anticipated, finally overcame technical obstacles and were put to widespread use, with both intriguing and appalling results.

Toward the end of the 1980s and the early 1990s, acoustic guitars saw a revival in popularity, helped along by MTV's popular Unplugged series of televised concerts. Viewers were treated to such unthinkable sights as the rock band Kiss, without makeup, performing their 1970s coliseum favorites on acoustic guitars. It was a trend that foreshadowed an appreciation of the guitar's roots that would continue throughout the 1990s.

The early 1990s saw a great revival in guitar-based music, based largely on the grunge rock movement. Sales of electric and acoustic guitars and basses soared, and once again new companies, large and small, were drawn into the industry. Many players favored leaner, stripped-down amplification, abandoning the enormous racks of electronic gear that were popular in the 1980s. Lo-fi tones and altered tunings became fashionable, and players began to re-explore vintage instruments, amplifiers and effects with a new appreciation for their capabilities.

Along with this trend came a vigorous market for antique electric instruments and associated paraphernalia. This even extended to 1970s-era Fenders, which have become quite valuable, making those of us who remember seeing them hanging, new, in music stores "not that long ago" feel somewhat vintage ourselves.

The 1990s saw small manufacturers continue to turn out high-quality progressive designs, especially in the area of pickups and tube amplifiers. One surprising reason for this is the fall of the Iron Curtain in Eastern Europe. In the early 1990s, former Soviet vacuum tube manufacturers began selling their products in the West, just in time to meet the demand created by a great revival of interest in the sound of vacuum tubes in guitar amplification, recording equipment, and home stereos. Vacuum tube manufacture has all but disappeared in the US and Western Europe, and the availability of Russian brands has helped insure that tube amplifiers, whose tone and response is so important to the sound and technique of the electric guitar, will be around for a long time to come.

Another interesting fact of the 1990s is that the large American guitar companies saw a revival in quality and prestige. Both Fender and Gibson benefited from new ownership, rebuilding their names with high-quality reissues of vintage models, new designs, and pricey custom shop instruments. Both companies have benefited from a strong demand for high-end models by professional players and collectors alike.

Electric bass achieved a high degree of design sophistication in the 1990s, as manufacturers made the innovations of the 1970s standard features, and began to produce very good modern versions of vintage models. Five, six- and seven-string basses, which started to gain popularity in the 1980s, became common. Bass players have tended to be more accepting of innovation and new design, a fact illustrated by a history of new features appearing on basses first.

In the late 1990s, many guitar players finally noticed the extra strings on basses and followed suit, using 7-string guitars to great effect in a revival of metal-based rock. The tones created by both electric guitars and basses were strongly influenced by the digital revolution, as computer-based recording, sampling, and inexpensive home recording equipment turned players into producers. Electronic music, which has been predicted to replace guitars since the late 1960s, made great advances in technique and popularity in the 1990s, and at one point in the middle of the decade many industry pundits were again predicting doom and gloom as the grunge movement ran its course. As usually happens, the new styles provided fresh musical ground for electric guitars and basses to explore. It seems that people will never tire of the gratification of picking a string, regardless of what sound comes out.

Constructing a 6-String Electric Guitar

Tools and Materials

Explanation of Tools

The tools needed to build an electric guitar are common to most woodworking shops and available at home centers and hardware stores. Moreover, many of the procedures in this book can be accomplished in varying ways using a variety of tools. Some tools and jigs may be made from scratch or improvised for a special situation. Generally, if you have some basic hand and power tools you will need only a limited range of extra equipment to build most instruments. Naturally, power tools expedite the process enormously. Using hand tools can take more time, especially in the milling stages, but with some perseverance, success is insured. Overall, a balance of hand tools and power tools is the best. Both types require some practice and skill to master.

1 Router

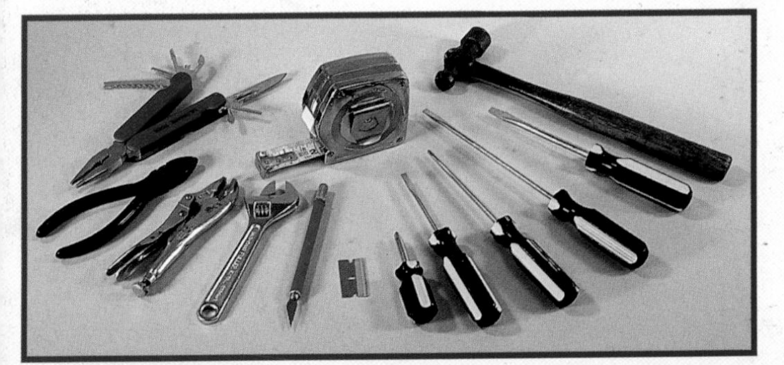

2 Basic hand tools

You may mill the initial wood stock by machine, usually at the place of purchase or with your own equipment. Thereafter, the router (Fig 1) becomes an important tool for the beginning steps of making the body (see p 8). As you proceed to more detailed work, hand tools become the requirement. A good collection of basic shop tools such as screwdrivers, X-acto knives, scissors, wire cutters, tape measure, hammer, pliers, wrenches, etc. (Fig 2, 3) are indispensible.

RULERS

A variety of drawing tools for making the master drawing, preparing templates, and marking wood include rulers and straight edges of various lengths, French curves, squares for right angles, a compass, and other implements, shown below. Transparent plastic rulers are useful for lining up parts and other measuring procedures (Fig 4).

SAWS

You need two types of saws–one designed to cut straight lines and one to cut curved lines. For cutting straight lines, use a sharp handsaw, table saw, radial arm saw, or band saw. Skill saws and jigsaws may also be useful for such operations (Fig 5). A small backsaw is particularly useful for hand sawing smaller pieces of wood. Curved or irregular cuts may be executed by hand with a coping saw or fretsaw (not the one used for cutting fret slots but for making ornate cuts). Use band saws and jigsaws for complex cutting such as shaping the body form and fashioning ornate head stocks as well as for cutting smaller pieces of wood.

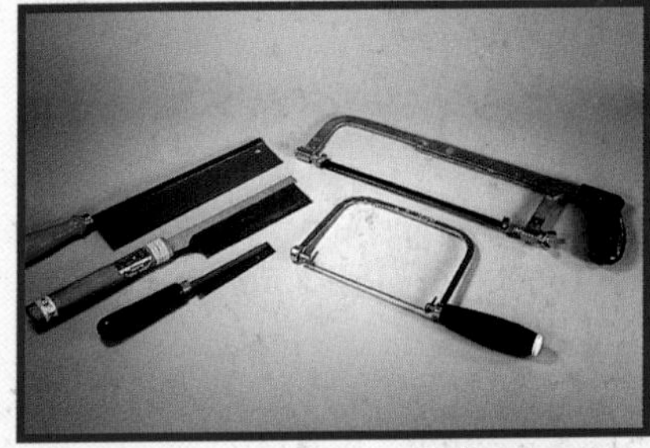

5 Handsaws

A band saw (Fig 6) is fairly indispensible for this project (in

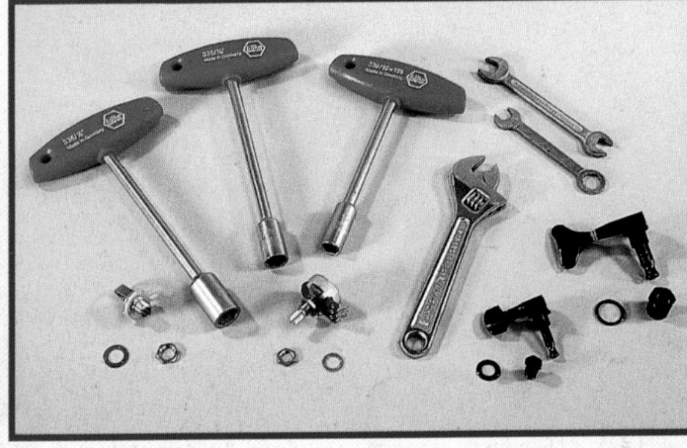

3 Wrenches

4 Drawing tools

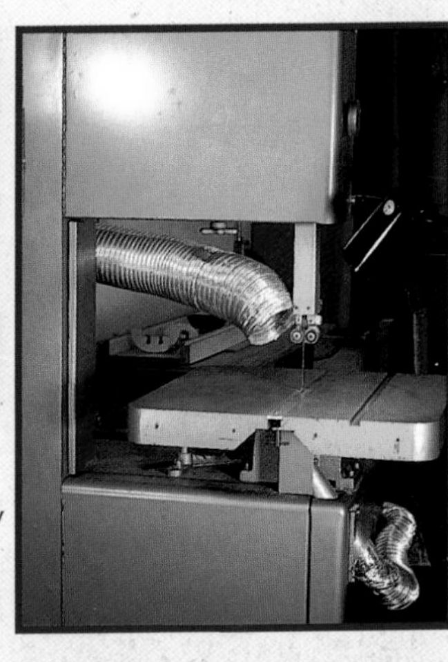

6 Band saw

particular, cutting out the body and neck shapes), and easily the most efficient tool for general sawing. Band saws are sold in various sizes depending on the application (the standard 14 in is sufficient). If you do not have access to a band saw, contact a local woodworking enterprise or friendly woodworker for assistance.

DRILLS

A manual twist drill, brace and bit, electric hand drill (Fig 7), or drill press (Fig 8) are needed for making accurate holes. There are many excellent brands of inexpensive hand-held electric drills available. Electric guitars require drilling many holes for components, tuners, etc. (our guitar features a total of 67 holes!). A stationary drill press is the preferred tool for the most accurate drilling processes. The necessity for precision, and size and logistics of hole drilling, may dictate which tool is best to use.

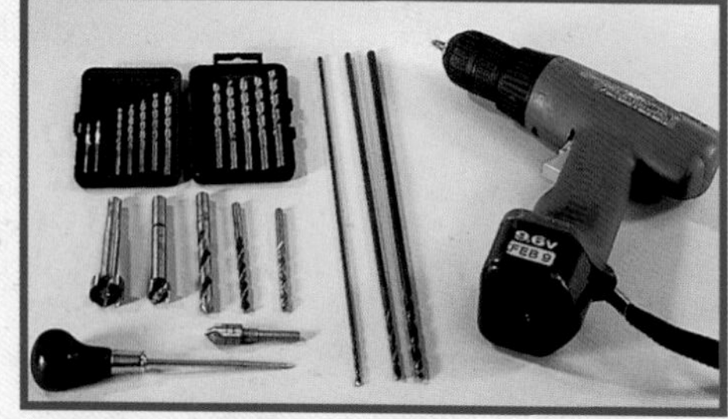

7 Electric hand drills and drill bits

PLANES AND SPOKESHAVES

Hand planes, electric thickness planers, jointers, and electric sanders can adjust the thickness of wood and smooth surfaces to accurate dimensions. Industrial planers and jointers are recommended for the initial milling of raw wood (Fig 9). Your local lumber store or woodworking shop can help in this preparation. Hand planes come in a variety of sizes and styles designed for specific purposes (Fig 10) and require some practice to master. Use a block plane and jack plane to plane by hand. Power sanders such as an oscillating spindle sander (Fig 11) and bench-top belt/disc sander (Fig 12) make for efficient work but require a light touch because they remove wood very quickly. They are, however, expensive and by no means essential. Hand scrapers (Fig 13), electric palm sanders, and sandpaper blocks (Fig 14) are important for leveling and smoothing wood when there is not too much to remove.

A draw knife is good for quick wood removal from curved surfaces, especially for shaping the neck (Fig 10). Spokeshaves (small planes with handles on the sides), come in various configurations. Curved and flat-face types are particularly useful for contouring the body and neck and getting into tight places.

10 Wood shaping tools

KNIVES AND FILES

Sharp knives, one or two chisels, and a mallet are useful for removing small areas of wood (Fig 10). Files come in a wide array of sizes, shapes, and degrees of coarseness. For general use, we recommend a standard 8 in half-round, bastard-cut wood file and an 8 in rasp for faster wood removal. A flat mill (metal-cutting) file is good for fretwork.

CLAMPS

Clamps are important for holding wood stable while cutting and gluing. Spend some time examining various kinds (Fig 15) and ask other woodworkers about their preferences. A bench

8 Drill press

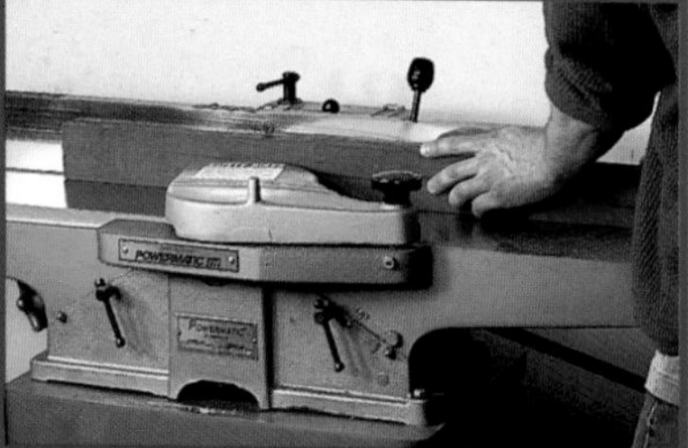
9 Jointer

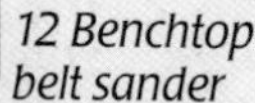
12 Benchtop belt sander

11 Oscillating spindle sander

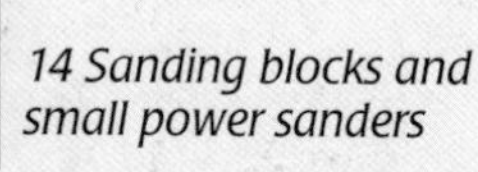
14 Sanding blocks and small power sanders

13 Hand scrapers

vise or Black and Decker Workmate are also useful in these roles. Companies that deal in specialty tools feature a wide variety of clamps, vices, and other tools designed for specific purposes to make the building process easier and more efficient.

SPECIALTY TOOLS

See a guitar maker's catalogue for hundreds of specialized tools for instrument makers and tool freaks. A few of these are extremely useful and are worth purchasing for building even one instrument. Others are only economical when used for more extensive production.

Considered indispensible are a fretsaw to cut fret slots (unless you buy a pre-slotted fingerboard), fret-end nippers for trimming the ends of freshly installed frets flush with the fingerboard, and a fret file for rounding the tops of the frets after leveling (Fig 16).

ELECTRONICS TOOLS

A soldering iron (45 watts is ideal, too much power can damage fragile components), rosin-core solder with a low melting point, and a wire cutter/stripper (Fig 17) will be necessary for installing the electronic components. Alligator clips, a hemostat or a similar device may be used for a heat-sink, clipped onto the wires of capacitors, resistors, etc. to divert the heat of soldering away from these sensitive parts.

15 Clamps

We use small copper clips with a length of stripped wire soldered on, as these conduct heat well without being heavy enough to bend the parts that they are clipped onto. Test leads are wires with clips at either end, useful for experimenting. You may want to make specialty versions of these, such as a length of coaxial cable with a ¼ in jack at one end and two clips at the other, for testing instruments before they are fully wired. Lengths of heat-shrink tubing are indispensable for insulating exposed wires, capacitor legs, etc. Lastly, a digital multimeter is an inexpensive tool whose uses extend far beyond instrument making.

GLUES

Most any modern wood glue will give good service if properly applied. Each glue type has its own properties and requirements: follow label directions. *Natural animal-based* glues have a long-to-medium drying time, dry clear, and can be softened with heat and moisture in case disassembling is needed. These come in dry form and need mixing with water and heating. *Modern hide* glue is now available which doesn't require this preparation. *White glues* are also widely used in instrument making. Recently *Aliphatic* or yellow glue has become prevalent since it dries fast and holds extremely well. However, yellow glues tack quickly allowing little time for positioning and clamping. Except for waterproof varieties, these can be softened for disassembling with the patient application of water and heat. *Epoxy* is a word that covers a wide range of products that are generally useful where a strong bond or filling property is desired. They come in a variety of types for highly specific applications, most of which are not useful for instrument making, except those specifically designed for laminating tropical, oily, or hard-to-bond woods for which other glues are not suitable. Never use rubber cement or contact cement for laminating. *Hot Glues* and *Krazy Glues* may be used for specific applications. *Polyvinyl acetate, powdered resin*, and *resorcinol* glues are also useful in special cases. Research other specialty glues as needed.

TAPES

Drafting tape is useful to protect surfaces from scratching or marring. Unlike masking tape, it doesn't leave a residue.

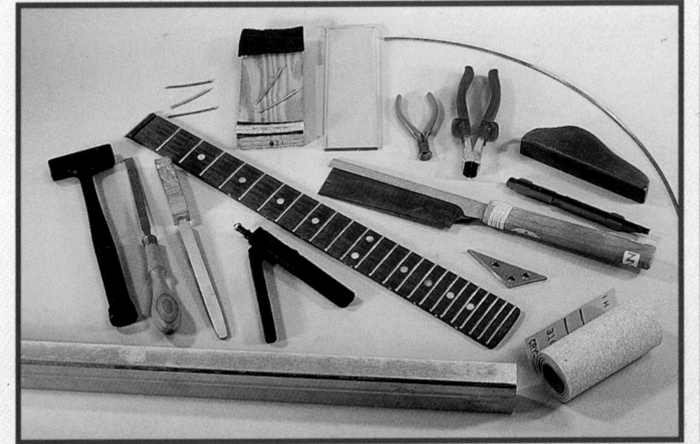

16 Fretting tools

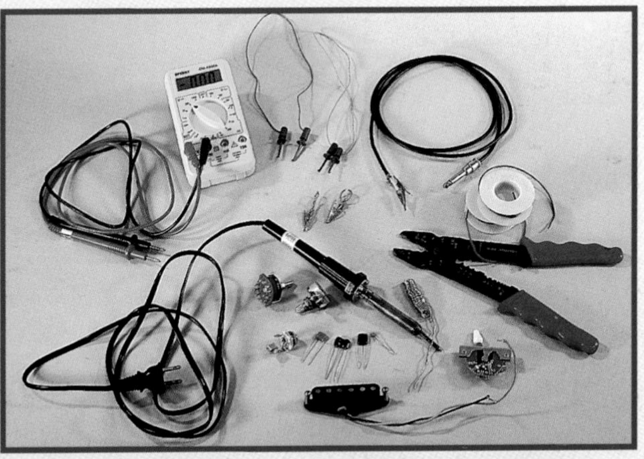

17 Electronics tools

Double-sided carpet tape (Fig 18) is used to temporarily adhere jigs and templates to parts. It is often better than clamps because it will not slip or create obstructions on the working surface. The thicker cloth types are best.

SAFETY EQUIPMENT

Safety equipment for protection of eyes, ears, and lungs is essential (Fig 19). Use safety glasses, hearing protection, dust masks, and dust removal equipment.

Jigs, Templates, and Router

Spend time and effort to make good jigs and templates. The success of each step is determined by the precision of each preceding step.

The router (p 9) is a versatile and powerful tool that is essential but requires some familiarity before launching into intricate and complex cuts. For specific router instruction consult your local bookstore. Experiment with the router on scrap wood before you begin the project.

You will need at least two bits for the guitar project. Use a straight bit with a bearing top for templates when cutting out the cavities for pickups, electronics, etc. This bit is 2 in long, has a straight ⅜ in diameter cutting edge with ½ in long blade, ⅜ in diameter roller bearing, and 1½ in long shank. The roller bearing will follow the template. The longer-than-standard shank is necessary for the required depth of cut. Use a round-over bit to quarter-round the edges of the guitar body.

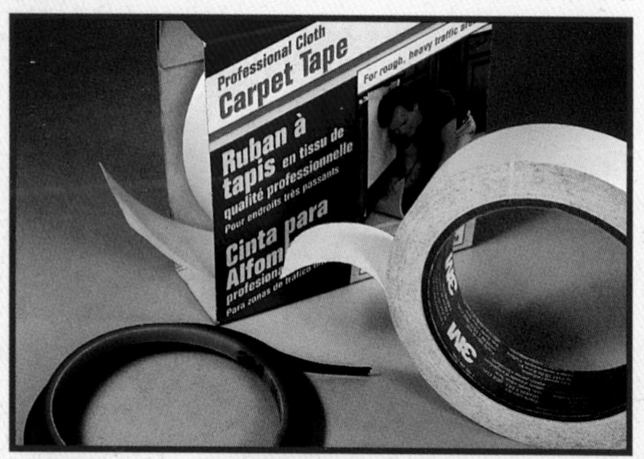

18 Tapes

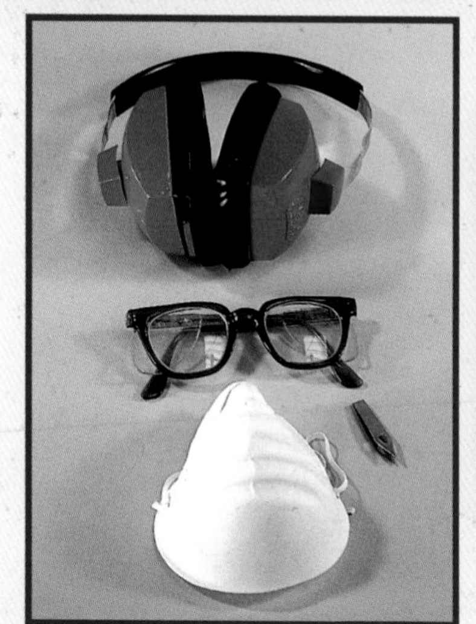
19 Safety equipment

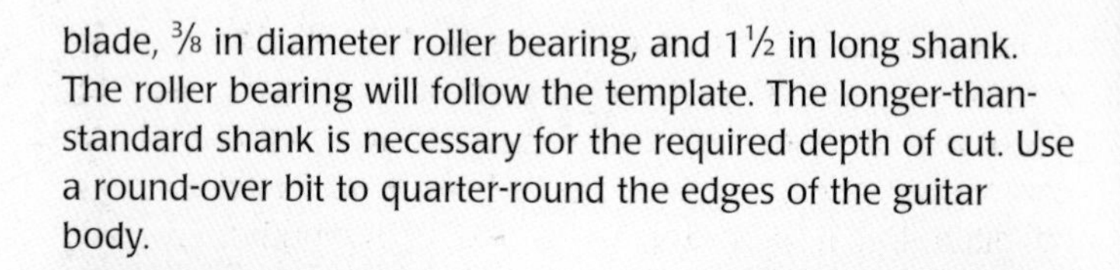

HARDWOODS AND THE ELECTRIC GUITAR

Our electric guitar is made from three pieces of wood (Fig 21): body (mahogany), neck (maple), and fingerboard (ebony). Many hardwoods, and even some softwoods, are suitable for making electric guitars and basses. Maple, mahogany, alder, and ash are probably the best woods for general use, while oak is rarely used because of its open grain and tendency to develop checks and cracks. Sycamore, poplar, walnut, cherry, beech, and birch can also be used. (*See* Appendix for a discussion of Wood and Tone, p 89.)

Exotic woods, highly figured woods imported from tropical regions of the world, are often favored by professional makers of fretted acoustic instruments because of their hardness and beautiful deep colors. Varieties such as rosewood, zebra wood, cocobolo, and ebony may be used but their expense, sometimes toxic nature, and issues of extinction of endangered species are worth considering. Makers use these woods for electric guitars for their striking visual qualities even though their tonal qualities vary. Exotic woods and highly figured maple are costly and difficult to work, thus not recommended for the novice.

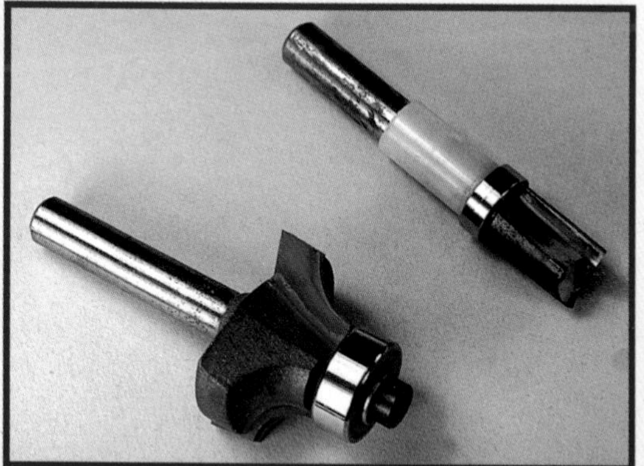
20 Router bits

21 Wood used in our guitar

Before you begin your plan, consult your local hardwood dealers to find what woods are most available in your area, ask woodworkers about wood characteristics, and experiment with scrap samples of each type.

HUMIDITY

Humidity is an important consideration in the making and maintenance of instruments. Wood in most commercial lumberyards has already been dried in large kilns to a degree of usability. Nevertheless, be sure to inquire about how the wood has been dried and what moisture content to expect. After milling the lumber, we usually let it condition in our workshop before we begin working it. After each main component has been cut from a plank, stack the pieces with strips of wood between them so that air may circulate around each piece. Since the stability of the neck is critical, we usually precut the wood near to its final shape and allow it to stabilize at least a few weeks in an environment of moderate humidity. It can then be trimmed to its final shape with confidence.

POINTS TO WATCH

1. Wood expands when humidity is high and shrinks when humidity is low.
2. 50% humidity (or a little drier) is a good working atmosphere.
3. It is better to work in a dry atmosphere. A completed instrument will swell without much harm, but shrinkage due to dryness may result in separations and cracks. Try not to glue or laminate on rainy or excessively humid days.
4. Use an inexpensive humidity gauge (hygrometer) during the building process. Invest in a dehumidifier or humidifier if necessary. Protect the finished instrument from extremes of humidity and temperature.
5. When wood contains too much moisture, the tone will suffer. If it gets too dry, the wood will shrink. A guitar stored in consistently moderate humidity will hold its setup better, avoiding frequent adjustments, especially regarding the truss rod.

GRAIN CONFIGURATIONS

The grain configuration (*see* right) makes the guitar body visually attractive. Most wood cut in modern mills is passed through a saw so that the resulting face grain pattern is whorled or irregular and the end grain passes from edge to edge rather than from face to face. This slab-cut wood is fine for the guitar body.

Quarter-sawn wood with a grain configuration of long straight parallel lines and an end grain of vertical annual rings is sometimes preferable for the neck for its stiffness, especially when using a softer wood such as mahogany. Quarter-sawn boards are difficult to find because the milling procedures used today yield wood mostly cut on the slab. Laminated necks can be arranged to orient the grain vertically, even when made from slab-cut boards, as in our bass. *See* Appendix (p 89) for more information on Wood and Tone.

Note   Wood is sold in nominal measurements. The actual measurements of the board are somewhat less due to wood shrinkage and wood removed through the milling process.

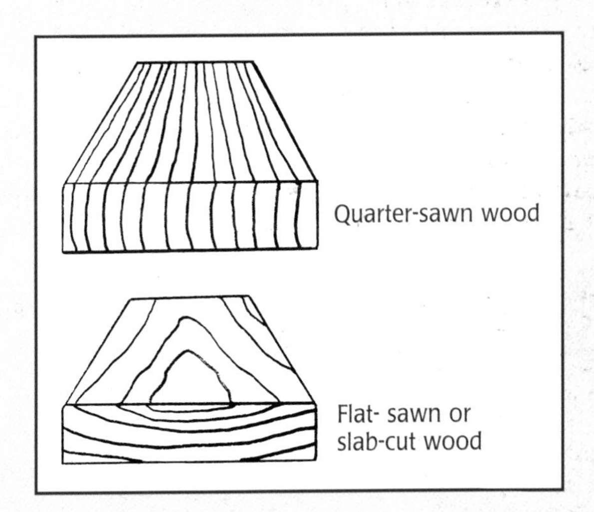

Design Considerations and Preparation

Body Shape

The choice of instrument design is based on aesthetic and functional considerations. The most enduring designs have been those that successfully combine visual appeal and playability.

The Fender Stratocaster and its many imitations have been produced in greater numbers than any other electric guitar. Its timeless shape has passed nearly five decades without looking dated, and is right at home among today's curvy automobiles and consumer goods. This futuristic design was based on careful considerations of comfort and playability, an ergonomic approach that was far ahead of its time in the mid 1950s. Variations of this shape were used for Fender's Precision and Jazz basses (Fig 1).

The Stratocaster body is derived from the classic acoustic shape, rounded with a central waist dividing it into upper and lower bouts. The upper bout has large cutaways on either side of the neck, forming a pair of horns. This shape accommodates all the important points of interaction with the player's body. If you plan to design an unusual body shape,

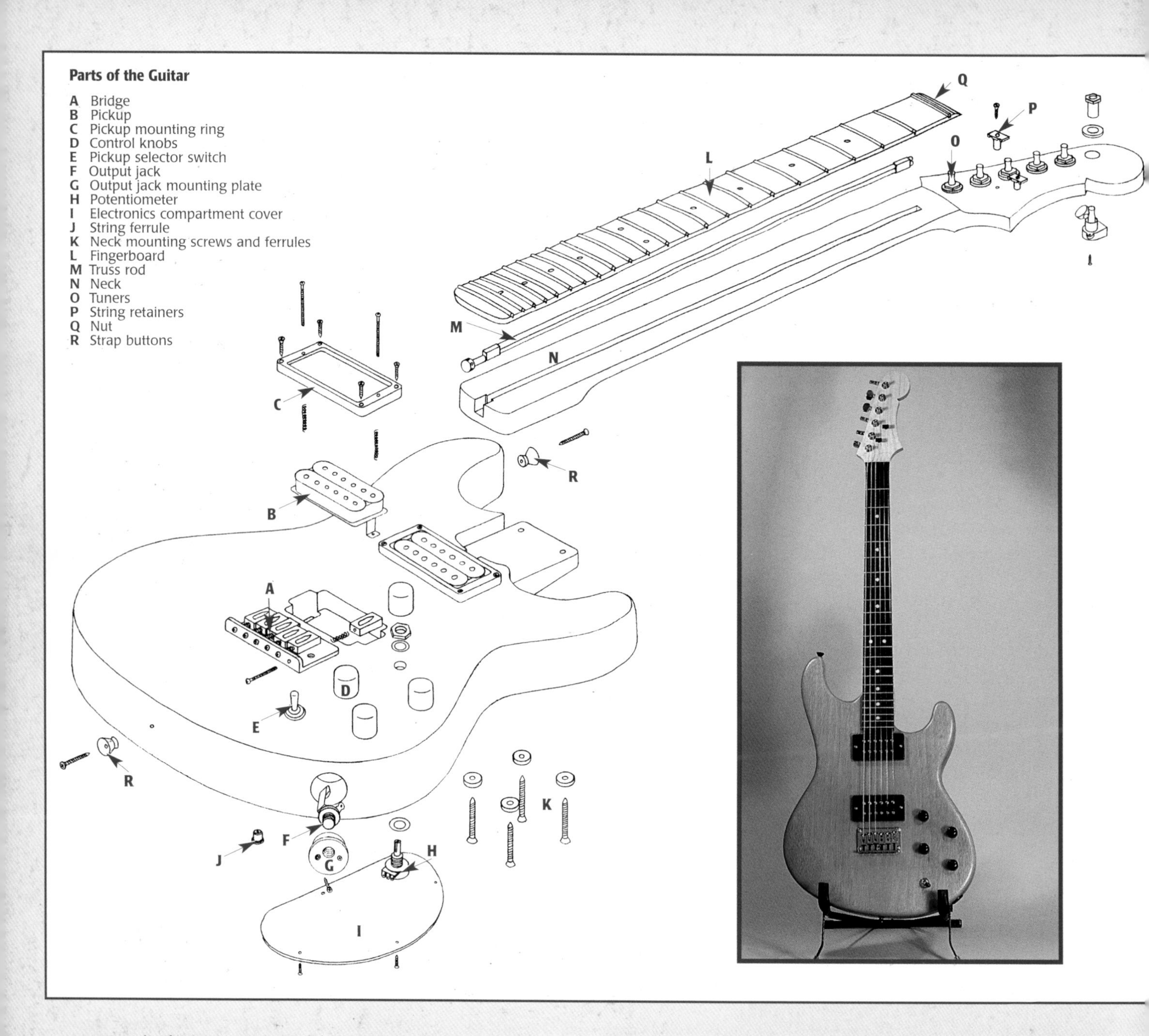

compare its features to those of a traditional body style to avoid unanticipated problems with balance and playability (Fig 2 & 3). Also *see* drawing Body Shape, p 15.

LOWER BOUT, BASS SIDE (A) Picking arm rests here. Shape and beveling here determine where the hand is positioned over the strings. The Stratocaster design pioneered beveled edge for added comfort.

LOWER BOUT, TREBLE SIDE (B) Best site for the main electronics, reachable, but out of way of picking area. Design should allow room for desired electronic components.

WAIST, BASS SIDE (C) Here, instrument body has greatest contact with player's body. The Stratocaster design pioneered a contour in the back. Its shape and size, combined with position of waist in overall shape, can be designed to provide for optimal playing position, sitting or standing.

WAIST, TREBLE SIDE (D) Most common place for guitar to contact player's leg when sitting. We usually leave the back edge somewhat unrounded to keep instrument from slipping forward on leg. Placement and shape of waist will determine instrument's position when played sitting, and should be optimized for balance and playing posture.

HORN/CUTAWAY, BASS SIDE (E) Length of upper horn determines placement of strap connector, which influences balance and positioning of instrument when played standing. The Stratocaster design allows instrument to hang with its headstock slightly closer to the player's body than previous designs, which for many players makes for better left-hand technique. It also eliminates neck-heaviness, an important consideration for basses, especially those with more than four strings. Ideally, instrument should hang in desired playing position without neck having to be held up by the left hand.

HORN/CUTAWAY, TREBLE SIDE (F) Cutaway allows full access to upper frets. Horn completes shape of waist, allowing alternate place for instrument to sit on player's leg.

The design of the Stratocaster does not work for everybody. Some players prefer the "grab" of sharper edges, or a neck that sits farther from the body. The arched top and back of a Gibson Les Paul provide an effective alternative to the Stratocaster's contours. Heavier body woods may balance well with a shorter bass-side horn, or none at all, but basses almost always balance best when the neck-side strap connector is positioned closer to the neck, in the area of the 12th to 15th fret.

When working out the final shape of the instrument body, it is helpful to include the placement of the pickups, knobs and switches, as well as the bridge. These components, with their geometric shapes, interact visually with the outline of the body.

Headstock Design

The headstock's main purpose is to provide a place for the tuning machines. The arrangement of tuners determines how the strings pass through the nut slots. Ideally, it allows the strings to pass in a straight line as they cross the nut, reducing tuning difficulties caused by friction in the nut slots. At the same time, the strings must have ample down-bearing pressure at the nut to achieve proper tone and to avoid being pulled out of their slots when bending strings.

Fender headstocks put all the tuners on one side, allowing the strings to pass straight through the nut, and putting the tuners in an easily reachable location, if somewhat tightly spaced. Traditional headstocks using even numbers of tuners on each side allow for more comfortable spacing, but usually require that at least some of the strings make an oblique angle through the nut. Some designers avoid this by angling the sides of the headstock toward a point at the tip, creating an arrowhead shape that brings the tuners farthest from the nut closer to the centerline. The design we chose for our bass has a slightly tapered shape that minimizes unwanted string angle while retaining a more classic look.

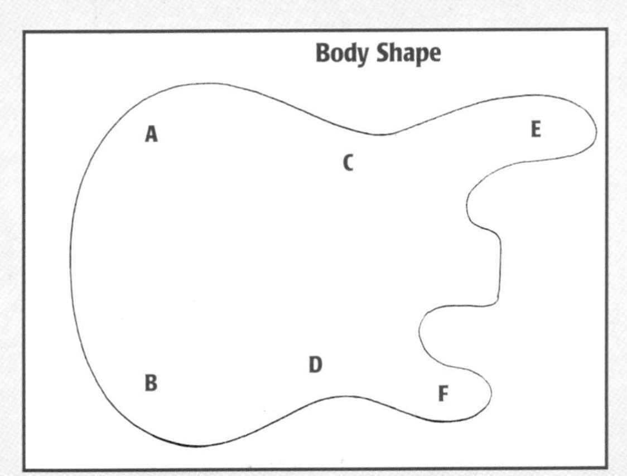

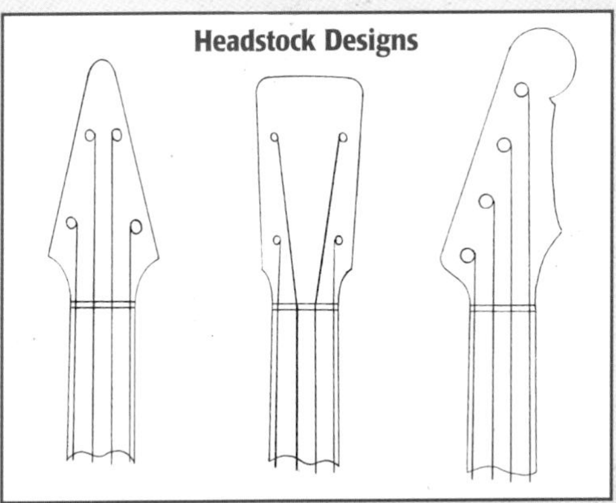

1 Jazz Bass and Stratocaster bodies

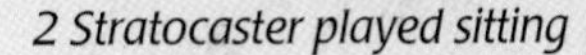

2 Stratocaster played sitting

3 Stratocaster played standing

Another option in headstock design is the angle of the peghead in relation to the neck. Traditionally, headstocks angle back from the neck to achieve proper string tension over the nut. This requires that a joint be made between the neck and headstock pieces (A, B, and C) or that the neck be carved from a thick enough piece of wood to fit the headstock (D and E). Headstock angle can vary, ranging from about 10 to 20 degrees depending on the desired characteristics. A sharp angle will create a strong downward tension across the nut, strengthening tone and sustain in the open (unfretted) strings. However, it also increases friction through the nut slots and exaggerates the tendency of the strings to saw their slots deeper over time, especially when used with a vibrato bridge. Shallower headstock angles offer better tuning stability, and many builders feel they produce an open-string tone that is more consistent with the sound of the fretted strings.

One drawback of angled headstocks on an electric guitar or bass is that when the instrument is laid on its back it rests on the end of the headstock. This flexes the neck in the same direction as the pull of the strings, causing a possible warp. If the instrument is dropped or knocked over and lands on its back, the tip of the headstock usually hits first and can result in a crack or break. Necks whose truss rods are accessed at the peghead can be especially susceptible to breaking if they use a hex nut for adjustment, which requires that enough wood be removed from this critical area to allow a wrench to fit over the nut. The problem can be avoided by locating the adjustment nut at the body end of the neck, or by using a truss rod with an Allen-wrench type of nut, which only needs a small hole or channel for access. Additionally, the neck-headstock joint can be strengthened with a volute, a feature that leaves the wood thicker in this vulnerable area. These measures create a very strong headstock that will survive almost any fall.

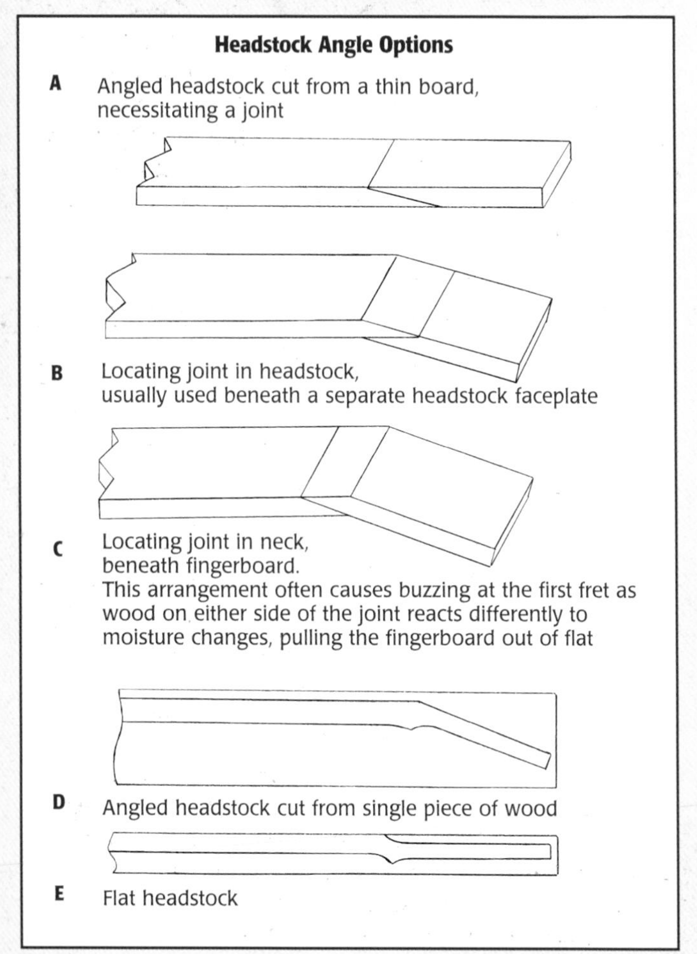

An alternative to angled headstocks is the type used on Fender guitars and basses. These headstocks are parallel to the neck, set back about a half inch from the surface of the fingerboard (*see* E at left). The neck may be made from a piece of wood just under an inch (when a separate fingerboard is used) without having to use a glue joint as with an angled headstock. When the instrument is laid on its back the entire neck remains elevated with no pressure on the headstock. The disadvantage of this design is that the strings will not have enough downward pressure on the nut unless they pass beneath a retainer between the nut and tuners. Fender guitars use a pair of T-shaped metal retainers (string trees), each holding two strings (the E and A strings tuners are close enough to the nut to have enough angle without these). Fender basses use one retainer for the D and G strings. These retainers are currently available in low-friction models, some with small wheels and others made from a self-lubricating graphite compound. Standard metal string trees may be lubricated with graphite from a pencil, drawn onto the point of string contact. As an alternative to these retainers, tuners are available with graduated-height string posts: they get shorter as they get farther from the peghead, providing just enough downward pressure at the nut. This is a feature of the 6-in-line version of the Sperzel Trim-Lok tuners, which also use a mechanism to lock the strings to the posts, avoiding slippage.

The most untraditional headstock option is none at all. This is done by mounting tuners on the body or, more commonly, using a bridge with tuners built in. The main reason for this design is sonic: the headstock mass influences tone and sustain unevenly up and down the fingerboard. The reasons for this are mostly because the headstock is an isolated center of mass at the end of the neck, causing the neck to vibrate inconsistently at different frequencies and as the strings are fretted to various lengths. By doing away with the headstock altogether this complex interaction is greatly simplified, leading to a more consistent tone and sustain. Some of the benefits of headless necks can be achieved by designing a conventional headstock as light as possible. Keep in mind that tonal consistency is only a good thing if you want it; some players prefer that each note have its own distinct character.

Neck Considerations

SHAPE

Small variations in neck shape can cause noticeable differences in feel and comfort. Carefully consider where your thumb rests on the neck, how different string spacings work with your fingers (both with chords and single-note runs), and how different finishes (gloss or satin) feel on the back of the neck. Also make a note of how the neck shape should change over its length in order to reflect the change in wrist angle and hand position between the lowest and highest frets. You may find that you like how one neck feels near the nut but prefer another above the 12th fret, and may want to shape your neck to make a transition between the two (Fig 4).

Keep in mind that the neck shape should allow for comfortable playing over extended periods of time. Choose a shape that will allow the fretting hand to be as relaxed as possible while maintaining just enough pressure on the strings; tone suffers when the neck is squeezed too tight.

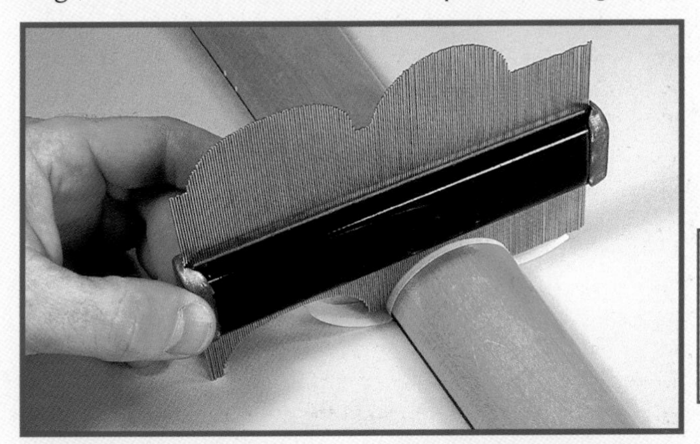

4 A feeler gauge can make a cross section of a neck (mask the neck to avoid scratches). Trace the shape from the gauge onto paper or cardboard, and cut this out to use as a template.

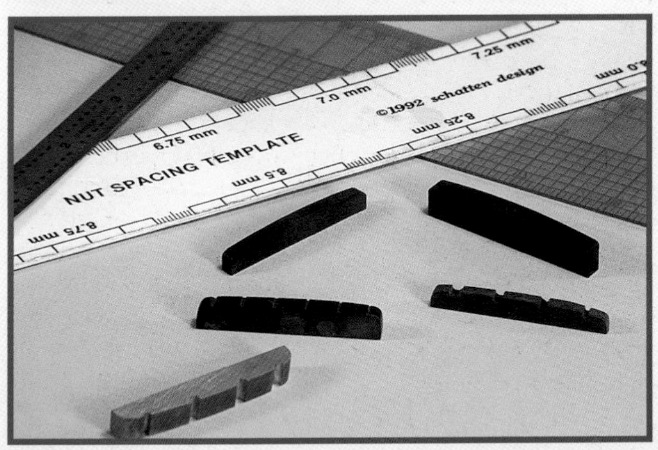

NUT WIDTH

The width of the neck at the nut determines the spacing of the strings (Fig 5). Electric guitar nuts are usually about $1\frac{5}{8}$ in wide, while those on acoustics are $1\frac{11}{16}$ in. Bass nuts with four strings are between $1\frac{1}{2}$ in and $1\frac{5}{8}$ in. Nut width variations have a larger effect on the spacing of the four strings of a bass than on the six on the guitar. Choose a nut width that provides enough space between the strings for your fingers, but narrow enough for comfortable movement between adjacent strings. Consider a wider string spacing if you bend strings a lot.

Be sure to consider how much space to leave between the outside strings and the edge of the fingerboard–usually $\frac{1}{8}$ in at the nut. Some prefer more space for bending; others leave as little as possible (without causing the strings to slip off the edges of the frets) to have the narrowest fingerboard for a given string-spacing. This is also a consideration when choosing the angle of the bevel on the ends of the frets.

FINGERBOARD ARCH

Fingerboards are usually made thicker in the middle than at the edges to give a more comfortable hand position when playing chords. The arch is measured by the radius of the arc that describes it (*see* below). It varies between $7\frac{1}{2}$ in (high arch, as on early Fenders) and 20 in (nearly flat). Classical guitars use a completely flat fingerboard. One drawback to a high arch is that strings that are pulled across the fingerboard will fret out, or rattle against the higher frets, if the action is set up for a low string height. Flatter fingerboards don't have this problem.

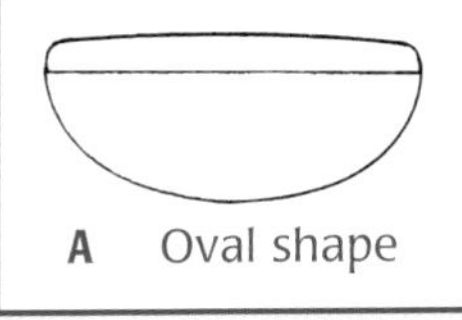

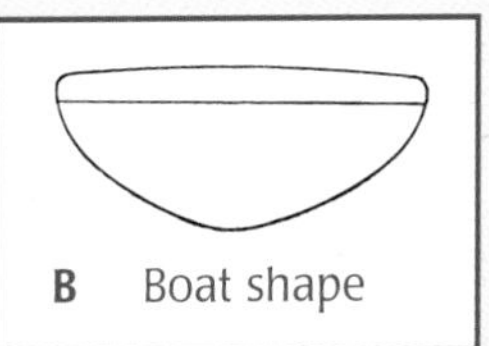

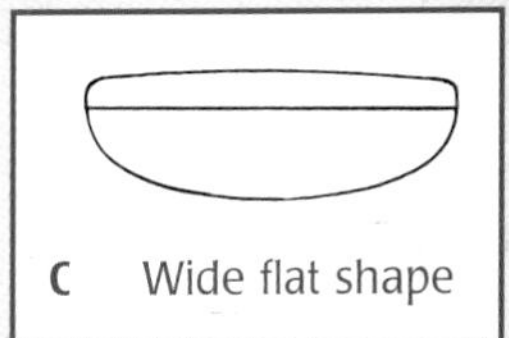

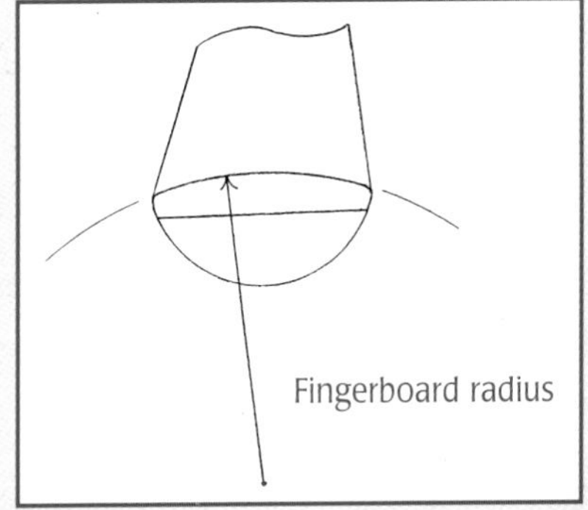

TRUSS RODS

The truss rod is a mechanism inside the neck that counteracts the forward bend created by the pull of the strings. It allows the neck to be adjusted to have a very slight curve, or relief, that is optimal for achieving a low, comfortable string height at each fret. The amount of relief depends on string gauge (thickness), the desired height of the action, and personal playing preferences (*see* Strings and Setup, p 48). Truss rods bend the neck but do not actually

5 Nuts and nut spacing template

stiffen it or correct the sonic shortcomings of a neck that is too flexible. A bowed neck will not transfer vibrations as efficiently into the body, because the strings have more leverage and will put energy into flexing the neck rather than creating sound.

Truss rods are made in several different designs (Fig 6), available from guitar builder suppliers. They consist of stainless steel rods placed into a channel inside the neck, with an adjustment nut at one end that varies the amount of flex as it is turned (*see* photo below). Access to the adjustment nut is at either the headstock or the body end of the neck. Some truss rods, such as the one we used in our guitar, have the ability to flex the neck forward as well as backward, allowing for correction of backbows sometimes caused by moisture variations in the neck wood. Backbows are rare, however, in a properly built neck made of seasoned wood.

Truss rods can use one rod or two. Single-rod types are the oldest and most traditional. (Fig 6C, 7C) They are placed deep in the neck, sometimes in a curved channel, and work by compressing the back of the neck to impart the desired flex when the nut is tightened. One-piece truss rods can be designed to provide a forward flex to the neck as well, by using a threaded steel anchor plate at either end, one with reverse threads (Fig 6D, 7D). The truss rod itself is threaded and screwed into these anchors, and an adjustment nut is welded to one end. The assembly is then mounted into the channel in the neck with the anchors firmly attached, but the rod itself left free of glue or other obstructions. As the adjustment nut is turned the entire rod turns with it, driving the anchor plates closer together (to flex the neck back) or farther apart (to flex forward).

Double-rod types make use of an over-and-under configuration. The two rods are connected at one end, and at the other end the bottom rod passes through a hole in a block that is attached to the top rod (Fig 6B, 7B). The bottom rod end is threaded where it protrudes from the block, and a nut is placed on it. When the nut is tightened against the block, the entire mechanism bows back. Unlike the single truss rod design, which relies on compressing the neck to achieve this bow, the dual-style truss rod creates its bow independently of the neck by flexing against itself. Double-rod types may be built to provide forward flex as well by using a block at either end, with a reverse-thread arrangement similar to that used by their single-rod counterparts (Fig 6A, 7A).

Both types of truss rod are manufactured in a number of variations. Some allow for a more shallow channel in the neck, a good choice for those who intend to carve a thin neck for use with small hands. One type of truss rod used by the Martin Company and others features an inverted "U-channel" (a U-shaped length of metal into which the truss rod is placed) in lieu of the top rod in a double-rod system, as shown. Several suppliers offer U-channels made of carbon fiber providing additional stiffness to the neck.

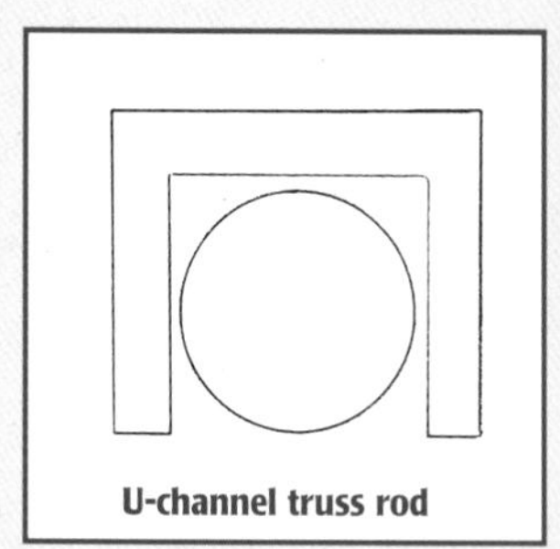

U-channel truss rod

Single-rod or compression truss rods are inexpensive, lightweight, and may easily be made rather than bought. Simply thread the end of a stainless steel rod and put a sharp bend in the opposite end at the appropriate length (Fig 6C). Heating the rod with a torch is helpful to make this bend. A $\frac{3}{16}$ in diameter rod is the most common for guitars and a $\frac{1}{4}$ in rod is sometimes used for basses, especially those with more than four strings or a scale length greater than 34 in. The truss rod may be covered in heat-shrinkable plastic tubing or wrapped in plastic tape to help prevent a rattle that sometimes happens if the truss rod is under little or no tension.

Compression rods are chosen to recreate the sound of a vintage instrument. Their lighter weight and compression they

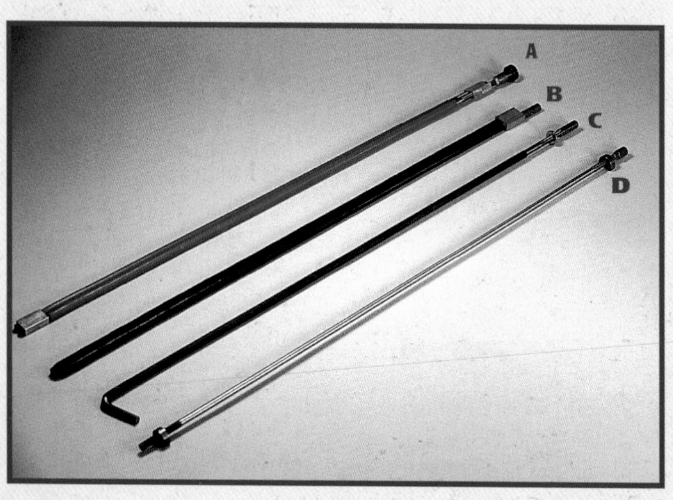

6, 7

A Double rod, 2-way adjustable

B Double rod

C Single rod

D Single rod, 2-way adjustable

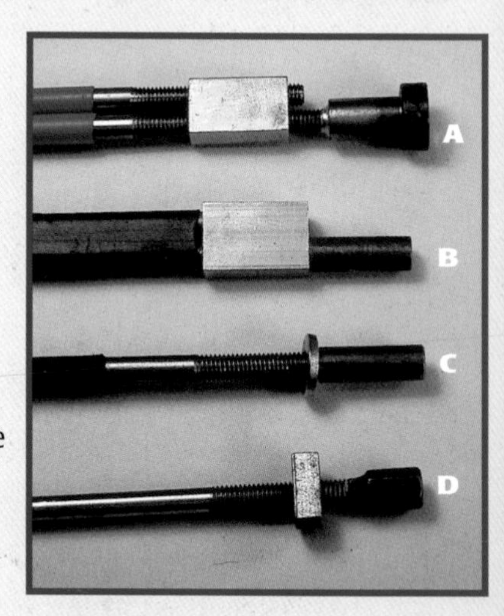

place on the neck contribute subtly to the tone of the instrument. This type of truss rod is somewhat more difficult to install (especially when using a curved-bottom channel) and almost impossible to replace if it breaks. Truss rods that use a hex-head nut require a large access area, which weakens the nut/headstock joint if placed there. A volute at the back of the nut will provide some insurance against breakage.

The instruments described in this book use double-rod types which are the easiest for the beginning builder to install. They are also removable (as long as the neck is designed to allow this and they are not glued in place) in the unlikely event of breakage or stripped threads. Double-rod truss rods can exert a great deal of force in the desired direction of flex, and it is rare to encounter a warp that they cannot correct. In extreme cases these truss rods can crack the backs of necks or cause a fingerboard to pop off. A volute and a properly glued fingerboard will help prevent this.

Occasionally builders will elect to use two truss rods in one neck. This is most common in basses with five or more strings, or in seven- or twelve-string guitars. The advantages are that more force is available to counter the increased string pull, and the neck may be adjusted to correct a twist, which cannot be fixed with a single rod. Additionally, when setting up the neck, slightly more relief may be used beneath the lower strings to compensate for their greater range of movement. Disadvantages are that more wood must be removed from inside the neck, reducing stiffness, and space must be made for the two adjustment nuts.

Neck/Body Connection Options

1 GLUED-ON (OR SET) NECK In this most traditional method of neck attachment, the base of the neck is shaped to fit into a pocket in the body, and glued there permanently. This provides a solid joint when it is designed to have sufficient surface area where the two pieces connect. The heel (the back of the neck-body joint) may be carved to provide access to the upper frets, as long as enough wood is left for proper strength. However, replacing a damaged or warped neck is very difficult.

2 BOLT-ON NECK This attachment style (Fig 8) was chosen by Leo Fender as a way to simplify production. The neck fits into a pocket in the body and is held there by bolts (usually screws). This allows a neck to be switched for replacement or experiment. Bolt-on necks provide a solid connection if made well, with less inherent flex than some set-neck designs. However, they require a relatively bulky heel that can be difficult to reach around. They are the easiest to make and recommended for a first attempt at neck building.

3 NECK-THROUGH-BODY Here the neck wood (Fig 8) runs the entire length of the instrument, passing through the body that is made of separate pieces (sometimes called wings) glued onto either side. This design provides the most solid neck/body attachment, since both bridge and fretboard are on the same piece of wood. The heel can be carved to the most playable shape of the three types since there is no joint to weaken by removing too much wood. However, a damaged neck is almost impossible to replace; the best one can do is saw off the body sides to use again. While these are more complex to build than a bolt-on, they are relatively straightforward and may be considered by the first-time builder.

We chose a bolt-on neck for our guitar and a neck-through for our bass. These are the best suited to the beginning luthier and are the designs that we prefer. Neck-through body construction is more common in basses than in guitars, but it is a fine choice for either instrument when taking a no-compromise approach to tone and playability. The joinery and carving involved will appeal to experienced woodworkers, and while it isn't any more difficult than that on the other designs, there is more of it. Bolt-on necks are an excellent choice for a first instrument, and have been used on many of the best guitars and basses.

Neck/Body Angle

When laying out an instrument, an important consideration is the alignment between neck and body. This determines the height of the strings at the bridge and must be matched to the chosen bridge type. Bolt-on necks are set parallel to the body, elevated slightly above it, as shown in A, p 20. They are usually used with bridges that place the strings approximately ½ in above the body. The use of a taller bridge, such as the Gibson-style Tune-o-

8 Bolt-on neck and neck through body

Matic (approx. $\frac{5}{8}$ in to $\frac{7}{8}$ in), will necessitate routing the neck pocket at an angle to the body surface. Neck-through designs may be made with an elevated fingerboard, but more often feature a slight angle between neck and body, shown in B. Use the bridge when laying out the side-view of your instrument to insure that this angle is calculated accurately.

A Neck parallel to body

B Neck angled back from body

Neck to body angle

Bridge Types

Many types of bridges are available for electric guitars and basses. Electric instruments that lack a soundboard may use heavier bridges than those used for acoustic instruments with independent, fully adjustable saddles for each string. This allows for much more accurate intonation and optimal playability.

Different weights and designs of bridges have different sonic characteristics and may be chosen to enhance or fine-tune instrument tone. Also, electric instruments may use bridges that allow the tension of the strings to be changed while playing, raising and lowering their pitch. These are known as tremolo bridges, although the real name for what they do (fluctuating pitch) is vibrato. Bridges of this type are often called whammy bars, after the lever that attaches to the bridge to raise and lower pitch (Fig 9).

The design of any instrument bridge is critical to the sound that it produces. The bridge performs the vital task of coupling the strings to the body, and must provide a solid connection while also performing the tasks of anchoring the string tension and allowing the necessary adjustability.

Bridges fall into two general categories: those for use on flat-surfaced bodies and those that can be mounted on an arched-top instrument. Flat-top bridges are patterned after the models designed by Leo Fender for his Broadcaster/Telecaster, Stratocaster, and Precision and Jazz basses. They have simple construction: a flat plate is screwed to the body, with the edge opposite the neck bent vertically, about $\frac{1}{4}$ in above the surface of the body (Fig 10). Separate saddles for each string are attached to the vertical part of the plate with screws, which allow the saddles to be adjusted to change the length of the string slightly, for proper intonation. Small springs around the screws keep the saddles from moving. The strings are individually adjustable for height with two small screws in each saddle. Strings are attached either through holes in the vertical bend of the bridge plate (bass models, generally) or by passing through holes in the bottom of the bridge to the back of the body, where they are held by ferrules (Fig 11).

Bridges of this type, especially those with strings passing through the body, are considered to be among the best-sounding bridges for electric guitars and basses. Fender-style bridges usually have a string spacing that is on the wide end of the range, at $2\frac{7}{32}$ in between the outside strings. The bridge we chose for our guitar has a $2\frac{3}{32}$ in spacing, making it compatible with a wider range of pickup models (Appendix: Electronics, p 71).

Arched-top guitars utilize bridges that sit above the surface of the body, usually on two posts screwed into the body. Gibson's Tune-o-Matic is the most common example (Fig 12, 13). It uses a separate stop tailpiece mounted just behind the bridge to hold the tension of the strings, and has separate saddles for each string, individually adjustable for intonation. Overall height is adjusted by turning the mounting screws on either end of the bridge. The saddles are not individually height-adjustable, but rather are set to a fixed 12 in radius. These bridges place the strings higher above the body than

9 Tremolo or whammy bar bridge

10 Telecaster-style bridge

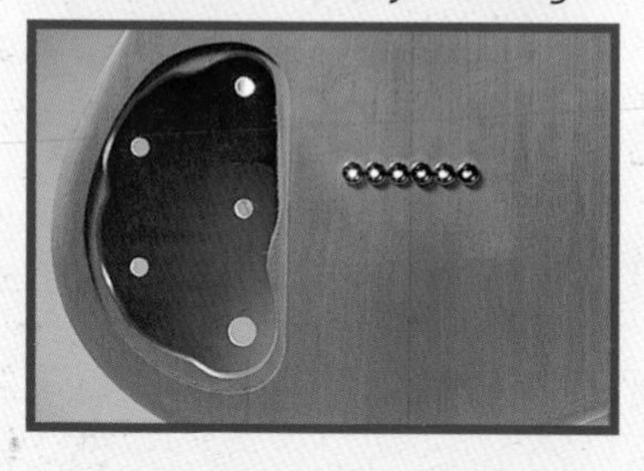

11 String ferrules

the Fender type, requiring a greater angle between neck and body (*see* Neck/Body Angle, p 20). Tune-o-Matic and similar bridges usually have an overall string spacing of 2 1/16 in.

12 *Tune-o-matic bridge*

13 *Variation of Tune-o-matic bridge. Stop tailpiece is equipped with fine tuners, and the bridge saddles are small rollers, allowing adjustment of the string spacing for use with a wide range of pickups. Roller saddles have a slightly detrimental affect on tone.*

Gibson's Les Paul Jr uses a bridge related to the Tune-o-Matic. It is a single bar, spanned between two large mounting screws, for both bridge and tailpiece (Fig 14). Strings pass through holes in the neck side of the bar, emerge out the back and wrap over its top, where they pass across ridges in the metal that form the actual saddles. The metal ridges are staggered for improved intonation over a single straight saddle (such as on an acoustic guitar) but are not individually adjustable. Further, the stagger is arranged for a wound G string, rather than the unwound one found on most modern, light-gauge string sets. These bridges have had a resurgence in popularity in the late 1990s, and their tone is favored by many guitar builders and collectors. Recently, an updated version of this bridge has become available, with limited adjustment for intonation.

14 *Les Paul Jr.-style bridge*

Many suppliers offer specialty variations of the above bridge types, which are cast or machined from brass, steel, or aluminum. They are designed to make use of the sonic characteristics of these metals, and offer options for fine tuning. Adding mass to the bridge area enhances bass and midrange, and can improve sustain, but usually does so at the expense of some of the sound of the instrument wood. Brass bridges are heavy, and may be helpful in filling out the tone of a thin-sounding instrument. Aluminum is lightweight, and helps bring out the maximum tone of the wood, although it may add a slight ping of its own. Many companies offer bridges of mixed materials (steel base with brass saddles, for example) or after-market saddle sets for modifying existing bridges. One popular type of the latter is the graphite String Saver saddles offered by the Graph-Tech Company. They are made of a low-friction composition to minimize string breakage, and have a favorable effect on tone and sustain without adding weight to the bridge.

Expensive specialty bridges offer interesting alternatives, but are not necessarily better than traditional models. The bridges that offer the best tone are those with a minimum of extraneous parts and a simple, straightforward design.

15 *Fender Stratocaster tremolo*

Tremolo bridges for guitar are available in a number of styles and models. Those that perform best are based on the original Fender Stratocaster bridge (Fig 15).

This simple bridge uses a base plate much like the Fender types, but mounts to the guitar body with six screws in a line along the neck-side of the bridge, each in front of a bridge saddle. A bent metal arm (the whammy bar) screws into a hole in the treble side of the bridge and extends across the face of the guitar (Fig 9, p 20). When the arm is pressed toward the body, the bridge plate pivots on its six mounting screws, lowering tension on the strings and dropping their pitch (Fig 16, 17). Pulling the arm away from the body raises the pitch, although the range in this direction is limited.

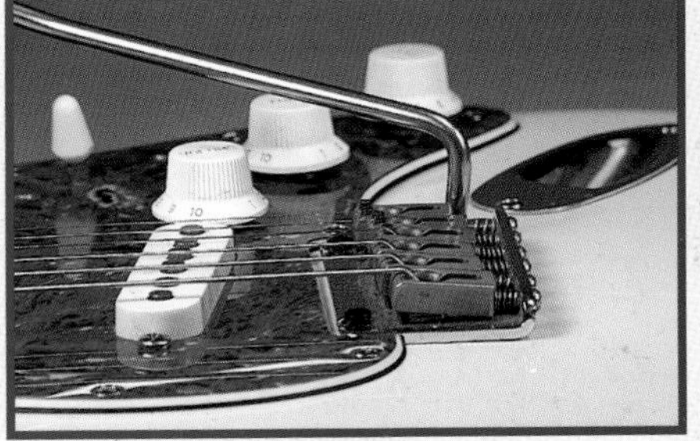

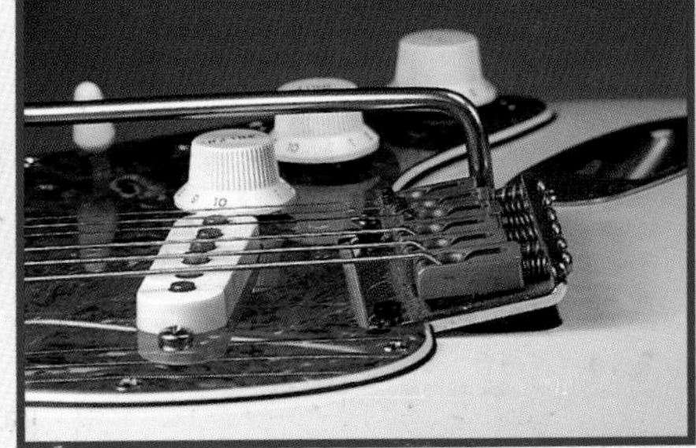

16 *Stratocaster-style tremolo, with brass replacement saddles.*
17 *Tremolo with bar depressed*

Beneath the bridge, a steel block extends through a cavity to the back of the body (Fig 18), where it attaches to a variable number of springs. These extend across the back of the body in a shallow cavity, providing a counterbalance to the strings (Fig 19). As tension is lowered in the strings, it is increased in the springs, which pull the strings back into pitch when the bar is released.

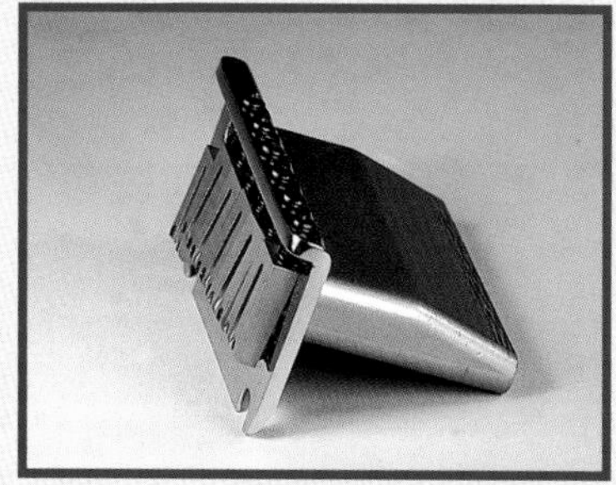

18 Tremolo bridge out of the guitar

The standard Fender tremolo goes out of tune with heavy use, probably caused by friction in the instrument nut or string retainers (which grab at the string as it slides past), the windings slipping on the tuner posts, or friction between the bridge and its mounting screws. Nuts and retainers are available in a low-friction material, and work very well. Tuners that lock the strings to the post have also eliminated most of this source of trouble. Friction at the bridge screws can be minimized by adjusting the screw heights to allow the bridge to pivot freely without its front edge lifting off the face of the guitar.

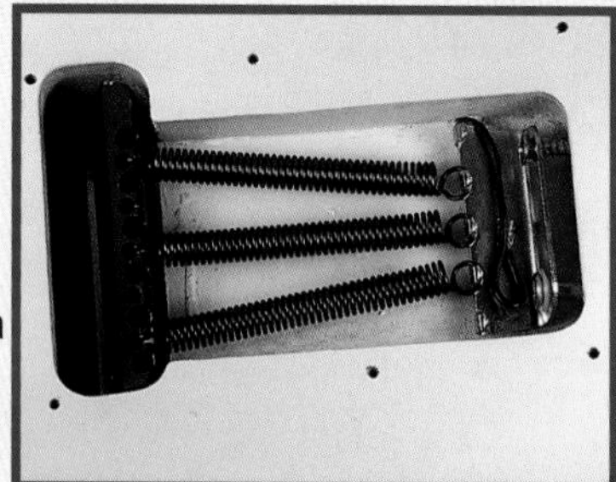

19 Tremolo springs

Newer variations of the Fender-style tremolo achieve a smoother action by replacing the six mounting screws with two large studs, one on either end of the bridge (Fig 20). The Floyd Rose tremolo and its many licensed copies, popular in the 1980s, use a nut that clamps the string in place, avoiding any tuning problems at the headstock. Tuning when the nut is locked is possible with a set of fine tuners on the bridge itself. The locking nut arrangement has become less popular with the common use of low-friction nuts and locking tuners, which are far less cumbersome.

20 A modern variation of Fender-style tremolo

While these modern tremolos are effective at staying in tune, they do not allow the guitar to sound as full and powerful as the original Fender design. The choice of which system is right for your instrument depends on your playing style and individual preferences. Tremolo systems come with diagrams showing the size and placement of the necessary body routs, and routing templates are available from guitar shop suppliers.

Creating a Full-Size Pattern

A full-size pattern will act as the template for the body and the neck. The following discussion is specific to the guitar. Many of these procedures apply to the bass as well. Remember to procure components (Fig 21) before determining a body shape to make sure everything fits in its appropriate place.

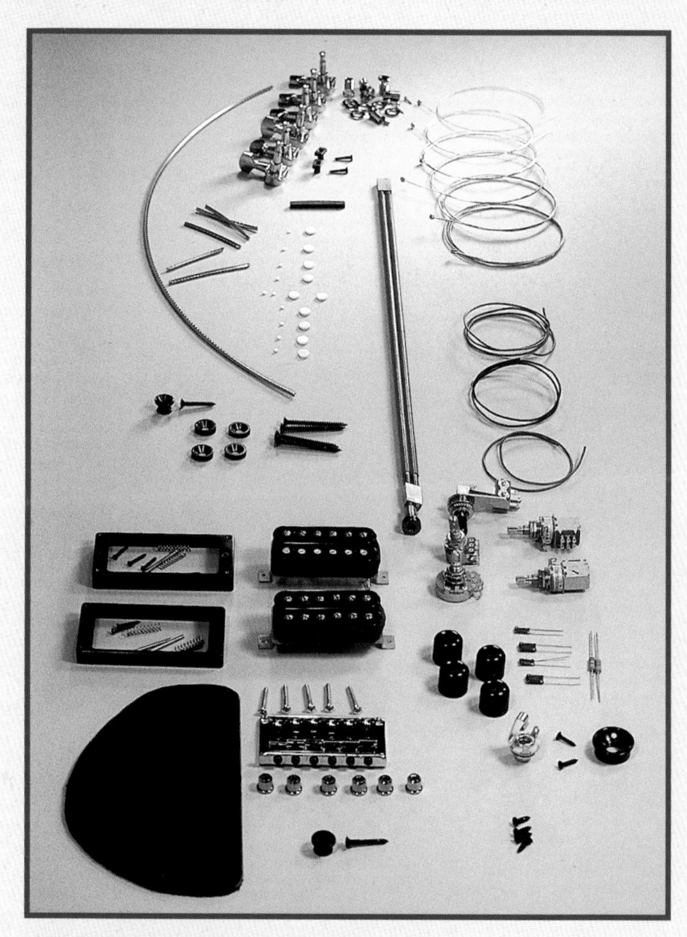

21 Components used in the guitar

Transfer the drawing to a large piece of paper or posterboard (*see* Appendix: Master Guitar Pattern, p 62). Two sheets of 18 in x 24 in drawing paper taped together will accommodate the full-size dimension (longer for the bass).

Draw a centerline through the middle of the drawing paper as a reference. Plot the nut and the bridge first. Mark a point along the centerline, approximately 8 in from the end of the paper. This point, where the strings break the saddle, is to be referred to as the bridge. All other measurements will use this as a point of reference.

Along the centerline, mark the nut placement 25½ in from the bridge. This is the scale length (25½ in is standard Fender length; 24¾ in is standard Gibson length). Longer scale lengths are higher in tension; richer in harmonics.

Make nut width 1⅞ in (our guitar) and mark along the centerline (Fig 22).

Mark neck pocket 7$^{3}/_{32}$ in from the bridge. Measure and mark 7$^{19}/_{32}$ in from the bridge as the position of the 21st fret. The width of the neck/fingerboard at the 21st fret is 2$^{3}/_{16}$ in. Draw this line (Fig 23). Draw the edges of the neck and fretboard by connecting the points between the ends of the nut and 21st fret (Fig 23).

Draw the shape of the end of the neck (which is also the shape of the neck pocket) by using the full-size pattern provided here. Be sure to achieve the correct curves, as shown in Fig 24.

22 Marking the main points along the centerline

23 Drawing the 21st fret and sides of neck

24 Drawing the end of the neck/neck pocket

Neck Pocket Pattern actual size

Transfer the pattern outline to a master drawing (do it freehand, with an enlarged pattern, or trace an actual guitar). Check to see that proportions between parts are visually balanced in relationship to each other. Make adjustments where necessary. Place the various electronic components and other items on the drawing to get a sense of the final look (Fig 25).

Draw the headstock pattern in the same way as the body shape. Place the tuners (we use six on a side design) on the drawing, as shown, to make sure of alignments of strings, tuning knobs, etc. (Fig 26).

Draw lines representing the outside strings (approx. ⅛ in for guitar) in from the edge of the neck, through the nut, and use these lines to locate tuners. Draw the rest of the strings. Strings must pass without contacting other tuner posts.

25 Using the hardware in the design process will give a clearer view of how the shapes work together visually

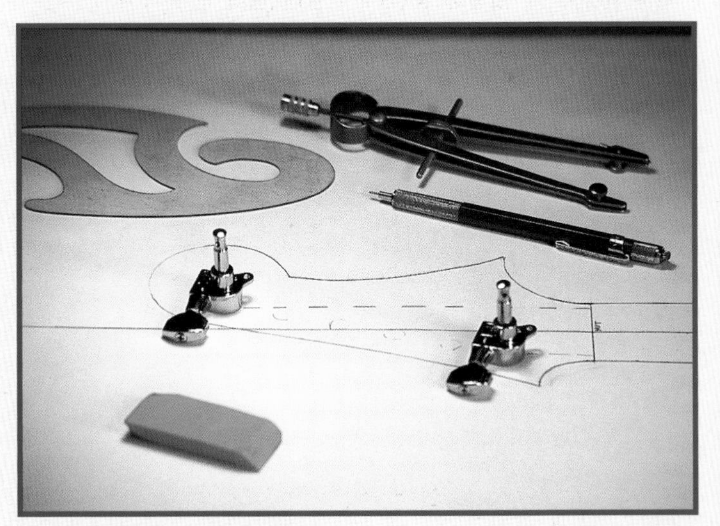

26 Laying out the headstock

The Guitar Body

Preparing Wood Stock

Make a copy of the outline of the body from the Master Drawing and cut it out to use as a working template.

Shop for wood for the wood stock in a specialty store that will allow you access to their stock and will help you find appropriate wood. If possible, take an informed woodworker who knows your needs with you. If there is no local supplier, consult both guitar supply catalogues and mail order wood dealers. The body may be built from one or several pieces of wood depending on the wood available. When selecting wood for its aesthetic effect, consider how the grain works with your shape. Direction of wood grain and changes in wood coloration, shown at left, may be important in your decision (Fig 1).

1 One-piece bodies from same board with opposite grain orientation

If wood of your choice is not available in large enough pieces, glue together two or more pieces (as shown in the drawings). Joint pieces or have surfaces trued at a woodworking shop. You can hand plane or sand to achieve a perfect joint, but this is much more difficult. Test joint by holding the pieces together in front of a bright light to detect flaws. Glue boards together. Follow the manufacturer's directions for glue use.

Pre-draw lines on the wood perpendicular to the joint for accurate clamp placement. Use larger clamps, such as bar clamps or pipe clamps, and place at right angles to the joint so pieces will not be pushed out of alignment. Arrange clamps for even distribution of pressure. Mill the body blank perfectly flat to a thickness of 1¾ in. Cut body blank to approximately 14 in x 20 in.

Establish a centerline on the body blank. If you use a 2-piece body, utilize the center joint line as the centerline. On a 3-piece body, the centerline will be down the center of the middle piece. Match centerlines of the body pattern to that of the wood.

Trace around the body shape (Fig 2, 3). Do not cut out body at this time.

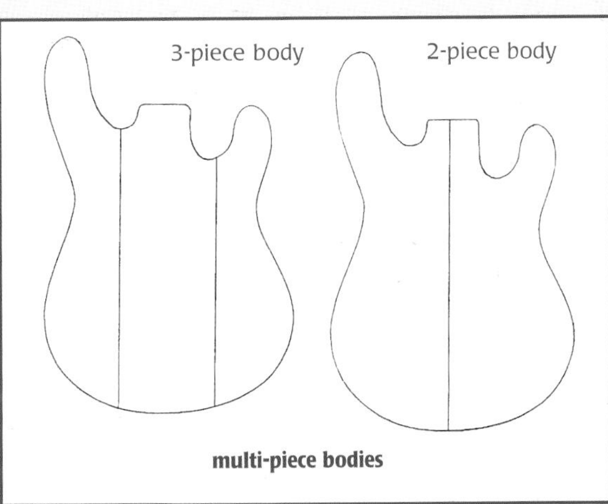

multi-piece bodies

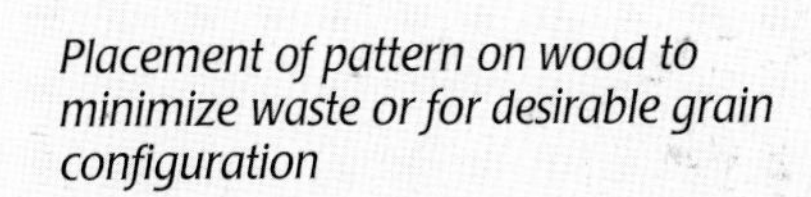

Placement of pattern on wood to minimize waste or for desirable grain configuration

2 Transferring body pattern to the wood

3 Body outline drawn on wood

4 *Drawing the pickup outline on template*

5 *Rough cutting template with a jigsaw*

7/8 in

B

A

$2\frac{13}{16}$ in

$3\frac{7}{32}$ in

$1\frac{9}{16}$ in

$3\frac{3}{8}$ in

$1\frac{15}{32}$ in

Pickup Cavities Pattern actual size

A main pickup cavity and B area under pickup legs

Making the Pickup/Neck Pocket Master Template

The Master Template is used for routing the neck pocket and two pickup cavities in the guitar body. We make it from ¼ in thick masonite because it is inexpensive, available, and easy to work. (If you wish, guitar supply companies sell pre-machined templates). Buy enough masonite for two thicknesses of template material, necessary to complete the routing procedure.

Routing will be made with a ⅜ in straight router bit with a matching ball bearing guide and a long shank capable of cutting 1⅝ in deep (*see* Jigs, Templates, and the Router, p 12).

Cut one thickness of masonite 20 in x 14 in. Mark a centerline on this template blank. The centerline will insure that the neck pocket and two pickup cavities line up so that the strings will pass over the correct point on each pickup. Trace the outlines of the pickup cavities (pattern below left) and neck pocket (pattern p 23) onto the masonite to be used for the Master Template (Fig 4).

Rough cut the outlines in the masonite with a jigsaw or coping saw using a pre-drilled hole to start the cut.

Carefully file and sand the template (Fig 6) to specification (sanding blocks and dowels are helpful). Avoid angling or rounding walls of template.

Note A labor-saving alternative to hand cutting the entire Master Template is to handcut the neck pocket hole, then make a second template with a single pickup hole using the procedures described (Fig 7). This is used in

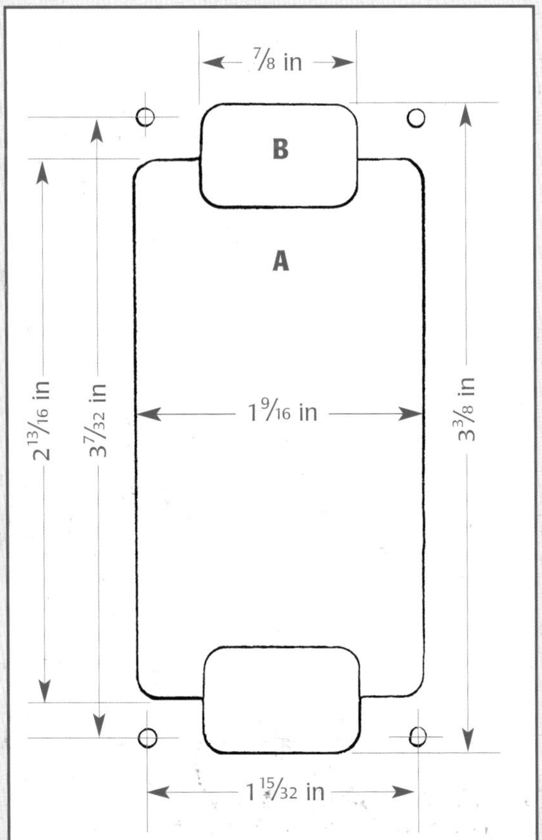

6 *Sanding the neck pocket to its final shape using small sanding block to keep lines straight*

7 *Making a pickup template to use for routing pickup holes in master template*

turn to rout the two pickup holes in the Master Template which saves a significant amount of handwork and insures that the pickup holes are identical.

Secure the single pickup template in position on the Master Template with heavy duty two-sided carpet tape (cloth-backed, not cellophane tape) or clamps. Be sure to carefully align centerlines of the two templates. Move the router through its entire range of motion to insure that it has enough clearance to cut the hole without interference (Fig 8). The router blade bearing will ride along the inside of the single template and cut an identical pattern in the Master Template, as shown (Fig 9). Carefully file and sand any irregularities.

Finally glue the $\frac{1}{4}$ in Master Template to another $\frac{1}{4}$ in thick piece of masonite. The extra template thickness is necessary for the bearing guide to be in contact with the template during the first shallow cuts for the neck pocket and pickup cavities. Rout out the holes in the second masonite layer, as shown (Fig 10). This completes the Master Template (Fig 11).

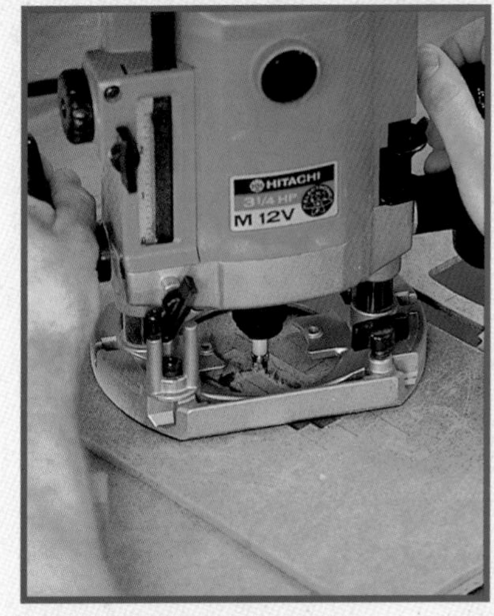

8 Routing pickup holes in Master Template, saving the time of hand-cutting two pickup holes

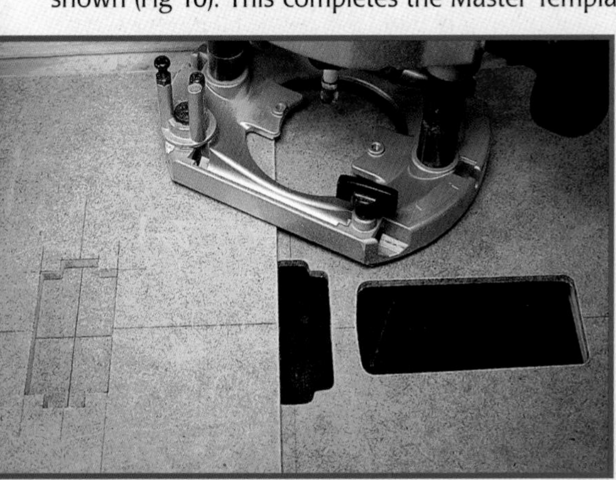

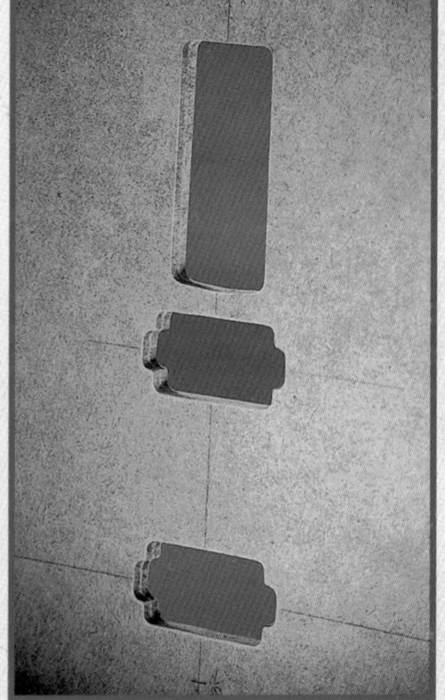

9 (lower left) Preparing to rout the second pickup hole in the Master Template

10 (lower middle) Routing the second thickness of masonite

11 (right) Completed Master Template

Routing Process for Pickups and Neck Pocket

Place the Master Template onto the body so that the centerlines match. Trace outline of each cavity onto body to double check placement and alignments (Fig 12). Secure the Master Template to the body with double-sided carpet tape, screws (providing they are put in areas outside the guitar outline and are recessed), or clamps.

The neck pocket will be $\frac{11}{16}$ in deep. Four or five passes of the router are necessary to reach this depth. Plan accordingly and remove only a little wood at a time.

The cavities for the pickups will be $\frac{7}{8}$ in deep. (If you use a higher bridge, this depth will be less.) The feet of the pickups

12 Tracing the outlines of the cavities on the body will allow you to check their placement, and be sure that nothing slips during the routing process

13 Routing the cavities

require an additional cut to a depth of 1 1/8 in (*see* Pickup Cavities Pattern, p 26). These cavities will be deep enough for all available Humbucker models.

Proceed, step by step, removing only a small amount of wood at a time (Fig 13). Chisel and sand all the recesses uniform.

Cutting and Shaping Body

14 Bandsawing the body shape

15 The body completely cut out

Cut out the body shape using a band saw with a sharp, medium-fine set 1/4 in blade (Fig 14). A quality jigsaw can also be used. Test jigsaw to insure it will cut a curve in a thick piece of wood without the blade angling. Careful cutting will lessen the filing, sanding, and scraping later. Take your time and always cut outside the pencil line (Fig 15).

Smooth all rough areas with files, sandpaper, and scrapers (p 10). Use adhesive sandpaper on sanding blocks of various contours to smooth tight curves. Stick sandpaper to a flexible eraser for fine contouring. Rough sand the sides with an electric spindle sander if you have one. Otherwise, proceed methodically around the entire periphery. Do not file or sand sides so much that they fall out of square with the face.

Expect to spend some time, perhaps several sessions, gradually working out imperfections. It is important to establish the exact final shape or outline of the body at this stage but not necessary to sand out all the scratches.

Round all the edges of the body with a quarter-round router bit (Fig 17, 18). To keep the router blade bearing from burning hard-to-remove marks in the sides, wrap masking tape around the sides where the bearing will ride.

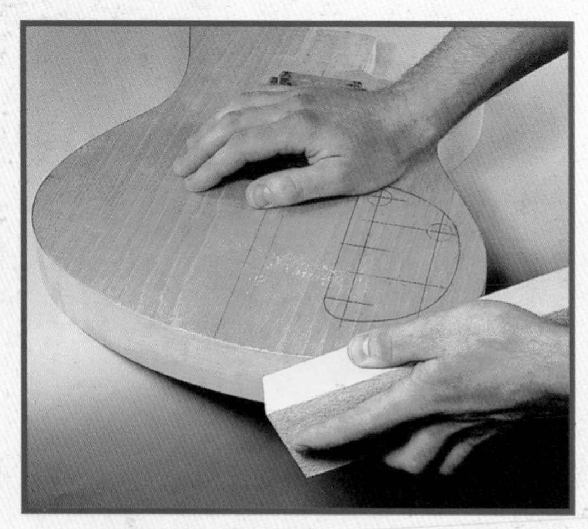

16 Sanding the sides to final shape

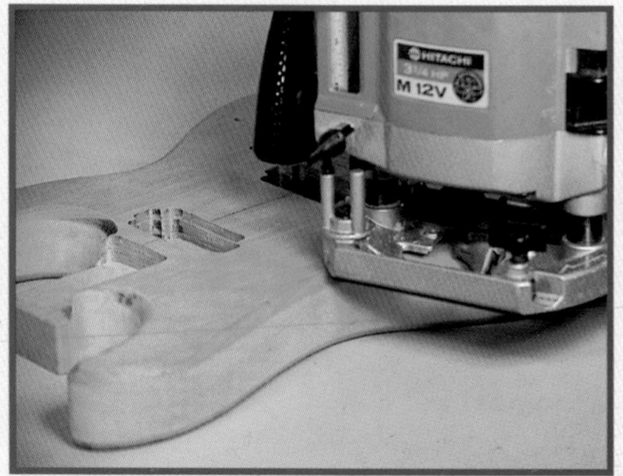

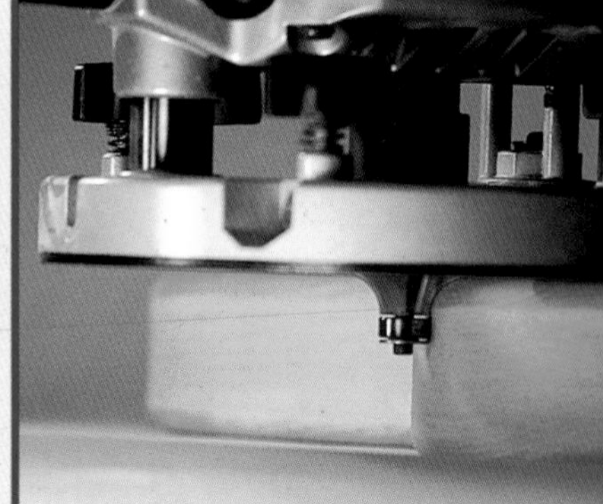

17, 18 Rounding the body

Routing the Electronics Compartment

19, 20 Plotting the electronic components

It is now time to place the knobs and switch that will control the electronics. Carefully position the control knobs in a practical and ergonomic (Fig 19, 20) arrangement. *See* Electronics in the Appendix, p 77, regarding their placement.

On the face of the body, measure and mark the exact point of each control knob and switch (Fig 21). Be sure that each corresponding internal component has enough space (especially the output jack with the cord plugged in) (Fig 22).

On the front of the body draw the outline of the electronics compartment and its cover to make sure they encompass all the internal components. Remember that the actual compartment is smaller than the cover that will eventually enclose the compartment. The cover rests on a ledge that surrounds the compartment cavity. If the ledge is less than 3/8 in wide, make accommodation for four small screws that hold the compartment cover in place by widening the ledge at the screw placements. Be sure these don't interfere with internal components. Make a pattern for the cover using tracing paper and transfer to the back. Double check all alignments.

21 Marking out the components positions

22 Test-fitting the internal components

Drill holes for the stems of each component (Fig 23). Drill these holes completely through the body to help place the compartment cover and monitor the depth of the compartment as you rout it.

Rather than having to make two templates for the electronics compartment (one for the cavity, one for the compartment cover), carefully freehand the cavity with the router leaving a margin for the ledge on which the cover will rest. If you are nervous to rout freehand, make a separate template for each step. Rout the compartment to a depth that leaves 3/16 in to 1/4 in of wood, as seen in the holes drilled for the electronics.

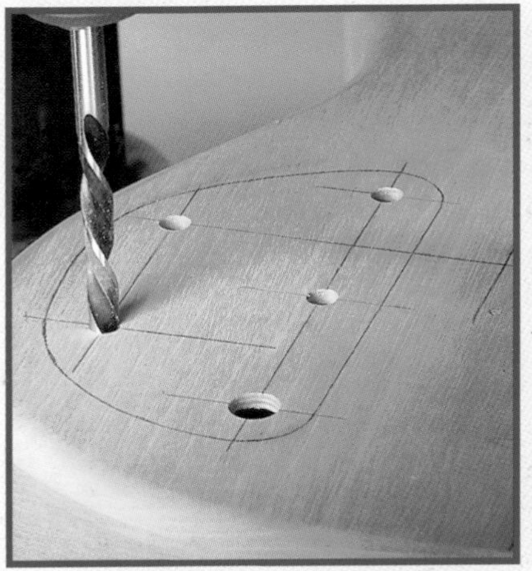

23 Pre-drilling electronics holes

24 Routing the electronics compartment cover recess

Make a masonite template (as you did for the neck pocket and pickup cavities) for routing the recess for the electronics compartment cover (*see* pattern, p 30). This template is crucial in making a recess with neat edges and will also be used in tracing the outline of the cover itself. Carefully put the template in place with double-sided carpet tape and rout the cover ledge to the depth that matches the thickness of the cover material (Fig 24). *See* photographs for finished electronics compartment (Fig 25, 26).

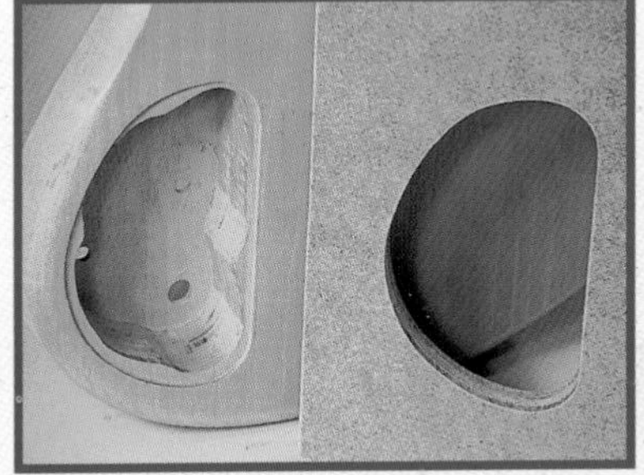

25 Routed electronics compartment and template

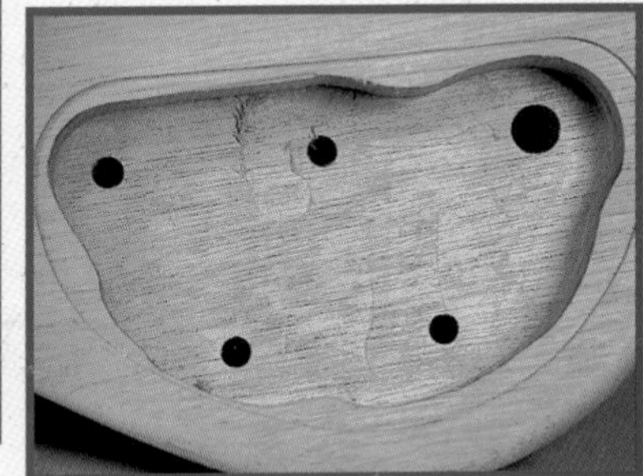

26 Electronics cavity interior (right)

27 *Placing and squaring the bridge*

28 *Screwing the bridge to the body*

Bridge Placement

You may choose to delay placing the bridge until the neck is mounted on the body in order to insure proper alignment. The bridge is mounted on the centerline of the body, oriented with the two outside string saddles equidistant from the centerline, (Fig 27).

Place the bridge so that the end of the scale length (25½ in from the nut), called the bridge point, is located exactly at the spot on the bridge where the saddles are adjusted to their fullest extension toward the neck. This will allow the best range of adjustment for intonation.

Once you have accurately determined the bridge location, carefully mark the points for the bridge mounting screws by drawing a circle inside each mounting hole and marking the centerpoints with a scratch awl. Pre-drill the screw holes to the full depth of the screw length, with a bit that is just smaller than the threads of the mounting screws.

Temporarily mount the bridge to use as a guide for drilling the string holes (Fig 28). Choose a drill bit just under the size of the string holes in the bridge plate. The string holes in the body must be drilled accurately to insure they are centered under the holes in the bridge plate. If the bridge overlaps these holes at all, the string will catch when being pushed through from the back. This is especially problematic when reusing a string that has been on a guitar before and no longer has a straight end.

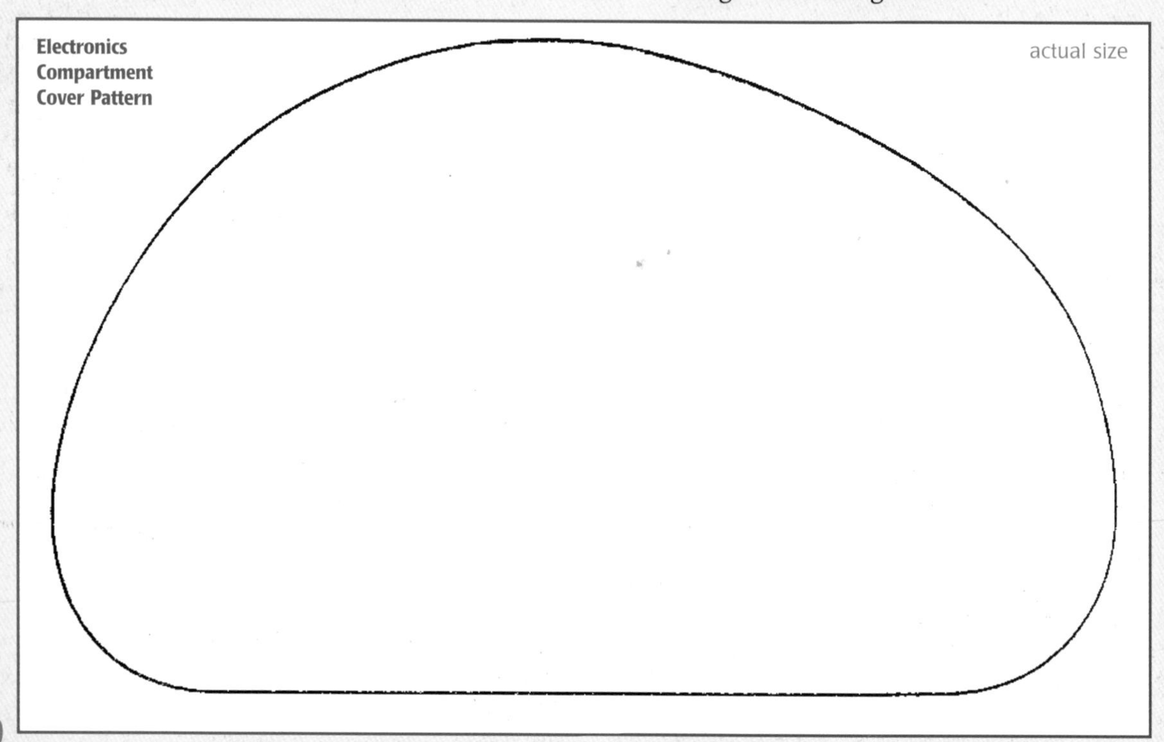

With the bridge mounted to the body, place the appropriate bit into the drill press chuck and align the body so that the first string hole is centered under the bit. With the drill press OFF, and unplugged for safety, hand-turn the drill chuck while gently lowering the bit into the hole, until the bit has just started to break the surface (Fig 29). Repeat this procedure for all six holes, being very careful not to chip the plating on the sides of the bridge holes. Remove the bridge and complete the holes, drilling them fully through the body (Fig 30). Drill slowly, clearing chips often to keep the bit from wandering.

On the back of the body, drill the six 5/16 in holes for the string ferrules (for our guitar, others require 3/8 in holes). Drill them just deep enough for the ferrule caps to sit flush to the body. Each ferrule should be centered exactly on its string hole for easy stringing. When completed, the ferrules sit very close together (Fig 31) and any inaccuracies in their placement are quite apparent. If you aren't totally confident in your drill press technique, you may make a template for these holes.

29 Marking string holes using drill press

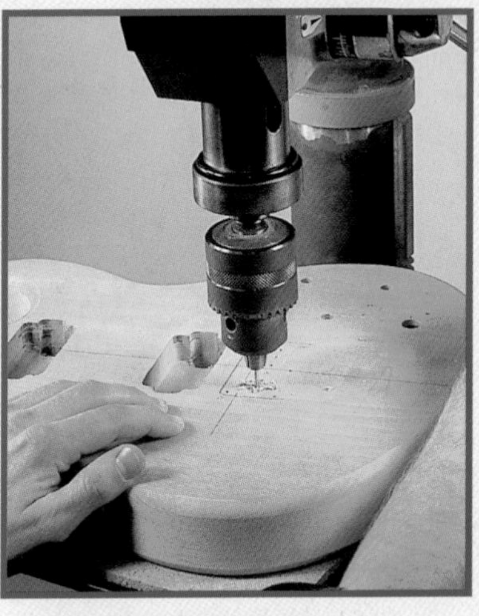

30 Drilling string holes

31 String ferrules

TEMPLATE Clamp a straightedge to the drill press table, a few inches to one side of the chuck (with the 5/16 in drill bit in it), to use as a fence. Using double-sided carpet tape, mount the bridge plate, with saddles removed, onto the straightedge, several inches over from the chuck. Align the bridge plate so that its string holes are parallel to the edge of the straightedge (Fig 32). Choose a small piece of masonite with at least one straight side for the jig. Place the straight side of the masonite against the straightedge on the drill press. Tape a clear plastic drafter's triangle to the masonite so that it rides above the bridge. Align this plastic indicator to the first string hole in the bridge plate. Clamp the masonite in place, making sure that it is snugly pressed to the straightedge, and drill a hole in it. Unclamp the masonite, move it along the straightedge until the indicator aligns with the next hole in the bridge plate, reclamp the masonite, and drill the next hole. Continue until all six holes are drilled.

32 Making a jig for aligning ferrule holes

Mount the completed template to the back of the guitar body with double-sided tape, centered over the six string holes. Place the body onto the drill press table with the bit centered in the first hole. Gently turning the drill chuck backward will help align the body precisely without damaging the masonite. Clamp the body to the table. Recheck alignment and drill the hole (Fig 33). Repeat for all the holes, using the drill press depth-stop to keep each hole at the optimum depth for easy stringing.

Once the ferrule holes are complete, slightly flare the string holes where they meet the ferrule holes using a small file. This will ensure easy passage of the string. Test-fit the ferrules (Fig 34).

33 Drilling ferrule holes using template

34 Test-fitting the ferrule holes

35 Determining the heel shape

Neck Screw, Ferrule Holes, and Truss Rod Nut Channel

36 Our body with uncarved heel, and a finished body. Ferrule holes are drilled when heel is still square, to position them evenly. Individual depths match heel contour.

Determine the shape of the heel chamfer and draw a guideline on the sides of the heel area (Fig 35). Do not remove too much wood around this area. A strong neck-body joint is important to the tone of the instrument (Fig 36).

Once the chamfer guideline is drawn, use it to mark the appropriate depth of each ferrule hole. Set the depth-stop on the drill press accordingly (Fig 37). Drill each ferrule hole with a ⅝ in Forstner bit, to the predetermined depths (Fig 38, 39). With a 5/32 in bit, drill a hole for each neck screw in the center of each ferrule hole, through to the neck pocket (Fig 40). Rout or chisel a small channel for the truss rod adjustment nut (Fig 41). If you wish, this may be done later, once the neck is ready to be fitted to the body.

37 Setting drill press depth stop

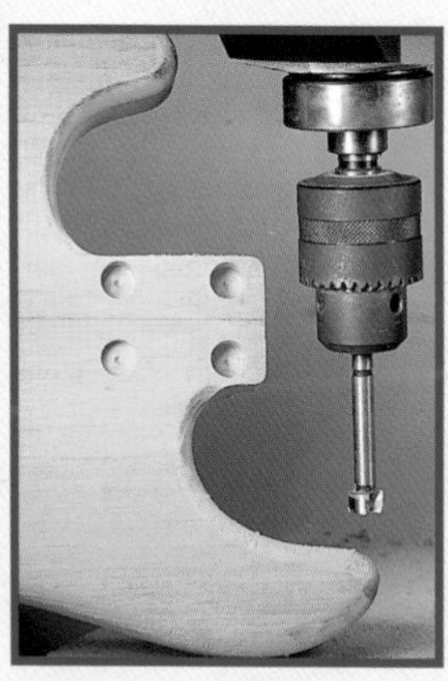

38 Drilling ferrule holes

39 Finished ferrule holes, with varied depths

40 Drilling neck screw holes

41 Truss rod nut channel

42 Marking the heel chamfer

Carving the Body Contours

Heel chamfer (Fig 42, 43, 44), back contour (Fig 45, 46, 47), and arm bevel (Fig 48) may now be carved using spokeshaves, drawknives, scrapers, and sanding blocks.

43, 44 Carving the heel chamfer

Test-fit each area for maximum comfort and playability (Fig 49). Final adjustments may be made once the instrument is assembled and test-strung before finishing.

45 Marking the back contour

46 Carving the back contour with a spokeshave

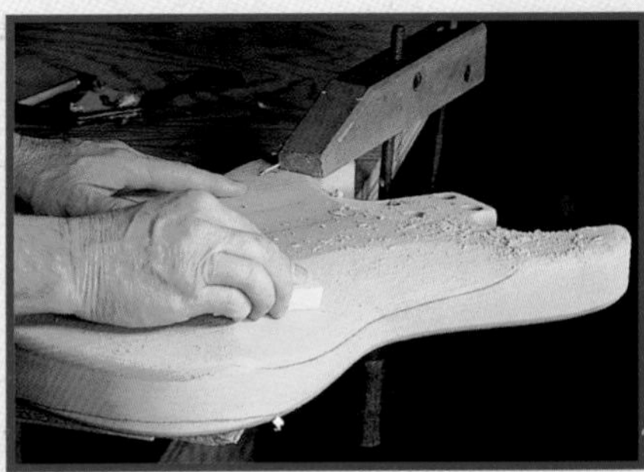

47 Sanding the back contour smooth with an eraser as a sanding block. Flex the eraser slightly for concave curves.

48 Carving the arm bevel

49 Testing the contours in playing position

Neck Pickup Wiring Holes

Drill four holes in the body for the electric wiring: (1) a hole into the electronics compartment for the output jack, (2, 3) from the electronics compartment into the pickup cavities, and (4) one from underneath the bridge to the electronics compartment for a ground wire.

The output jack hole passes straight through the side of the body at the lower bout. Drill the output jack hole with a 7/8 in bit (or one that suits cover). A Forstner bit is best for this job (Fig 50). Be careful not to chip the edges of the holes since the electrosocket jack mount cover has very little overlap.

Drill the hole connecting the electronics compartment and the neck pickup cavity with a 12 in long, 1/4 in bit (Fig 51). The bit passes through the output jack hole to keep it parallel to the top of the body. The hole should intersect the neck pickup cavity in the corner closest to the electronics compartment. Locate this point on the back of the body and draw a 1/4 in circle around it.

On the back of the body above the output jack hole, mark two lines representing its outside edges. Align a straightedge between one side of the 1/4 in circle and the output jack hole and draw a line. Repeat on the other side of the 1/4 in circle. These two lines represent the path of the bit. This hole is drilled 7/8 in from the top of the body to intersect the bottom of the neck pickup cavity. Our body is 1 3/4 in thick, and the hole is 7/8 in from the back of the instrument. Plot a point on the electronics compartment wall between the two drawn lines, 7/8 in in from the back. Draw crosshairs at this point and pre-punch it using an awl.

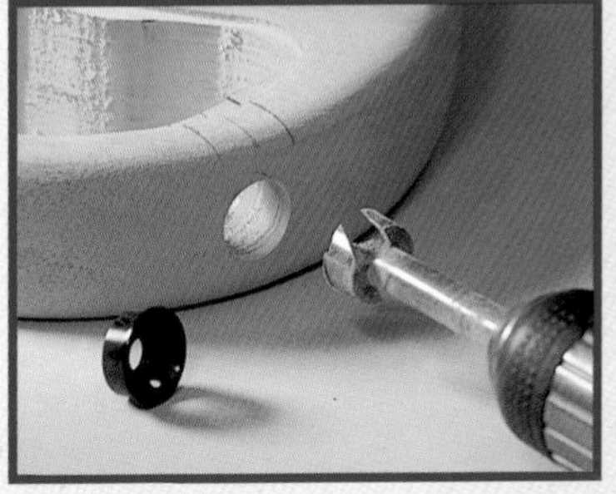

50 Output jack hole and Forstner bit

51 (right) Setting up to drill the neck pickup wiring hole. The circle around the entry point will let you see if the bit drifts off center as it starts the hole

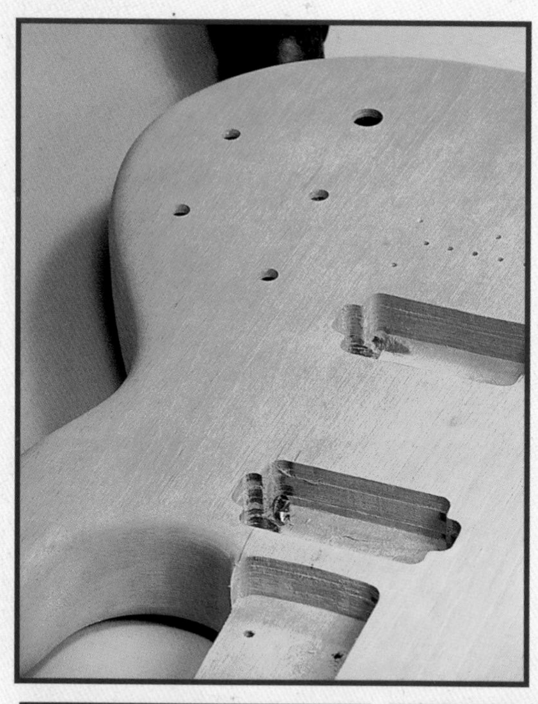

52 The bit emerging into the pickup cavity

Make a drill guide for the output jack hole to help control the long bit by covering the hole with thick tape (metal shielding tape works well) and cutting a ¼ in hole ⅞ in from the back (Fig 51).

Insert the drill bit through the hole in the tape and start it in the pre-punched hole. Be especially careful beginning the hole if the compartment wall is at more than a slight angle to the trajectory of the drill bit. Just after the bit breaks the surface, check the crosshairs. If the bit has been deflected off center, compensate with the same deflection at the taped output jack hole.

Once the hole is begun, turn the body over to see when the bit emerges into the pickup cavity (Fig 52). Drill slowly and clear the bit of chips frequently so the drill bit will come out at the right place.

Drill another connecting hole from the bridge pickup cavity to the electronics compartment. Use the 12 in long bit, maintaining as low an angle as possible without hitting the opposite edge of the pickup cavity (Fig 53). This hole is about 2 in long. Drill slowly as the drill breaks into the electronics compartment to minimize chipping.

The last hole is drilled from beneath the bridge into the electronics compartment, this time using a 12 in long, ⅛ in bit. The hole is located between the string holes and the neck-side edge of the bridge, towards the electronics compartment (at left). Since the hole is at an extreme angle, there is a danger of the drill bit skipping over the face when attempting to start the hole. Use a vertical ¼ in pilot hole ⅛ in deep to help prevent this.

53 Drilling the bridge pickup wiring hole

54 Drilling the ground wire hole

Neck and Headstock

Wood Preparation

Visit your local hardwood dealer to select wood for the guitar neck or find a mail order company that carries specialty woods. Choose the wood carefully (*see* Appendix: Wood and Tone, p 89). Make a one-piece neck with a separate fingerboard. This produces excellent results with minimum difficulty. We use maple for our guitar neck.

Draw an actual-size side view and top view of the neck on paper or posterboard to use as templates. The neck blank should have a final thickness of 1 in. Depending on the headstock design, the overall neck length is between 26 in and 27 in. Leave an extra 5 in for a working margin for a total stock length of 32 in. A 4 in margin should be left at the body end of the neck blank to help support the router when eventually routing the truss rod slot. Cut the neck blank to length. The width of the neck blank should accommodate the width of the headstock design.

Note Since retailers measure wood in its rough-sawn state, thickness is expressed in quarters of an inch, i.e. 6/4 in equals 1½ in. This is a nominal thickness; actual is usually less. For 1 in thickness, you may have to buy a 5/4 in piece.

Plane the board to a 1 in thickness making sure the fingerboard side is perfectly flat. Joint the bass side edge of the blank. Place the neck pattern on the neck blank to check how the neck design relates to the grain configuration.

Draw a centerline up the neck blank parallel to the jointed edge of the board. This will help in centering the neck properly and will act as a guide in routing the channel for the truss rod.

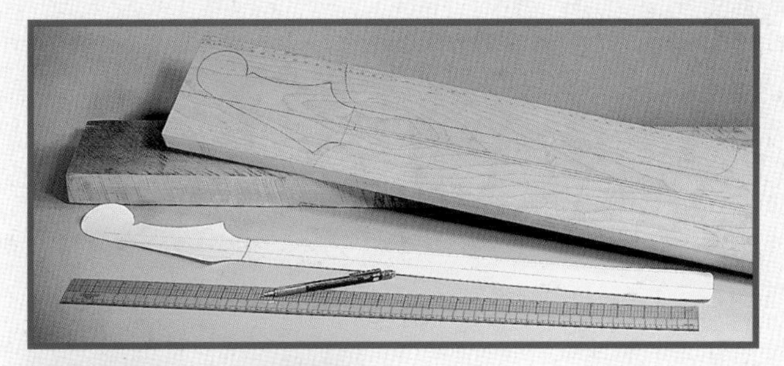

1 (above) Transferring neck outline to wood

2 Band saw either side of neck

The Neck

Using the neck template, transfer the neck design to the board itself (Fig 1).

Using the band saw, remove wood from either side of the neck between the nut to about 3 in from the end of the neck (Fig 2). The two ends of the neck are left full width for a later step in the process.

Leave a $^{3}/_{16}$ in working margin on either side of the neck outline (Fig 3).

3 Band saw neck outline

Use a drawknife and spokeshave to rough-carve the back of the neck, leaving $^{1}/_{8}$ in to $^{3}/_{16}$ in extra for later removal (Fig 4, 5).

Note Since most hardwoods will move slightly after cutting, latent tension in the wood will be immediately released at this point. A flat-sawn piece of maple will usually bow slightly back from the fingerboard side as the wood is removed from the back The release of internal tension will cause some of this movement immediately (Fig 6). Over a period of time, moisture equalization in the wood may cause a little more movement. Wait a few days for the neck to settle in. Many guitar companies wait months after rough-cutting necks before proceeding.

After carving the neck, lay a ruler or other straightedge along the face of the blank to check for warpage (Fig 7).

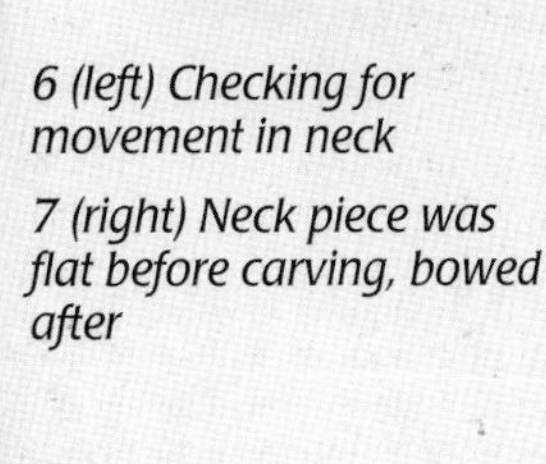

4 Rough-carving neck with drawknife

5 (above right) Rough-carving neck with spokeshave

6 (left) Checking for movement in neck

7 (right) Neck piece was flat before carving, bowed after

8 (right) Laying out truss rod position

9 (lower left) Channel is widened slightly at adjustment end

10 (lower right) Router guide in place on neck

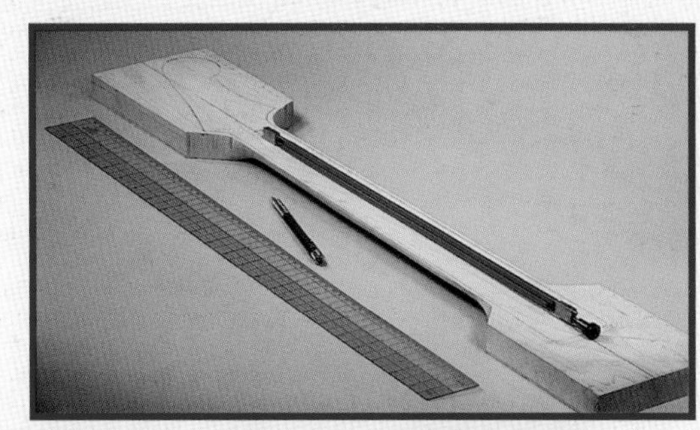

Check the neck periodically for movement. Once it has appeared to stabilize, resurface the top if necessary to insure that it is perfectly flat. A well-adjusted jointer or long sanding board are useful for this process.

Once it is flat, redraw the centerline and mark the length of the truss rod and truss rod channel on the wood (Fig 8).

Our truss rod requires a channel $\frac{7}{32}$ in wide and $\frac{7}{16}$ in deep with a small widening of the channel at the body end of the neck blank for the truss rod adjusting wheel (Fig 9).

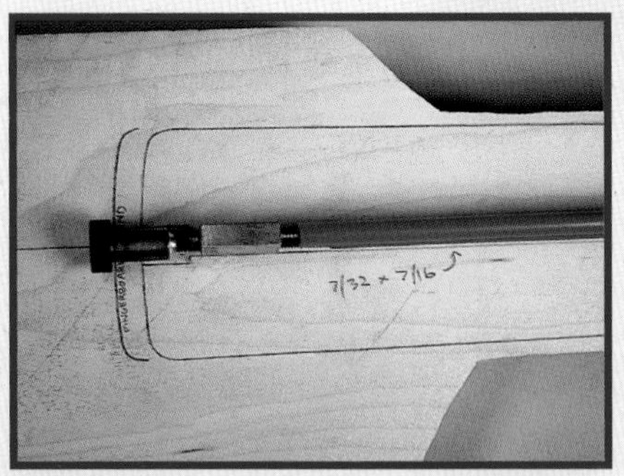

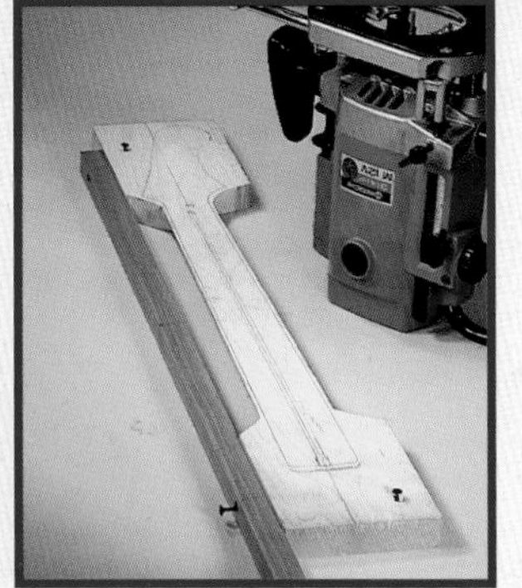

Set up a strip of wood as a fence exactly parallel to the centerline of the neck (Fig 10). The router edge-guide moves along this fence to insure a straight line. Screw the fence to the neck blank at a contact point outside the neck outline (Fig 11). The fence piece must have two straight parallel sides and line up perfectly with the neck centerline when in place. Double check and adjust with shims if necessary.

Secure the neck to the workbench. For best router clearance, rather than clamping the neck to the bench, screw the neck blank and router guide to a board that is then clamped to the bench (or use a cabinet maker's bench).

11 (left) Screws used to mount router guide and workpiece

12 (below left) routing the truss rod channel

13 (below right) Routing the truss rod channel, end view

Using a $\frac{3}{16}$ in bit, make several passes to achieve the final depth and width of the truss rod channel. Since the $\frac{3}{16}$ in bit doesn't match the width of the truss rod, set the router guide to align the bit to one side of the channel. Rout to depth, making several passes. Reset the guide to align with the other side of the channel. Rout (Fig 12, 13).

Cut the excess wood from the sides and end of the neck heel (Fig 14). Leave $\frac{1}{8}$ in working margin on the sides. Cut the back of the neck heel and block sand to $\frac{3}{4}$ in thick, parallel to the top of the neck (Fig 15). Rough-sand the end of the neck (but not the sides) so that the heel begins to conform to the neck pocket in the body. Final fitting will come later (Fig 16). Test-fit the truss rod in its channel. We widened the channel slightly around the adjustment wheel for proper clearance (Fig 17).

14 (bottom left) Trimming excess wood around heel

15 (bottom middle) Trimming back of heel

16 (right top) Shaping end of heel

17 (right bottom) Truss rod in place

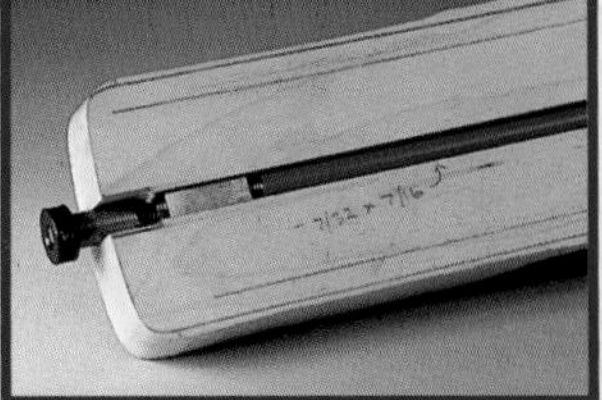

The Headstock

Draw a line where the nut will be installed (*see* Appendix Headstock Design, p 63). Segment it for six strings at the nut width. Draw lines representing the outside strings as they pass through the nut and onto the headstock. These will help determine the best placement of the tuners. When placing tuners, take into account the diameter of the tuner posts, drawn at right. Tuner holes should be centered to one side of each string line, half the width of the tuner posts (*see* drawing at right).

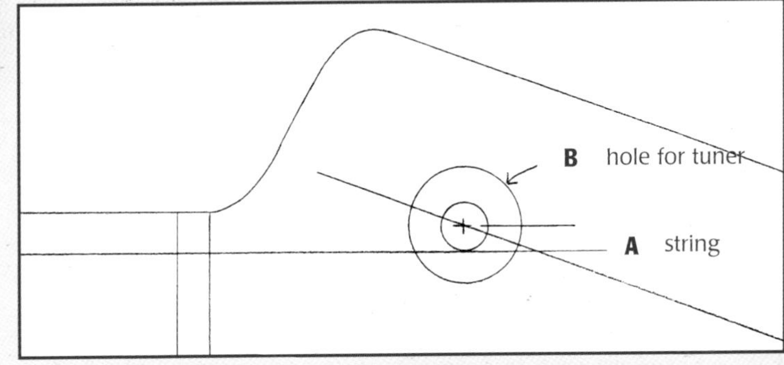

Center points of tuner holes are offset from string line by the radius of tuner string post, usually $\frac{3}{32}$ in

On six-on-a-side headstocks, tuners are usually placed $\frac{15}{16}$ in to 1 in apart, depending on the tuner style you use. The measurement from the center of the first tuner post to the fret side of the nut is usually around $1\frac{3}{4}$ in (Fig 18).

18 Locating tuners

19 Cutting straight side for tuner drilling jig

Mark the exact placement of all six tuners and drill their holes on a drill press.

Note Any misalignment of these holes will show. If you're not comfortable freehanding them, use the following procedure. Draw a line parallel to the centerline of the tuner posts just outside the actual outline of the headstock. This will act as a guide for drilling the tuner holes on the drill press. Cut along this line (Fig 19), then make any necessary adjustments with a file or sanding block to make sure it is parallel to the tuner line (Fig 20).

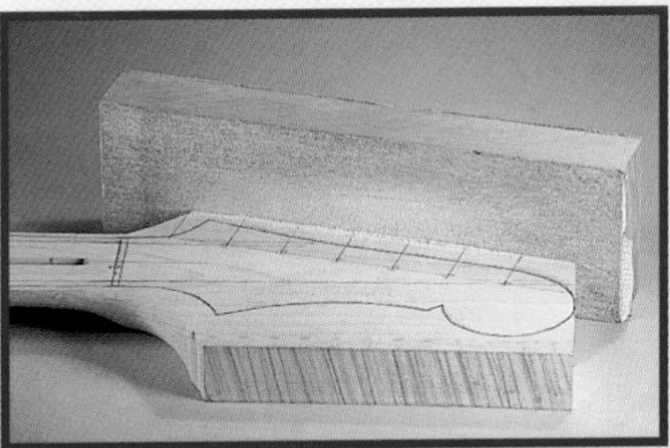

20 Sanding flat

21 Aligning headstock to marked fence

With a square, draw lines from each tuner centerpoint to the edge, perpendicular to the tuner line (Fig 21). Clamp the headstock to the drill press table with the drill bit positioned over the first hole. Clamp a straight piece of wood to the table to act as a guide fence for drilling. Make a mark on the fence at the point where the perpendicular line from the first tuner intersects it (Fig 21). This mark will align each tuner in turn. Using the drill bit that matches the tuners, carefully drill all the holes (Fig 22).

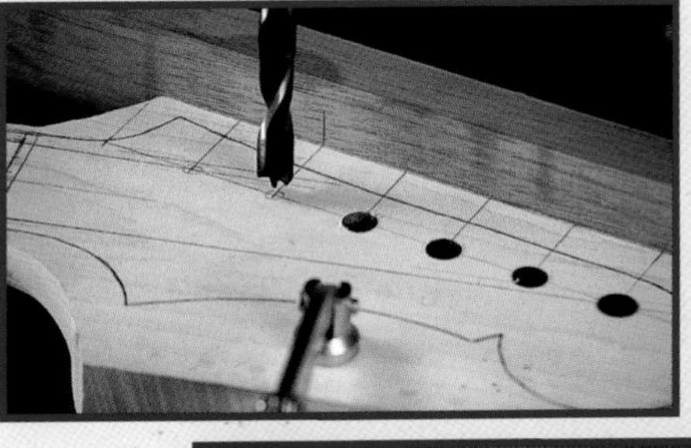

Prepare to remove $\frac{1}{4}$ in thickness of wood from the face of the headstock by marking on the side of the headstock (Fig 23). Mark the back of the headstock leaving room for a volute. The final thickness of the peghead is $\frac{9}{16}$ in. Use the band saw to remove excess wood from the peghead but do not cut the front and back pieces completely off. This leaves the pattern intact making it easier to cut the outlined shape of the peghead (Fig 24).

Band saw the outside shape of the headstock, removing all extraneous wood (Fig 25, p 38). Once the outline has

22 (upper left) Drilling tuner holes

23 (above) Marking headstock thickness

24 (left) Cuts for headstock thickness

25 Band saw headstock shape

26 Trimming excess

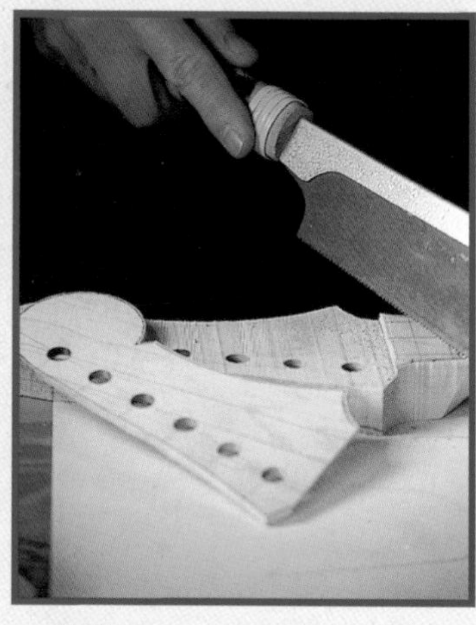

27 Excess trimmed

been cut, the top and back parts can be cut off with a handsaw (Fig 26, 27).

File and sand to refine surfaces and curves (Fig 28, 29). Do not sand the area just behind the nut on the fingerboard face of the neck. Leave a ⅝ in margin between the back of the nut and the beginning of the headstock ledge (Fig 30). This area will be finished after the fingerboard is attached.

File and sand the volute on the back of neck/headstock juncture (Fig 31, 32). The volute adds an ornamental touch and helps strengthen an otherwise vulnerable part of the instrument.

28 Shaping headstock

29 Shaping around volute with oscillating spindle sander

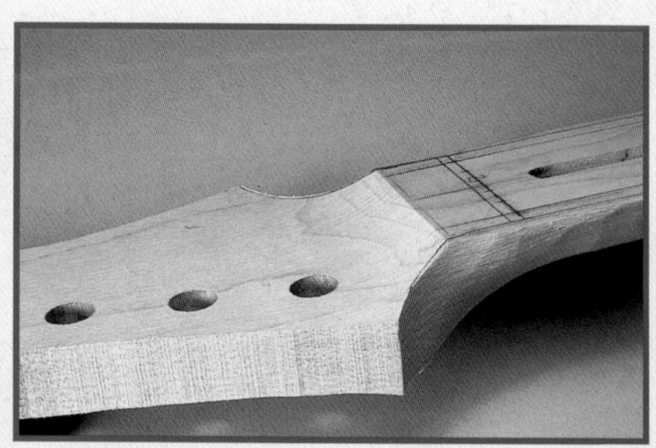

30 Pre-trimming around headstock-fingerboard interface

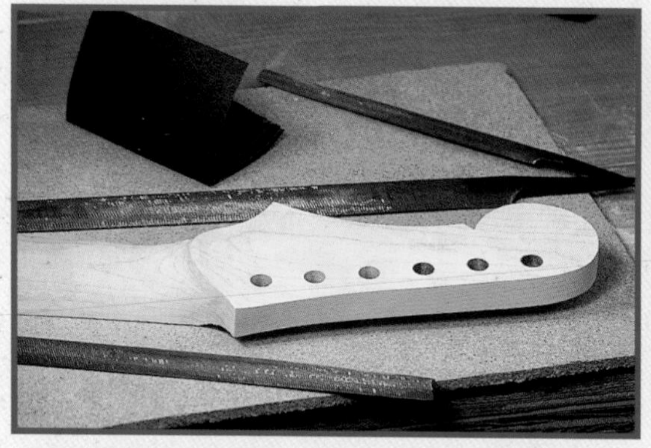

31 Shaped headstock

32 Contoured volute

The Fingerboard

1 Fretboards in various stages of construction

Preparation

The fingerboard, also called the fretboard (Fig 1), is a length of wood, fretted chromatically, and glued to the face of the neck. Rosewood, ebony, and maple are hard, resist wear and tear and are good woods for fingerboards. The advantage of these materials is that they are hard. Rosewood and ebony are fairly dark in color and look less soiled over time. Ebony, with its black color and close grain, makes a great background for mother-of-pearl inlays. Rosewood has beautiful dark, red and black grain patterns. Maple is inexpensive, easy to find, and has good tonal qualities. Fender pioneered the one-piece maple neck without a separate fingerboard where frets are mounted directly into the neck and the truss rod is installed from the back of the neck. As a less traditional choice, many of the harder, more flamboyant exotic woods such as wenge, zircote, goncalo alves, and cocobolo are also suitable for fingerboards. Our fingerboard is ebony and contrasts nicely with the mahogany body. Remember that wood choice affects the sound of the instrument (see Appendix: Wood and Tone, p 89).

Fingerboard woods are available from most wood specialty stores or through a guitar supply company. Purchase wood as raw stock from a wood store or as milled-to-size blanks from guitar suppliers. Specialty suppliers also sell blanks already slotted and arched.

You will need a square, fret saw, sharp pencil, and a small block of wood as a sawing guide. Specialty saws are available that exactly match the fret tang, the part of the fret which fits into the slot (Fig 2). The most common fret slot width is .024 in. Fret tangs can vary, however. Repair shops sometimes use thinner or wider fret tangs to fix a warp in a neck. Extra pressure in the fret slot forces the neck to flex back, a technique sometimes used to straighten older guitar necks that don't have truss rods. Conversely, narrower fret tangs may allow a back-bowed neck to straighten under string tension.

Guitar fret rules and other template devices are available for plotting common scale lengths. If you choose to use a nonstandard scale length, you can derive fret placements mathematically using the rule of eighteen. Divide the scale length by 17.817 to find the distance from the nut to the 1st fret. Subtract this distance from the whole, then divide the remaining distance by 17.817 again for the next fret and for each remaining fret placement. The 12th fret (one octave above the open string) should lie halfway between nut and bridge. And the 5th fret lies halfway between the nut and twelfth fret. Computer software is also available that will figure any scale length.

2 Fret-slotting tools

3 Marking frets

4 Sawing fret slots with fence

Fret	Distance
1	1.4312
2	2.7821
3	4.0572
4	5.2606
5	6.3966
6	7.4688
7	8.4808
8	9.4360
9	10.3376
10	11.1886
11	11.9918
12	12.7500
13	13.4656
14	14.1411
15	14.7786
16	15.3803
17	15.9483
18	16.4844
19	16.9904
20	17.4680
21	17.9188
22	18.3443
23	18.7459
24	19.1250
25	19.4828
26	19.8205
27	20.1393
28	20.4402
29	20.7242
30	20.9922
31	21.2452
32	21.4840
33	21.7094
34	21.9221
35	22.1230
36	22.3125

Fret distance from nut

Fret placements for a 25½ in scale length

Cutting Fret Slots

Make sure fingerboard wood is square and milled to specification: ¼ in thick, 2⅜ in wide, and 20 in long. Success in placing fret slots is determined by good preparation. One edge of the fingerboard needs to be perfectly straight since fret slots will be marked with a square placed against it. Our guitar uses a fingerboard that extends slightly beyond the heel end of the neck, allowing placement of one extra fret to provide a high D in standard tuning. Mill and prepare the fingerboard for fret slotting.

Mark the position of the nut. The nut slot is ⅛ in wide. Cut along the lines that define the nut width to a depth of 5/32 in. Carefully remove the remaining wood with a small chisel or file.

Mark the placement of each fret using an accurate square (Fig 3). The fretting measurements provided are based on the Fender 25½ in scale length. Practice making fret slots on scrap wood, of the same type as the fingerboard, until you feel confident enough to kerf the actual fingerboard.

Clamp a guide block carefully at the fret position. Hold the saw flat against the guide block and saw to depth (Fig 4). The depth of each slot should be slightly deeper (approximately .025 in) than the fret tang. Draw a pencil line on the saw at the desired depth as a general reference, if you wish.

Note If you can cut fret slots using a table saw or radial arm saw, specialty circular fretting blades designed to fit these machines are available from suppliers of guitar tools. Fret-slotting templates are also sold for use in this operation.

Fingerboard Inlays

After sawing all the fret slots, plot the placement of the inlay material. Dots of mother-of-pearl or abalone shell are the usual standard and can be bought ready-made from guitar supply shops in a variety of sizes, as shown. They are classic and by far the easiest to inlay for the novice since all that is needed is a matching drill bit. Custom shapes can also be purchased or you can cut your own shapes with a jeweler's saw. Consult specialty books about advanced inlay procedures.

Our guitar has medium-size mother-of-pearl dots, one dot each at the 3rd, 5th, 7th, 9th, 15th, 17th, 19th, and 21st frets, and two dots at the 12th and at the optional 24th fret (Fig 6).

Be sure to find a drill bit that precisely accommodates the

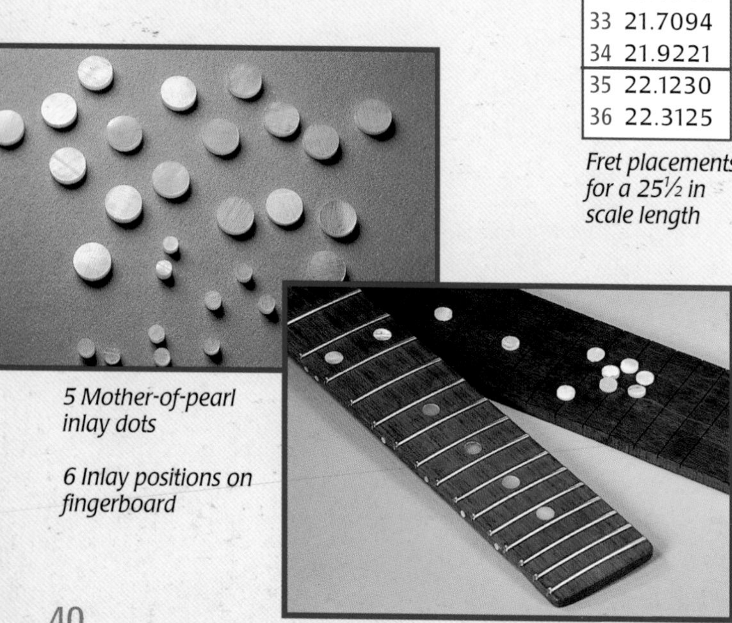
5 Mother-of-pearl inlay dots

6 Inlay positions on fingerboard

dot size. Experiment first on a scrap of fingerboard wood. Don't press the dot all the way in or it may be difficult to extract.

Draw a centerline on the fingerboard and mark the dot placements exactly between the appropriate frets. Double dots are offset from the centerline, often halfway between the centerline and edge of the fingerboard.

Set the depth of drilling on the drill press to accommodate the thickness of the dots. Proceed with drilling, being careful to line up the dots perfectly. We have made a drilling jig, as shown, to help to accurately guide the drilling process (Fig 7, 8, 9).

Glue the dots in place with white or yellow glue, epoxy, or one of the gap-filling cyanoacrylate (super) glues (Fig 10). If there are any gaps or chips around the inlay, mix the glue with some fingerboard sawdust to match the color.

Gluing Fingerboard to Neck

In preparation for gluing the fingerboard to the neck, trim and sand the end of the heel of the neck to its final dimension. Do not sand the sides yet. Trim the end of the fingerboard to its final shape. Remember that the fingerboard overlaps the end of the neck. The truss rod wheel should project just beyond the end of the fingerboard (Fig 11).

Temporarily clamp the fingerboard to the neck and make sure the truss rod slides in and out of its channel without jamming. This insures its easy removal and replacement in case it breaks, although this is unlikely with the truss rod we have chosen.

To maintain proper positioning while gluing the fingerboard to the neck, use small guide pins fashioned from shortened brads or other little pins or tacks. Nail two pins securely into the neck, one near each end, as shown (Fig 12).

Clip off the protruding end to about 3/32 in, or just enough to hold the fingerboard in place during the gluing process. Sharpen the end of each pin so they will penetrate the fingerboard when pressure is applied.

To insure even pressure over the entire fingerboard, use many clamps and a clamping block faced with cork to distribute pressure uniformly over entire gluing area(Fig 13). Check truss rod to ensure it doesn't get permanently glued in as you glue the fingerboard to the neck. Check that glue doesn't ooze into the truss rod channel and create an obstacle by making sure that the channel is cleared before clamping.

7 Aligning Inlay centering jig, testing on scrap wood

8 (upper right) Small section or ruler for centering between fret slots

9 A spacer (white stick) is used to drill for double dots at 12th fret

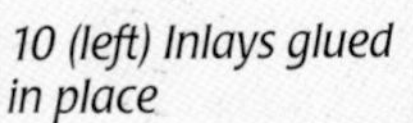

10 (left) Inlays glued in place

11 End of neck is sanded before fingerboard is attatched

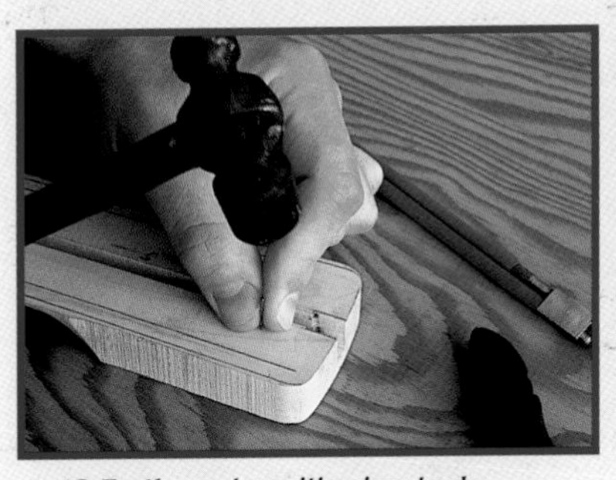

12 Fretboard positioning tacks

13 Gluing fingerboard: padded block keeps neck straight and pressure even

14 Trimming edges of fingerboard

15 Block-sanding rough neck shape

Trim excess wood from the sides of the fingerboard (Fig 14) and begin shaping and refining the neck/fingerboard combination to its final configuration. Keep back of neck flat by using sanding blocks (Fig 15).

Do not sand too much in the middle. Rounding the ends of the sanding blocks will help keep the neck flat all the way to the ends. Cardboard or paper templates of the preferred neck cross sections will help monitor your progress. Begin final sanding around the headstock (Fig 16).

16 Shaped fingerboard-headstock interface

Fingerboard Arching

The fingerboard now needs arching. Ours has an arc with a 12 in radius. Make a radius gauge with a compass, or purchase one, available in various radii, from guitar supply dealers (Fig 17). (*See* Fingerboard Arch p 17)

Place adhesive-back sandpaper on a flat block and begin sanding (Fig 18) to arch the fingerboard, as shown. Check progress with a radius gauge. Use a long straightedge along the length of the fingerboard to keep it perfectly flat. Start with 80 grit sandpaper and as you reach the final shape, use progressively finer grades of sandpaper. Alternatively, set up a simple jig with a radius sanding block that has been machined to the proper radius, available from guitar supply shops. A fence mounted parallel to the centerline of the fingerboard keeps the sanding block from wandering and accidently rounding the outside edges of the fingerboard too much, as shown (Fig 19).

17 Checking fingerboard radius

18 Sanding arch into fingerboard with full-length sanding block

19 Radiused sanding block with guide fence

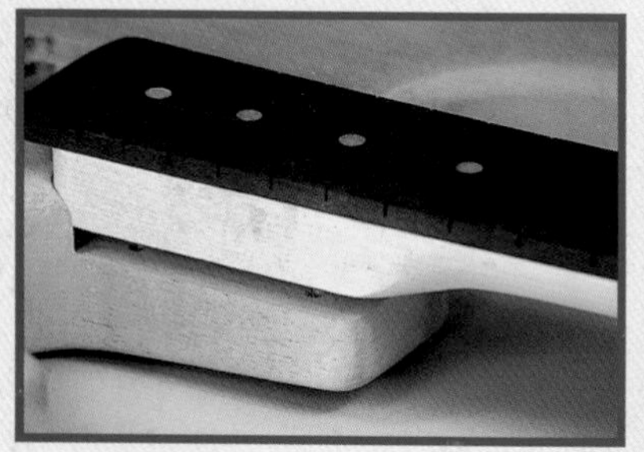

20 Fitting neck to body

Give final shape to the back of the neck. Use a contour template to help get the right curvature, but a good eye and feel are the best gauges. Try other guitars to get a sense of the range of neck shapes (*see* Neck Shape, p 17). Carefully fit the neck to the body.

21 Aligning neck to bridge

Use sanding block for neck sides and points where it contacts the neck pocket (Fig 21). Use a long straightedge to check the alignment between neck and body. Place the straightedge along the trajectory of an outside string, just in from the side of the fingerboard. Line this up with the outside bridge saddle (Fig 21). Repeat this process with the other outside string. Sand the neck at the heel area until the two outside strings are equidistant from the edges of the fingerboard.

Sand fingerboard to 400 grit sandpaper (taking care to not alter the arch or round the edges of the fingerboard). Polish with fine steel wool before the frets are installed.

Installing Frets

Fretwire comes in a variety of sizes for different instruments such as banjo, mandolin, and various acoustic and electric guitar types. It varies in width and height. Electric guitars and basses use a variety of sizes depending on players' preferences. Many modern guitarists prefer a larger jumbo fretwire for easier string bending and a fuller tone. Our choice is a medium fretwire traditionally used in Fender and Gibson guitars.

Using a fine triangular file, carefully dull the sharp edges of each fret slot with a few light strokes across the fingerboard. This eases fret entry, allows fret to seat properly, and helps prevent chipping when worn frets are removed for replacement. Fretwire is covered with a residue of machine oil left from the manufacturing process. The fretwire must be wiped clean. Use naphtha in a well-ventilated area.

Cut frets longer than the length of the slot on the fingerboard, as shown (Fig 22). Pre-curve frets to match the radius of the fingerboard by bending them gently by hand or use a special device, before they are cut into shorter pieces. Take care not to twist the fretwire. Carefully seat the ends of each fret in the slot.

Install frets by hammering into the slots with a minimum number of hammer blows. Use a small hammer or plastic-faced dead-blow hammer. Practice on a scrap of wood before attempting to install frets on the actual fingerboard.
Note An alternative to hammering frets is a system of pressing frets into their slots. Commercial varieties of a fret press include attachments for drill presses, stand-alone machines, and vise-grip systems. All of these work by using a caul that matches the fingerboard radius and holds the pre-curved fret while it is pressured evenly into the slot. Pressing the frets into their respective slots gives control over the process.

Our home-made fret press is shown at right. Carve two small curved pieces of hardwood or other durable material to a radius of 12 in, matching the radius of the fingerboard. Glue these to opposite ends of an 8 in long block, as shown (Fig 23). Position one piece over the fret to press it in, center the other over the fingerboard keeping the device parallel to the fingerboard. This keeps the fret from falling over and allows equal pressure over the full length of the fret as it is being pressed into place, as shown (Fig 24).

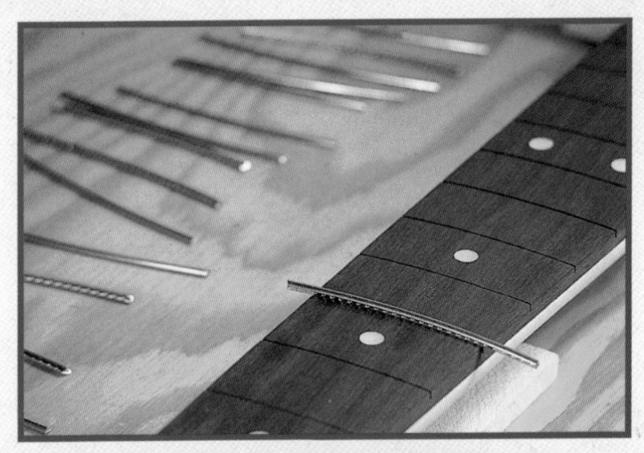

22 Frets trimmed to length for installation

23 Fret press. This one is made with milled phenolic blocks. Closer side presses fret, far side (with felt) rides on fingerboard

24 (left) Pressing frets

25 (above) Underside of neck must be supported directly below the fret. Here thin maple wedges are used, for easy height adjustment. Jorgensen clamp gives best control.

Use a Jorgensen clamp centered over the fret to exert more control over the distribution of pressure. Support the neck directly beneath the clamping point (Fig 25).

Match fret slots to fret tang size so they will press in easily. Be careful that the fret doesn't lean to one side as it is being pressed in. Do not over press. Clamps can exert a powerful amount of pressure and accidently indent the fret into the fingerboard.

A

Slot for
holding fret

Fret Press

Finishing Frets

Fret leveling and filing is crucial to the playability of your instrument. Clip frets as flush to the sides of the fingerboard as possible, being very careful not to chip the fingerboard. Use special clippers with a flat face to clip installed frets. Clip frets from sides to avoid crushing the fret tang. Squeeze the clipper handles evenly taking care not to pull the fret to one side or the other.

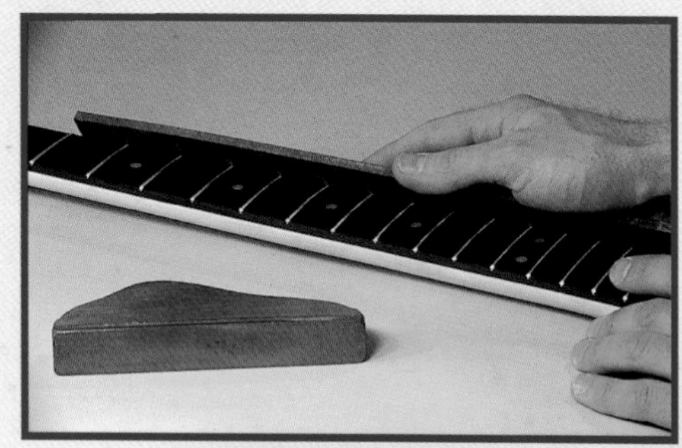

26 Beveling fret ends

Carefully file fret ends with a large mill file to bring them flush to the sides of the fingerboard, shown in diagram. Do not loosen frets. Bevel fret ends with a mill file, (Fig 26) Choose degree of angle shown in drawing below. Less angle leaves more playing area on the fret top; increased angle is more comfortable when sliding the playing hand up and down the neck. Be aware where the outside strings line up so the strings aren't inadvertently pulled off the ends of the frets while playing.

Fret end bevel positions

A

steep
bevel

B

shallow
bevel

C

rounded
bevel

Degree of Angle Options

27 Leveling frets

28 (right) Checking frets with straightedge

29 (below left) Leveled fret, taped off for recrowning

30 (below right) Recrowning fret with fret file

Adjust the truss rod if necessary until the tops of the frets are level. Level the tops of the frets. Use a fret/fingerboard leveler made from a fine sandpaper-covered flat length of wood or metal. (You may also use a long, perfectly flat mill file or a specialty fret file.) Leveler should be longer than the fretboard to level all the frets simultaneously. Holding it, as shown in Fig 27, prevents bending the neck while sanding as may happen when it is held on a bench. Check often with a straightedge as you file so as not to flatten them too much (Fig 28).

Place drafting tape (masking tape may leave a residue) on each side of every fret (narrower drafting tape is helpful for upper frets). Frets must be re-rounded where they have been filed flat (Fig 29). Use a specialty crowning file (available from guitar supply centers) (Fig 30), that matches curvature of chosen frets. Diamond-grit files, though expensive, are best. File just until the flat area left by the leveling file disappears. Over-filing will lower the fret in relation to the others.

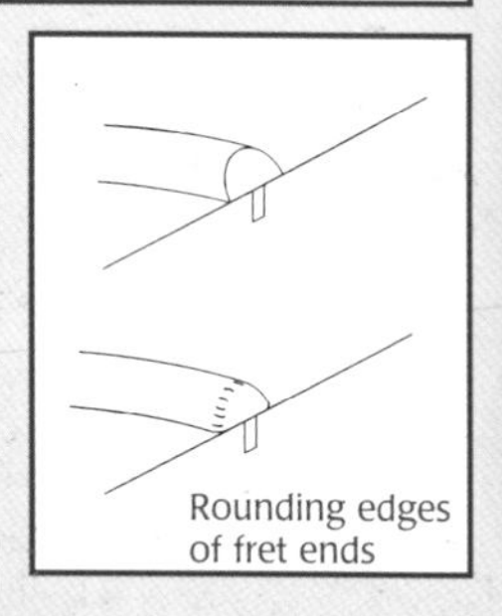

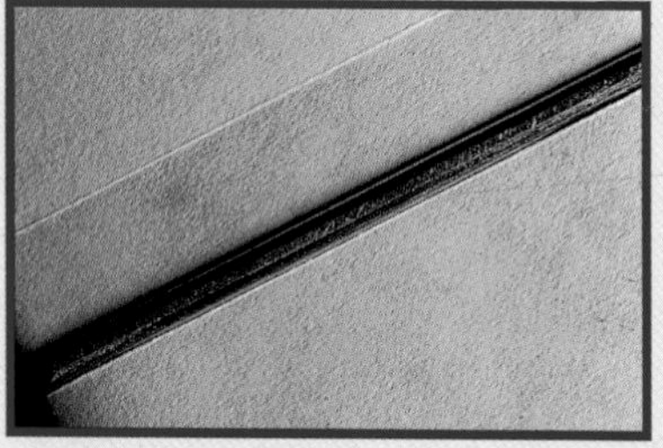

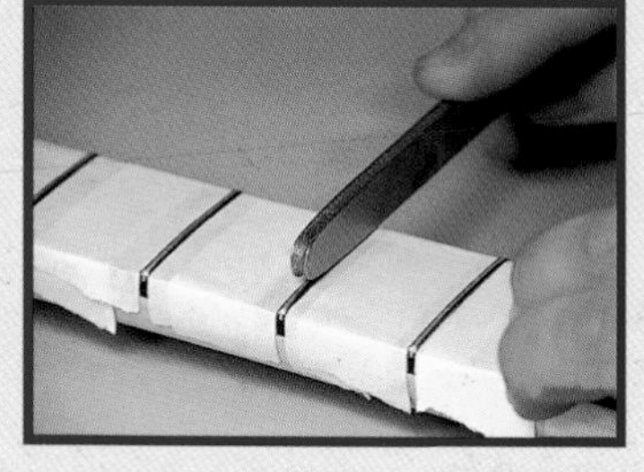

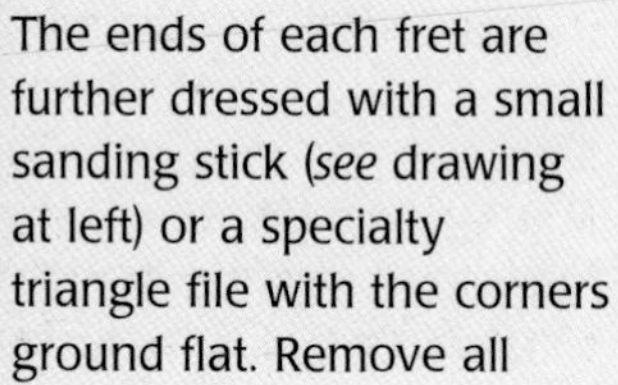

The ends of each fret are further dressed with a small sanding stick (*see* drawing at left) or a specialty triangle file with the corners ground flat. Remove all sharp edges. Slide your hand along the edges of the neck to find any sharp ends. Take care not to damage the fingerboard. Burnish frets with a light sanding with 600 grit sandpaper and a final buffing with fine steel wool.

31 Drilling for side inlays

Fingerboard Side Dots

Small inlay mother-of-pearl dots along the side of the fingerboard act as references to help the player find finger and chord positions. Their placements are identical to the inlays on the face of the fingerboard.

32 Side inlays in place

Find the exact center vertically and horizontally between the specified frets. Make a slight indentation with the awl to help position the drill bit and keep it from wandering. Remember that the double dot at the 12th fret is also doubled on the side.

Drill the holes with the appropriate-size drill bit. A brad point drill bit will center more easily on the nick made by the awl (Fig 31). Glue dots in place using a cyanoacrylate or white glue. Let dry and sand smooth with fine sandpaper (Fig 32).

Assemblage

If any major adjustment is necessary, it is best to find out at the assembly stage and correct it rather than later when adjustments may compound difficulties. Begin to fit the components together.

Fitting Neck to Body

Place the neck into the neck pocket and recheck its alignment to the body centerline. Holding neck firmly, push a 5/32 in drill bit through the neck screw holes in the body and twist by hand to make shallow pilot holes into the neck.

Remove the neck from the body and with a drill press using a 1/8 in bit (Fig 1), deepen each pilot hole to 3/4 in (the depth at which the neck and fingerboard join). Use the depth-gauge on the drill press to keep from drilling too far.

Put the ferrules for the neck screws into the body and place the screws into them. Some screws will need shortening since the back of the neck pocket was canted. Measure every screw carefully and cut them to a length just short of the neck/fingerboard joint (Fig 2, 3). The screws should stop short of the full depth of pilot holes to avoid cracking the fingerboard.

1 (left) Drilling holes for neck mounting screws

2 (lower left) Neck screws in place, untrimmed

3 (lower right) Trimmed neck screws

4 Attatching neck

Place the neck into the neck pocket and screw the neck to the body (Fig 4). Since the screws are different lengths, make sure to put them into their correct holes.

Tuning Mechanisms

Put the tuning mechanisms into their holes and secure them by hand-tightening the nuts. Mark and pre-drill the holes for the set screws. Put the set screws into place and fully tighten the nuts (Fig 5).

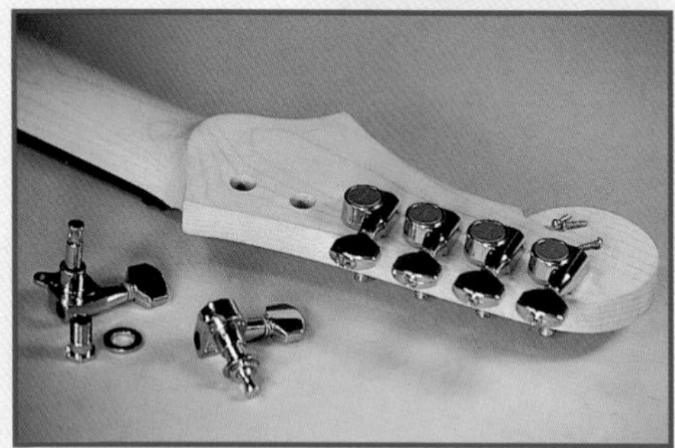

5 Aligning tuners in holes

The Nut

Nuts may be made from bone (traditionally), brass, plastic, or a number of specialty materials (Fig 6) available from guitar parts suppliers. Ours is made from graphite. Choose a graphite compound that minimizes friction, improving tuning stability.

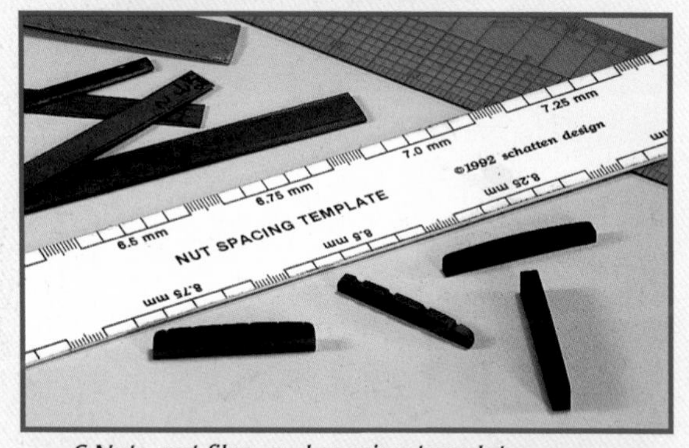

6 Nuts, nut files, and spacing template

Carve the nut material to fit the slot, arching the top to match the curvature of the fingerboard. Leave a height of about $\frac{1}{16}$ in to $\frac{3}{32}$ in above the height of the first fret.

Install the two outside strings and use them to place the positions of the outside nut slots, making sure that the strings are at the desired distance from the ends of the frets. File the slots with the appropriate nut files, just deep enough to hold the strings in place.

Carefully measure the positions of the remaining strings. Some players prefer strings that are placed equally between their centerlines, while others align them with equal spaces between strings, resulting in bass strings that are spaced slightly wider than the treble strings. Mark them by scratching a line on the nut, either side of each string, with a sharp hobby knife. File the remaining slots, leaving the strings a little high over the first fret. The nut slots will be filed to their final depth in the setup section. String up the guitar, and hear its first notes (Fig 7).

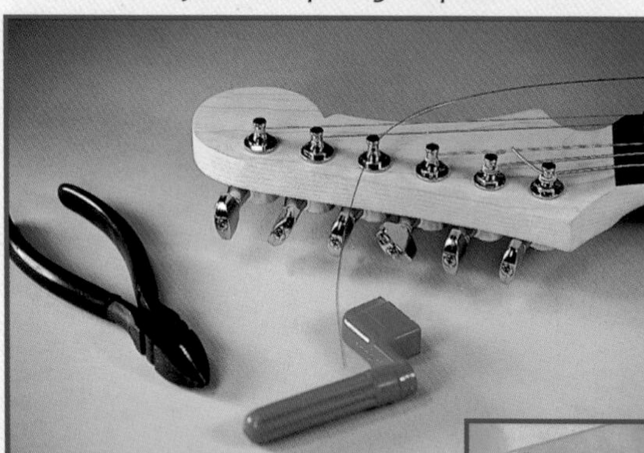

7 Stringing for nut slotting

Installing Pickups

8 Locating pickup rings

Place the pickups onto the face of the body by using the pickup rings to determine their exact location, centered and square to the bridge (Fig 8). Mark the point for each screw, being careful to keep them square (it is easy to misalign the pickup ring). Pre-drill holes for the mounting screws. Attach pickup rings to the pickups with the appropriate screws and springs (Fig 9) and fit each into their respective cavities, feeding their wires through the holes you drilled into the electronics compartment. Screw pickup assemblies to the body, as shown (Fig 10).

Cut an 8 in length of wire and strip one in of insulation off one end. Feed the unstripped end into the hole beneath the bridge and pull it through at the electronics compartment until just the stripped section is protruding from the hole at the bridge (Fig 11). Screw the bridge to the body, clamping the stripped wire to the body. This wire connects the bridge to the ground, and is necessary to avoid hum (Fig 12).

You may fully wire the electronics now (*see* Appendix: Electronics, p 71), although they will be removed for the finishing process. Conversely, you may temporarily connect the pickup leads to the output jack with test leads, in order to hear the guitar for the first time.

Finishing is the next step. Refer to p 48.

9 Pickups mounted in rings

10 (right) Attaching pickups in body

11 Bridge with grounding wire

12 Electronics compartment with pickup grounding wires

Electronics Compartment Cover

Use the routing template, p 30, and trace the shape of the electronics compartment cover on a sheet of plastic or wood (Fig 13). Rough-cut the shape on the band saw and trim to fit with a sanding block.

Mark the spots around the electronics compartment where the cover screws will be located (Fig 14). With the cover in place, drill the screw holes through the cover and into the body. Countersink the holes in the cover, and widen if necessary, as shown (Fig 15).

Shield the back of the cover with copper shielding tape and screw in place, as shown (Fig 16).

13 (upper right) Marking compartment door ouline

14 (middle right) Screw positions marked for drilling

15 (bottom right) Countersinking screw holes

16 Compartment door in place

17 Stringing

18 String retainers in place

19 Adjusting fret slot depth

20 Attaching strap buttons

Strings and Setup

After careful finishing, the final setup of the guitar can be done. String instrument (Fig 17) and install the string retainers (string trees) on the headstock (Fig 18).

Adjust the truss rod to achieve the desired neck relief. Usually this will be best with a very slight bow, so that when a straightedge is placed on the frets it shows a slight gap centered above the 6th fret. This may range from .003 in to .020 in, although some players prefer a neck that is absolutely flat. Set the height of the string action at the bridge by adjusting the individual saddles. String height depends on playing style. Hard playing needs a higher action to avoid fret buzz.

File the nut slots to their final depth (Fig 19). If you are using a low-friction nut, leave the strings a little high at the nut because these wear quickly. Trim the height of the nut until the strings are just above the top of the nut (about one-third the diameter of the string).

Set the intonation by adjusting the length of the strings at the bridge saddles. This is best done with an electronic tuner. When the open string and the fretted note at the 12th fret are in tune, the intonation is set. Or, you can match the fretted note to the octave harmonic by ear.

Set the height of the pickups beneath the strings. Most pickups fall in the general range of $\frac{1}{8}$ in to $\frac{3}{16}$ in below the strings (see Appendix: Electronics: Pickup Variations, p 74). Follow the manufacturer's instructions for your pickups. Install the strap buttons on the end of the bass-side horn and on the centerpoint at the end of the body (Fig 20).

Finishing

Finishing is largely a matter of personal preference and can be as simple or as elaborate as you wish. Every instrument maker has their own favorite finishing products and procedures developed through research and experience. Traditionally, luthiers spend as much time on the finishing stages of the instrument as on the actual making. Now as always, the finish will determine the final quality of the instrument.

There are several basic finishing steps that instrument makers follow: sanding and wood preparation, tinting or staining the wood, filling pores with grain filler for a perfectly smooth surface, sealing the wood against moisture, and applying topcoats. Makers vary this process for special finishing effects.

Finishes such as shellac, sanding sealer, and oil are designed to penetrate into the wood and harden to seal and protect the wood. Lacquer, varnishes, and wax are topcoat external finishes that provide more protection and a lustrous look. Finishes are applied through brushing, padding, or spraying depending on the product used and the finisher's resource and experience.

Depending on the outcome desired, the application of different products and the sequence of treatments may vary. We have tried to take a straightforward approach by employing readily available, easy-to-use products and minimizing the number of steps involved. For further options *see* Finishing Options, p 92.

Sanding

Prepare for finishing by disassembling the guitar and sanding and smoothing the wood (Fig 1), removing all scratches and other blemishes. Quarter-sheet, palm sanders help shorten work time and can leave a very good surface. Please use judiciously or they may create more imperfections than they remove. Sand carefully around pickup cavities and edges (Fig 2,3). Sanding involves repeated effort, each time using a finer grade of sandpaper. Scrapers may help with certain kinds of wood but require a bit of practice to be effective.

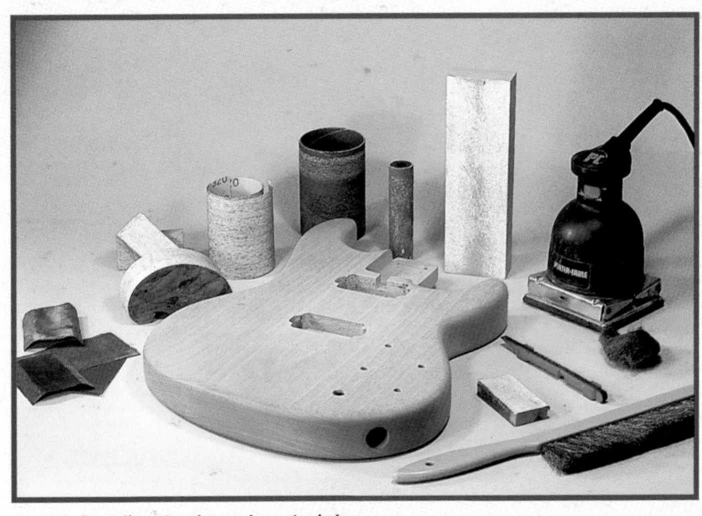

1 Sanding tools and materials

Surfaces made up of different woods will sand at different rates. Softer woods laminated to harder woods tend to dish out. Avoid this by using sanding blocks. Sandpaper wrapped around (or adhered to) a rubber drafting eraser leaves fewer scratches than a wood sanding block. Sand the instrument with 120 grit sandpaper to remove all glue smudges, level uneven surfaces, and smooth the surface of the wood. Sand again with 220 grit sandpaper to further smooth the surface. Sand the end grain. Your fingers can tell when the wood is beginning to be polished (Fig 4). Use finer grades of sandpaper for additional treatment. Sand headstock (Fig 5), and touch up the fingerboard, if necessary.

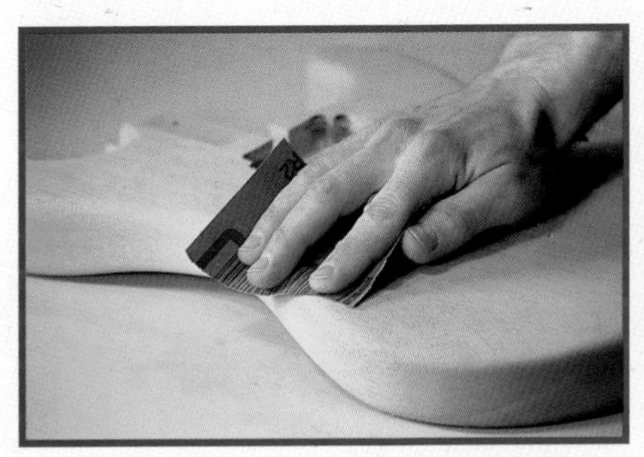

2 Sanding around edges with sandpaper stretched between fingers

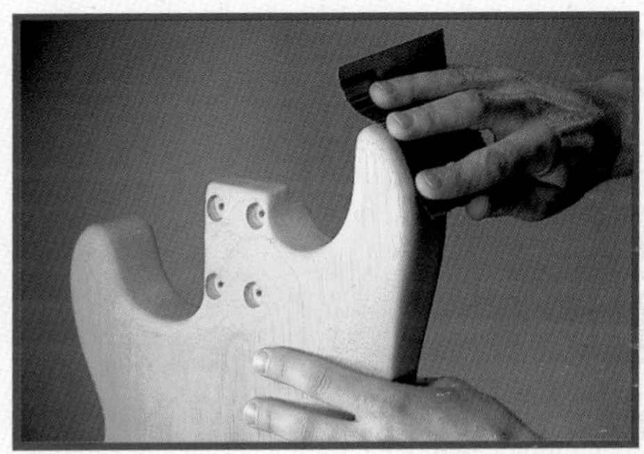

3 Sanding curves in upper horn

Wipe the wood with a dampened cloth, let it dry, and resand until smooth. Although this makes more work, it actually saves sanding time in subsequent steps.

4 (left) Sanding end-grain inside of horn

5 (right) Sanding headstock

Staining

The application of wood stain is optional. It is used to color and enhance the natural grain of the wood or create a visual effect (popular sunburst finish). Stains can be applied on bare wood before the sealing coat or mixed with the sealer. For maximum effect, stains are usually applied before a sealing coat.

Stains come in concentrated liquid and powder forms. They are mixed with water or alcohol for different shades. Stains mixed with shellac, varnish, or lacquer produce a more transparent look.

Stain scraps of wood of the same type as your instrument to test color. Stain is nearly impossible to remove. Rubbing surface with number 0000 steel wool will only lighten and highlight the finish.

Our guitar is not stained. The shellac and varnish used later in our process will deepen the inherent color of the wood and give the wood a natural look.

Sealing Wood

Sealing agents protect the wood against moisture and make subsequent coats of finishes take more effectively. Lacquer, sanding sealer, shellac, or oil are most commonly used for sealing wood (Fig 6). Stains may be suspended in sealing coats (make sure that the products are compatible).

Our guitar is sealed with shellac. It is a product of nature, sticks to most anything, has attractively subtle coloring properties, and dries fast and hard.

Purchase shellac in liquid or flake form and thin it with denatured alcohol. Sealer can be applied through brushing, spraying, or French-polishing. We applied a wash coat of shellac, reduced consistency (2 lb. thinned).

Subsequent coats may also be slightly thinned for easier application. Apply shellac evenly and quickly with as few strokes as possible (Fig 7). Let dry and sand smooth with 400 grit sandpaper.

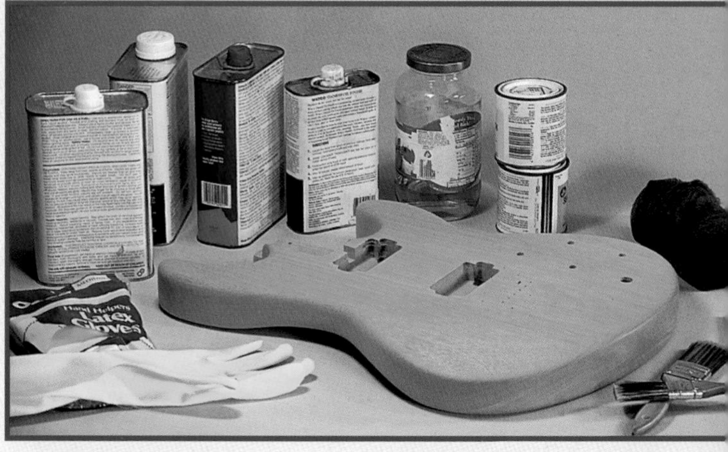

6 Finishing supplies

7 Applying first sealer coat

Grain Filler

Sealing agents and topcoats do not fill the pores of open-grained woods. Use special grain filler compounds to produce an absolutely smooth wood surface. Pores of woods such as rosewood, mahogany, and ash generally need filling. Nonporous woods such as maple, alder, and ebony do not. Some brands of grain filler have sealing agents and tints already mixed in them and may be applied in lieu of a sealing coat and stain. Follow the manufacturer's directions. More than one treatment may be necessary. Since we have sealed the wood beforehand with a coat of shellac, grain filling proceeds more efficiently.

Work the grain filler well into the wood pores and let dry overnight. Sand the wood and repeat this process if necessary. Apply a final sealing coat of shellac to fully prepare wood for the topcoats. Sand with 400 grit sandpaper to perfect smoothness.

Topcoats

Now consider special coloring treatments such as solid color coats, shading, sunbursting, and toning. Consult specialty books for this fascinating aspect of guitar making.

Dust the instrument well with a tack cloth or soft clean rag and find a dust-free environment to apply protective topcoats. Varnish has been a traditional finish for instruments for many ages. The great 18th century violin makers used oil-based varnishes exclusively. They provide a hard protective finish and beautiful luster. Although still available from luthier supply companies, they are seldom used today because of their extremely long drying time.

We use a high quality spirit-based commercial varnish for our topcoats. It is easy to use and ready to apply, and provides good protection from the elements. Spirit-based varnishes use paint thinner, mineral spirits, or turpentine as a base. They are often designated as interior or furniture-grade varnishes. They come in high-gloss, semi-gloss, dull-rub matte, and flat luster.

Some manufacturers suggest gloss coats for the foundation layers for transparency, with a final matte coat or two for visual warmth.

Poly varnishes can also be used. They are easy to apply, durable, and with some polishing produce a nice finish.

Eco-friendly, water-based varnishes are also easy to use and have the advantage of drying quickly and providing an easy-care surface. Always follow the directions suggested by the manufacturer.

Use a high quality brush. If cleaned up properly, it should last for a number of sessions. Plan the procedure you will use to apply the topcoats and how you will hang the instrument up for drying.

Depending on the brand of varnish you use, the first coat or two may be slightly thinned with mineral spirits. Each successive coat should be slightly heavier. Never apply the finish so thick that it will drip or curtain before it has a chance to set up and dry. Apply three or four coats. Let dry between coats. Lightly sand out imperfections between coats.

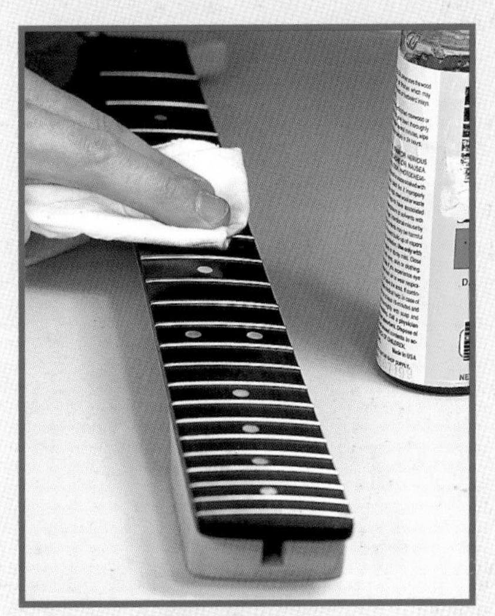

8 Oiling fingerboard

Rubbing Out and Polishing

After each coat, rub the surface with 400 grit sandpaper. Be careful not to sand through previous coats. Sometimes wet-and-dry sandpaper is used in conjunction with water or oil as a lubricant for more control during sanding. Dust well between each coat.

After the last coat of finish has been applied rub the surface lightly with a fine 000 or 0000 steel wool and buff with a soft cloth to add luster and highlight the finish. Or use a polishing agent for a higher gloss. Traditionally, choose pumice or rotten stone, hand-rubbed with oil or water as a lubricant. Buffing wheels with polishing compound are another option.

Finishing the Fingerboard

Use oil designed for wood (Fig 8). Specialty oils dry harder than furniture oils. Fingerboards are never varnished or lacquered, except for maple fingerboards that soil more easily than darker woods. Follow the manufacturer's directions.

Wax

Finally, a paste or liquid wax (carnuba wax is good) can be applied to give protection against extremes in humidity and provide extra sheen to the wood (Fig 9).

9 Our guitar is hand-rubbed to a high gloss. A wax coat protects against humidity changes.

Constructing a Bass Guitar

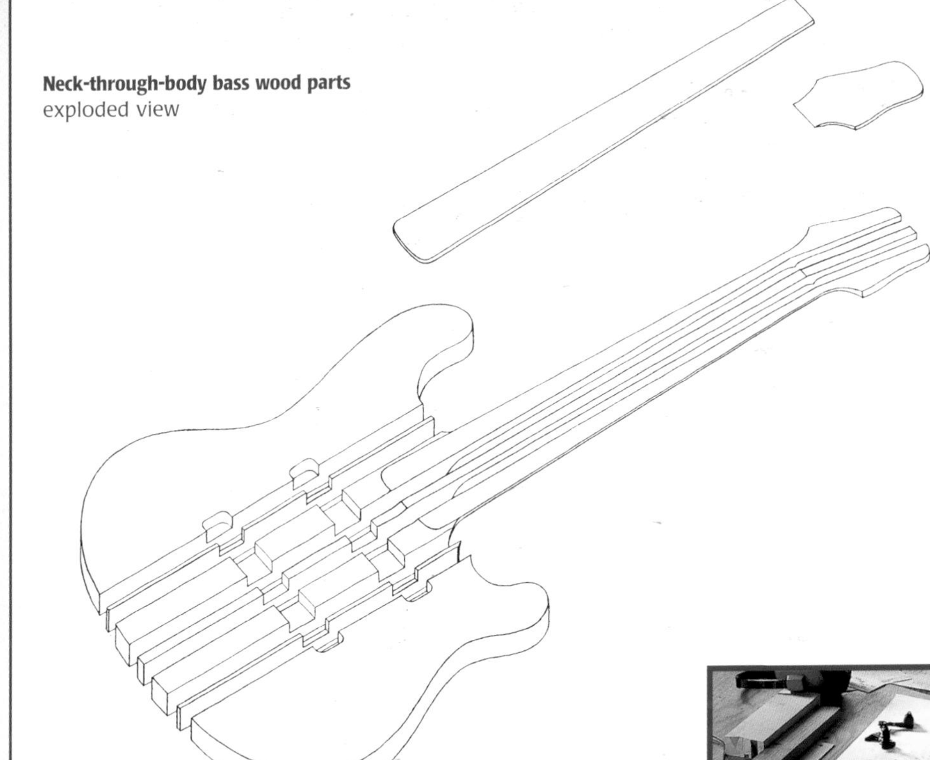

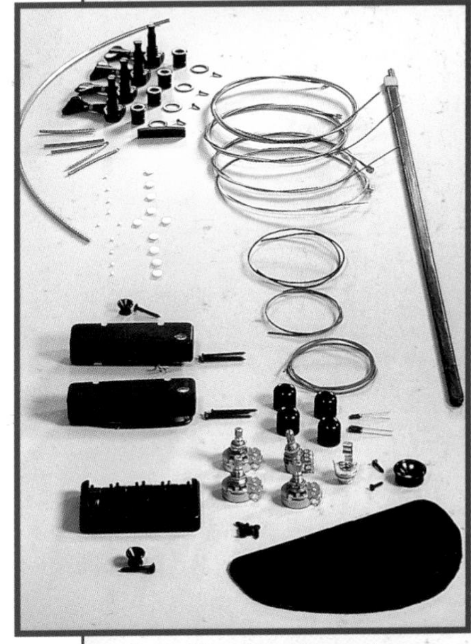

2 Parts and hardware for bass

Many procedures for making a bass guitar (Fig 1, p 52) are similar to those used in building the six-string guitar. The primary difference in our example is that we have used the neck-through-body design for the bass instead of the two-piece bolt-on design featured for the guitar. This means that the neck extends through the body and, in fact, becomes the central component of the body (*see* above drawing). The remainder of the body is then built onto the neck. This style offers tonal advantages and interesting visual options, but requires a good amount of sawing and milling usually done with a band saw and jointer. We also use a laminated construction for the neck to provide more rigidity and visual contrast by using maple and ziricote for the neck, and sapele (a species of mahogany) for the remainder of the body.

Prepare by reading Design Considerations and Preparation (p 13) and the Electronics (p 71) and Wood and Tone (p 89) sections in the Appendix. Procure all the necessary electronic parts and other hardware at this time so that your design will accommodate the actual components you will use (Fig 2).

The Neck

Draw an actual-size pattern (Fig 3) (*see* Master Patterns–Drawing Bass Pattern, p 64) or carefully measure an actual bass and make the modifications you wish.

We use a laminate construction for the neck. Determine the widths of the various laminate components. Color and grain contrast between adjoining laminates is a visually desirable effect. Make a list of the wood measurements for the number and widths of laminates and for the body wings, fingerboard, and headstock faceplate (if used).

3 Drawing bass pattern

Resaw, joint and plane the thickness of each neck piece to specification. Rough-cut the basic shape of each piece (Fig 4, 5). A vertical grain configuration of the two maple pieces adds to the neck's stability.

Level all gluing surfaces on the

4 Cutting maple neck laminates

5 Cutting ziricote center laminate and body laminates

1 (opposite page) Finished bass

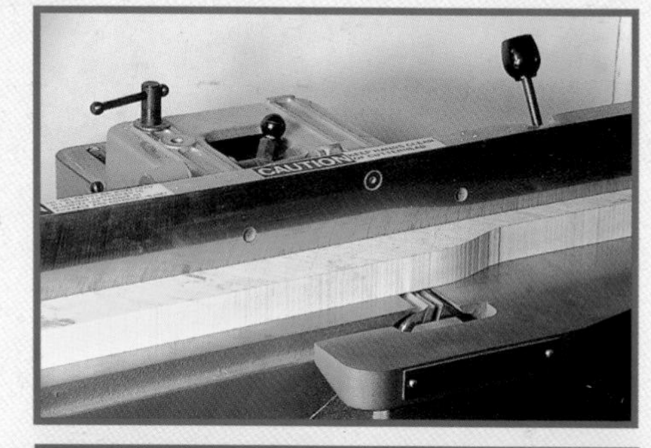

6 (right) Jointing maple laminates

7 Neck laminates

jointer (Fig 6). When a piece is to be glued on two sides, make sure to keep surfaces parallel. Pieces that will appear in mirror image (the maple neck pieces) should be kept at the same width for visual continuity (Fig 7).

Glue all neck components together (Fig 8), one piece at a time. Clamp. After the basic neck is assembled, trim the back of the neck to a thickness of 1 in. Joint or sand the neck face until it is perfectly level. Rough plane the headstock to its assigned angle at this point, (Fig 9) or wait until after the slot for the truss rod has been routed. The advantage of waiting is that a completely flat neck makes a better platform for routing the slot at the headstock end. The sides of the neck will be cut after the truss rod slot has been routed.

Based on the master pattern, draw the position of the nut, outline the neck taper, mark the position of the 12th fret, the end of the fingerboard, the bridge, and the termination of the body end of the neck (Fig 10).

8 (far left) Gluing neck laminates

9 (middle) Planing headstock for faceplate

10 (right) Marking layout on neck

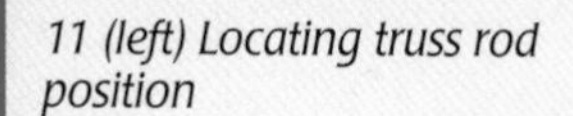

11 (left) Locating truss rod position

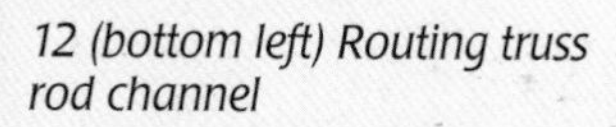

12 (bottom left) Routing truss rod channel

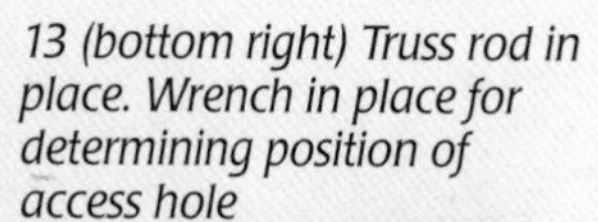

13 (bottom right) Truss rod in place. Wrench in place for determining position of access hole

Truss Rod, Headstock

Study the detail drawing of the neck/headstock/nut/truss rod conjunction (*see* Appendix: Master Drawings, p 65). Mark the placement points of each element of the actual truss rod on the face of the neck (Fig 11). The router is guided by a fence that rides against the side of the neck blank, so be sure that this is straight and parallel to the neck centerline. Patiently rout the truss rod channel by making several passes with the router, increasing the depth each time (Fig 12).

Note In the procedure for routing the guitar truss rod channel (described on p 36), we pre-carved the neck first to relieve tension in the wood, then re-leveled the surface before routing the truss rod channel. This is not necessary for this bass, because the vertically-oriented grain in the neck laminates do not flex when the neck is carved.

Saw and plane headstock to specification. Final arrangement of truss rod and headstock are shown in Fig 13. Prepare a headstock faceplate from 1/8 in thick ebony wood. Transfer

measurements to the faceplate to define the notch that accommodates the end of the truss rod and the access hole for the truss rod adjuster (Fig 14). Make any modifications necessary so the various components fit together properly.

14 Headstock faceplate, notched for truss rod block and drilled for adjustment wrench.

Glue the faceplate to the headstock (Fig 15).

Trim the back of headstock to a thickness to accommodate the tuning mechanisms (our measurement is 9⁄16 in). Remember to leave wood for a volute. Draw the headstock shape on the back of the headstock and cut out the basic outline on the band saw (Fig 16).

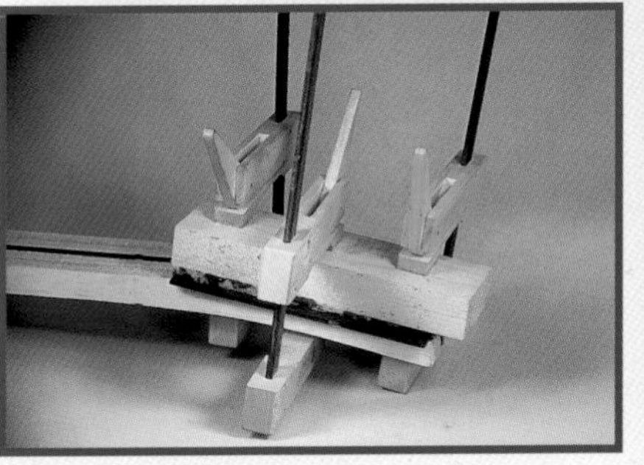

15 (above) Gluing headstock faceplate

16 (right) Bandsawing headstock outline

Plane and file the nut end of the faceplate level with the fingerboard. Insert the truss rod to insure that everything fits (Fig 17). Cut out the outline of the neck leaving 1⁄8 in extra on either side (Fig 18).

On the headstock, carefully locate the placement of tuner holes. Drill the holes on a drill press. A piece of wood pressed firmly to the underside of the headstock will minimize chipping as the drill bit emerges (Fig 19).

Begin contouring the back of the neck with a spokeshave, rasps, and files (Fig 20). The three neck cross-sections drawn on p 15 show the basic styles. Leave the neck a little oversize until the fingerboard is glued on. Make a simple template, as shown, to help gauge the shape (slightly oversize at this stage) (Fig 21).

17 Headstock faceplate trimmed to neck surface

18 Neck trimmed just wide of final width

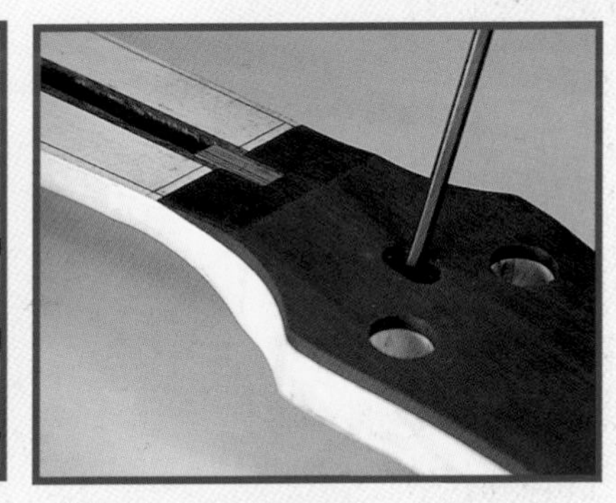

19 Tuner holes drilled

20 Rough-carving neck with spokeshave.

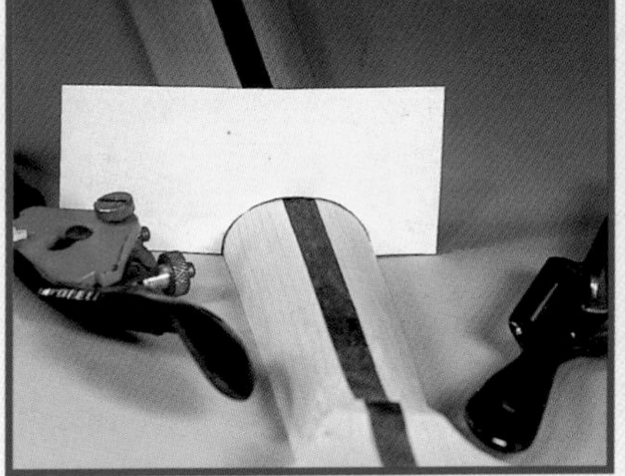

21 Template for neck carving

The shape of the heel (area where the neck meets the body) is determined by the joint between the outside portions of the body and the neck. This area will be more carefully contoured later, but remove as much material as possible while the body sides are unattached (Fig 22, 23).

22 (above right) Roughing-out heel with chisel

23 (bottom right) Shaping heel with drum sander

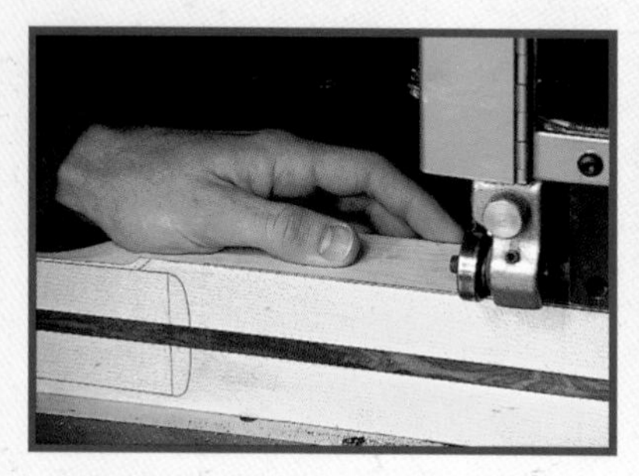

24 Trimming body portion of neck piece for neck angle

25 Measuring for neck angle with fingerboard and bridge in place

The body must be declined slightly to the plane of the neck to produce the correct string height at the bridge. Determine the height that is required and draw lines on the side of the body section of the neck assembly. Establish the amount the body section of the neck is to be trimmed to achieve the correct neck/body angle (*see* Appendix: Master Drawing, p 65). Band saw the excess wood from the top and back of the neck assembly (Fig 24). Sand these surfaces flat with a sanding block. Test for proper angle by putting the bridge and fingerboard in place. Adjust the bridge saddles to the middle of their height range. Rest a long straightedge on the bridge saddle and hold it above the fingerboard along the same line as a string (Fig 25). The straightedge should be at the height at which a string would normally rest above a fretted fingerboard, shown in drawing below.

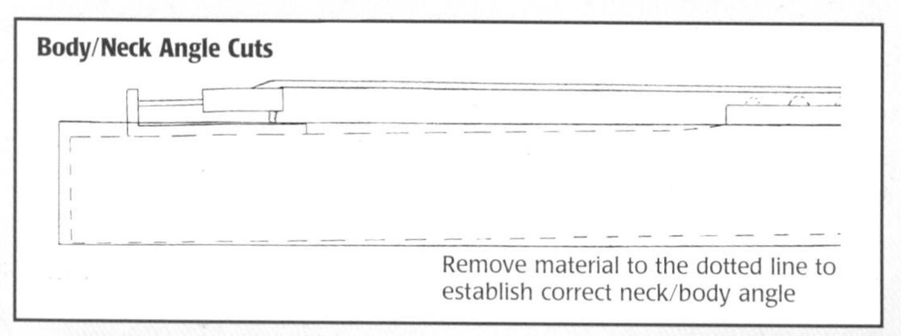

Fret distance from nut	
Fret	Distance
1	1.9083
2	3.7094
3	5.4095
4	7.0142
5	8.5288
6	9.9584
7	11.3077
8	12.5813
9	13.7835
10	14.9181
11	15.9891
12	17.0000
13	17.9541
14	18.8547
15	19.7048
16	20.5071
17	21.2644
18	21.9792
19	22.6539
20	23.2907
21	23.8917
22	24.4591
23	24.9946
24	25.5000
25	25.9771
26	26.4274
27	26.8524
28	27.2536
29	27.6322
30	27.9896
31	28.3269
32	28.6453
33	28.9459
34	29.2295
35	29.4973
36	29.7500

Fret locations for 34 in scale length

Fingerboard and Inlays

The construction of the bass fingerboard is the same as for the six-string guitar, *see* p 39. If you prefer, purchase a slotted fingerboard from a guitar supply company. We use rosewood for our bass guitar fingerboard.

26 Fingerboard with inlays

Scale length for a standard bass is 34 in. Place fret slots (measurements shown at left, and inlay fingerboard dots, Fig 26). Trim sides of fingerboard close to the final taper of the neck. Round the body end of the fingerboard and cut it to final width in the area where it overlaps the body (Fig 27). Test-fit the fingerboard with the truss rod in place to insure proper alignment. Re-check fingerboard surface of the neck with a straightedge, and relevel with a sanding block if necessary.

27 Fingerboard rounded at body before gluing

Make sure the truss rod is functioning properly before installing it. We do not glue it into the neck. Make any adjustments necessary to make it fit. If the channel is longer than necessary at the body end, fill the gap with a shim so the truss rod doesn't slide toward the body as it is being adjusted later. Put the truss rod in place and prepare to glue the fingerboard on top.

Install two small push pins or pins fashioned from brads into the neck to help secure the fingerboard and keep it from slipping during the gluing process (Fig 28).

Prepare several clamps and glue the fingerboard to the neck using a padded block to insure even pressure along the full span of the neck (Fig 29). Using this block will also insure that the neck remains straight as the glue dries. Trim excess wood from the sides of the fingerboard and begin shaping the final form of the neck (Fig 30).

Arch the fingerboard (we used a 12 in radius). If you purchase a pre-arched fingerboard, check the arch to make sure the fingerboard is perfectly level along its length. Sand to a high luster, *see* p 42, 43.

28 Fingerboard alignment tacks

29 Gluing on the fingerboard

30 Last chance to shape heel and neck before body wings are in the way

Installing Frets

Fretwire for basses is slightly higher and wider than is six-string guitar fretwire since wound bass strings wear frets faster. Narrow frets produce better intonation and are usually preferred for recording studio work. Try out various bass guitars to determine the feel you prefer. Purchase fretwire of your choice. *See* p 40 for fretting process.

The Body

Mill the wood for body to a thickness to match the neck. Transfer the pattern to the wood. Place the hardware on the body blank and determine the location of the pickups and electronics compartment (Fig 31, 32).

31 Laying out body shape on wood

32 Body ouline drawn on wood

Rough-cut the basic shapes of the two wings (Fig 33). Leave flat areas on the sides of the wings to aid in clamping them to the neck. The flat areas should be directly opposite each other so that the clamps are at right angles to the joint (*see* drawing) to prevent slippage when glued (Fig 36, p 58).

Before gluing the wings to the body, rout a channel in the jointed face of the treble (lower side) wing (Fig 34, 35) to carry the wires from the neck pickup to the electronics compartment (*see* Master Drawing, p 64). Routing now will save difficult drilling later.

Glue extra laminate

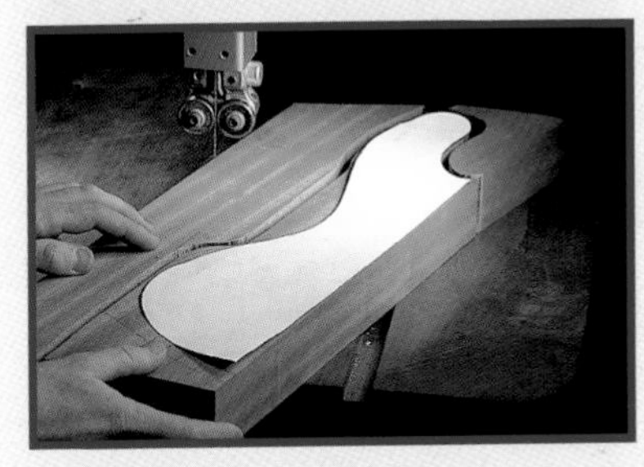

33 Band sawing body sides, leaving flat spots for clamping

Cutting body sides for perpendicular clamp alignment

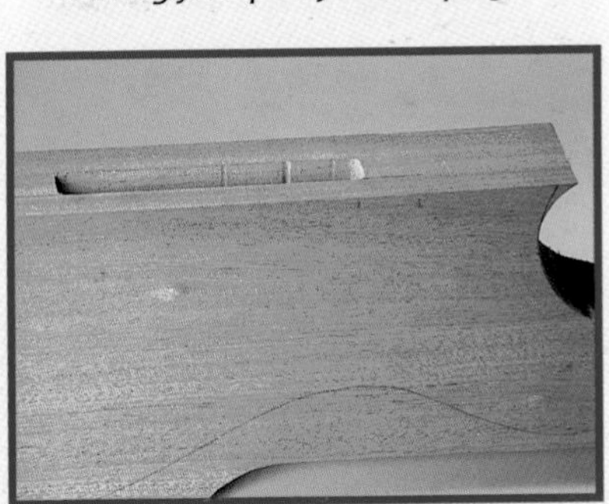

34 (left) Routing wiring channel

35 (right) Wiring channel

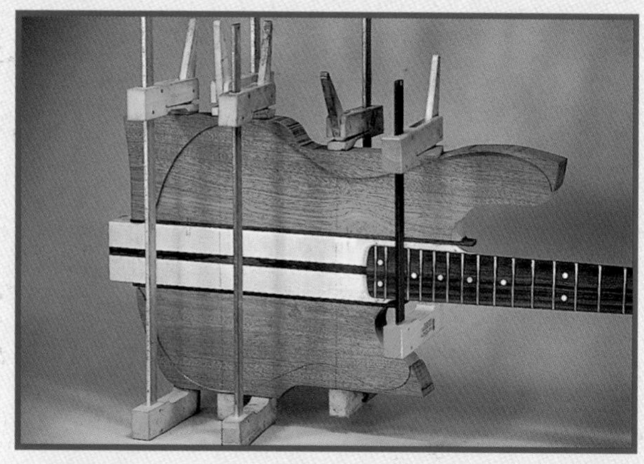

36 Gluing second body wing

pieces (as we have done) between body and wings to the wings. Trim them to the body thickness.

Cut body wings to their final shape before gluing them to the neck. Leave a little extra wood at each end of the joints for better contact at these points. Save the cut-off pieces to use as clamping cauls when gluing. Glue the wings to the body, one at a time, keeping the clamps straight. We use pins as in the neck/fingerboard joint. The alignment of these parts is important because discrepancies are difficult to correct.

When both sides are fully dry (Fig 37), trim the body around the ends of the joints to the final shape (Fig 38). Carve the areas of the body that intersect the heel (Fig 39).

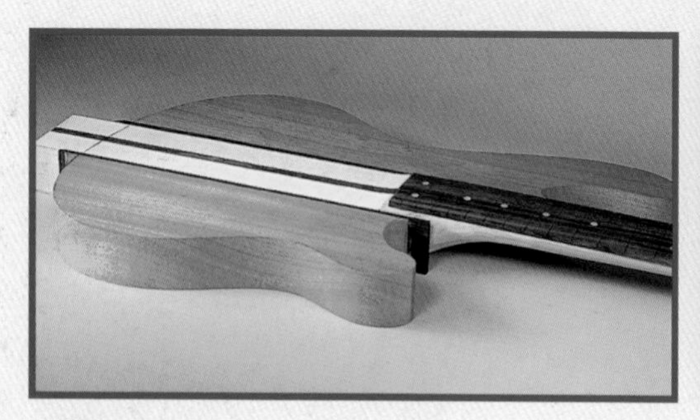

37 Body wings glued in place

38 Band sawing body ouline at joint

39 Carving heel into body wings

Assembling Body and Routing for Electronics

Lay out and position the electronic components on the face of the instrument in preparation for routing the pickup cavities and the electronics compartment. If you choose a different arrangement for the controls, adjust your electronics compartment shape accordingly. Avoid putting a potentiometer too close to the output jack, where the tip of the cord plug will contact the pot housing. Place knobs for accessibility and visual balance. Carefully position and mark the bridge placement (Fig 40).

40 Positioning knobs on body

Follow instructions on p 59 for making the routing template. This is actually for the compartment cover, not the main part of the cavity. The main cavity may be routed by hand or with a template cut to its outline.

Drill the holes for the control knobs (Fig 41) to prepare for routing electronics compartment on back of body. The stem holes will help act as a guide for routing the compartment to the appropriate depth. Drill out the bulk of the wood with a Forstner drill bit before routing. Finish the main cavity with the router, then rout the cover recess with the template (Fig 42).

41 Drilling holes for electronic components

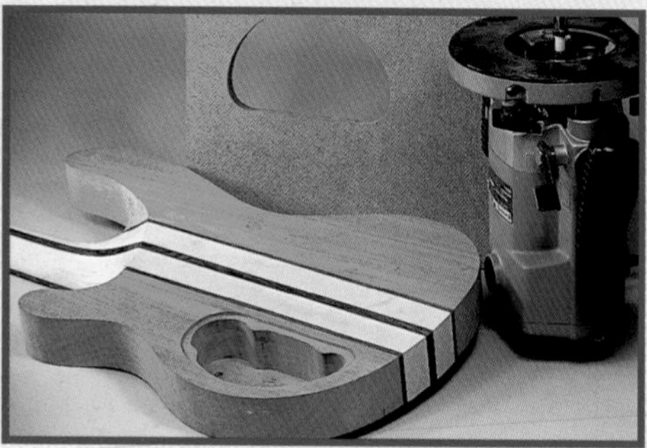

42 Routed electronics compartment and door recess

Pickup Cavities

Prepare a routing template for the pickup cavities (below). One template (*see* drawing) will do two cavities (Fig 43). Carefully clamp the template into place making sure to center it on the body laminates.

Rout the cavities in several passes until the appropriate depth is reached (Fig 44). The pickup holes should intersect with the channel routed earlier in the treble body wing (Fig 45). Unless the wiring channel already intersects with the electronics compartment, drill a hole between the two (Fig 46).

Drill a hole connecting the electronics compartment and the body face just below the bridge (use a 12 in long, ⅛ in bit), for the grounding wire (Fig 47).

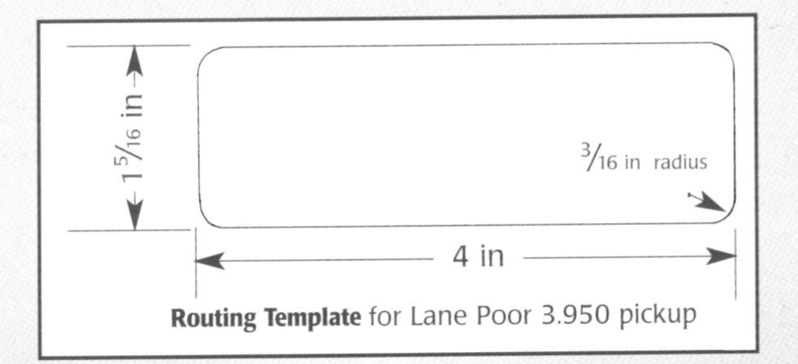

Routing Template for Lane Poor 3.950 pickup

43 Pickup cavities and routing template

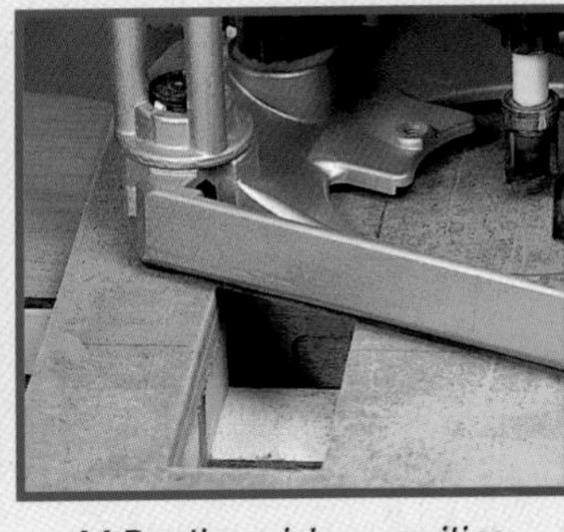

44 Routing pickup cavities

45 Pickup cavities and wiring channel

46 Connecting wiring channel and electronics compartment

47 Drillling hole for grounding wire

Body Roundover and Body Contours

Rout the body roundovers (Fig 48) described on p 28. Bevel the top of the body at the arm position until it feels comfortable. Carve the body contour with a spokeshave or drawknife. Finish with the eraser sanding block (Fig 49). These contours may be refined when the instrument is test-strung.

48 Rounding body edges

49 Carving body contour with a spokeshave

Fretting

Level and fret the neck, as described on p 35, 40. Take some extra care to support the neck when pressing in the frets, especially near the body end of the fingerboard.

50 Sanded heel and body contour

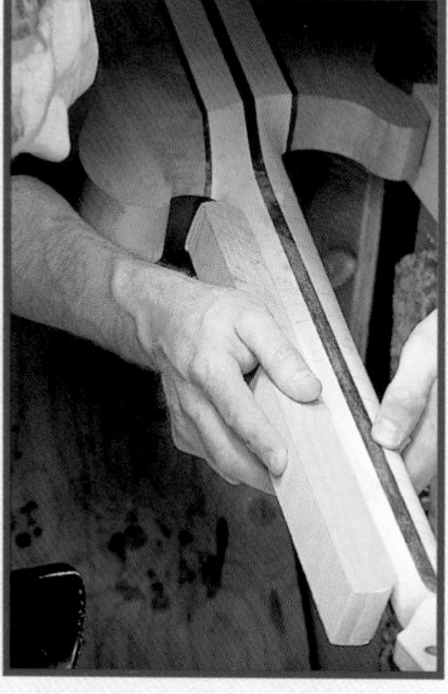

51 Block-sanding neck shape

52 Sculpting around base of fingerboard

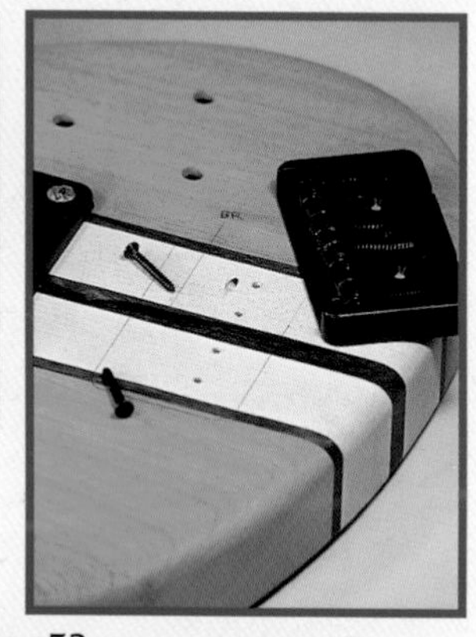

53 Installing pickups

54 Installing bridge

55 Finished bass, see p52

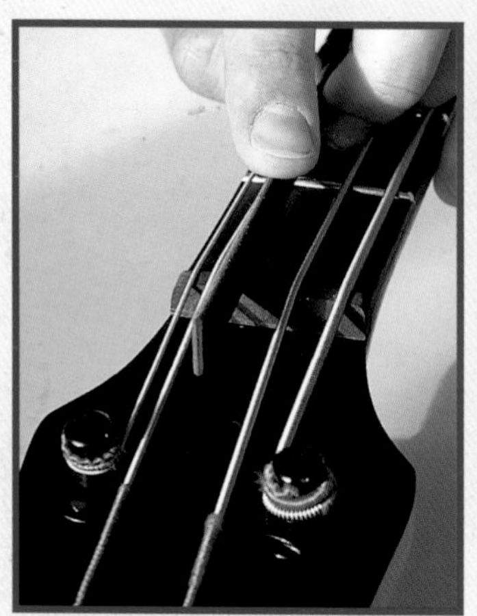

56 Filing nut slots

57 Strap button on horn

Prefinishing

Finish all basic sanding and contouring (Fig 50). Make a simple sanding jig from a perfectly flat length of wood with sandpaper glued to the edge for sanding and leveling the back of the neck (Fig 51). Sand carefully anywhere the different laminates join each other. Sand a gradual slope between the body surface and the neck/fingerboard junction (Fig 52).

Preassembly

Before finishing, assemble and string the bass to play and hear. Make any final adjustments to the neck and body contouring.

Attach the pickups, bridge, (Fig 53, 54), and tuners.

Cut a nut (*see* p 46). String it up and make preliminary nut slots (Fig 56). Tune to pitch. Tension the truss rod as necessary.

Clip the pickup wires to a test lead to hear the amplified tone.

Finishing is done now, *see* p 92.

Setup

String the instrument and adjust the truss rod as described on p 48, Setup. Set the string height at the bridge for the desired action.

Adjust nut slots to their final depths.

Adjust the bridge saddles for correct intonation.

Set the height of the pickups, usually 1/8 in to 3/16 in below the strings.

Install the strap buttons on the end of the horn and on the centerpoint at the end of the body (Fig 57, 58). *See* finished bass, p 52.

58 Installing strap button

Appendix

Master Drawings

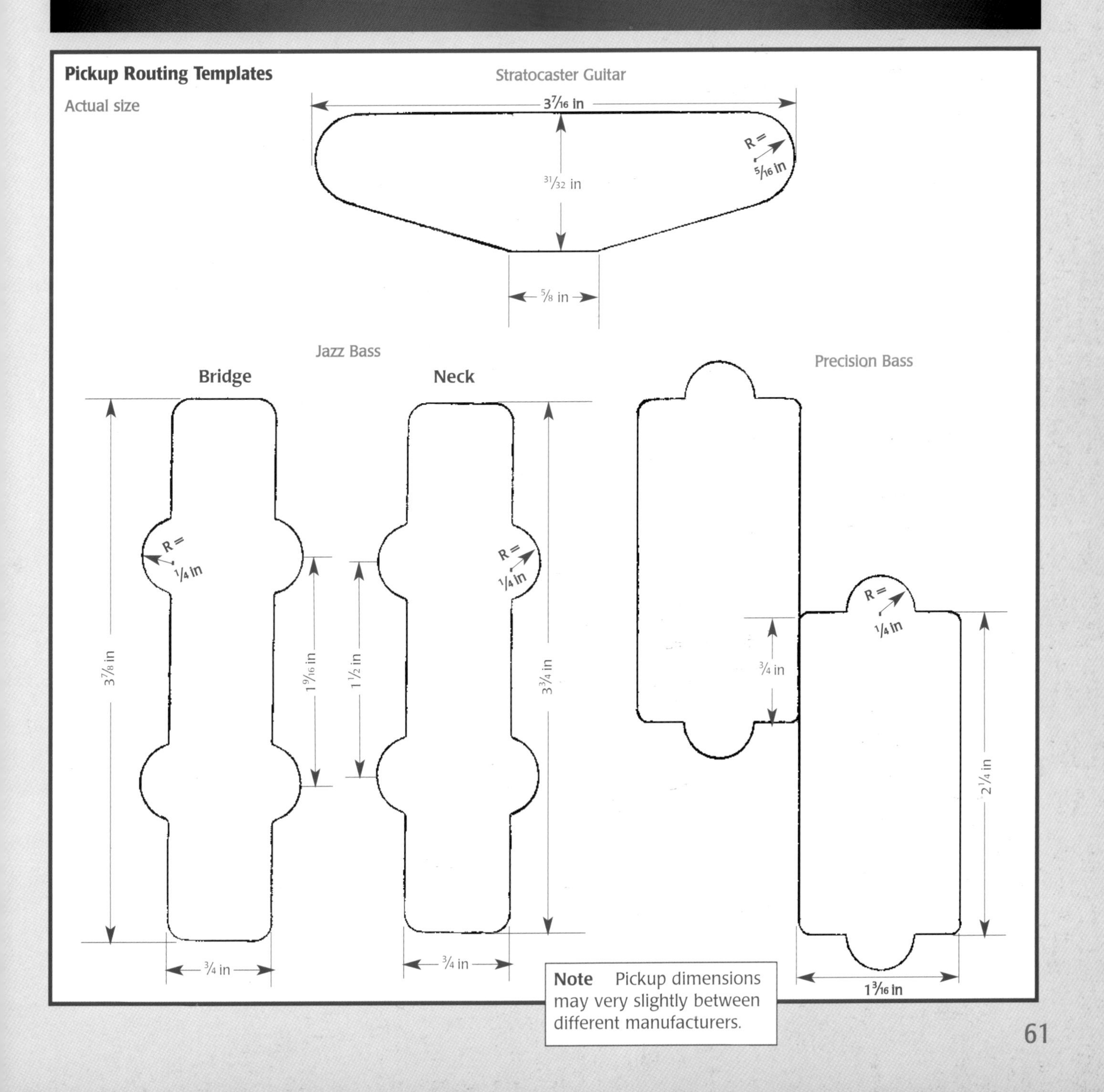

Note Pickup dimensions may very slightly between different manufacturers.

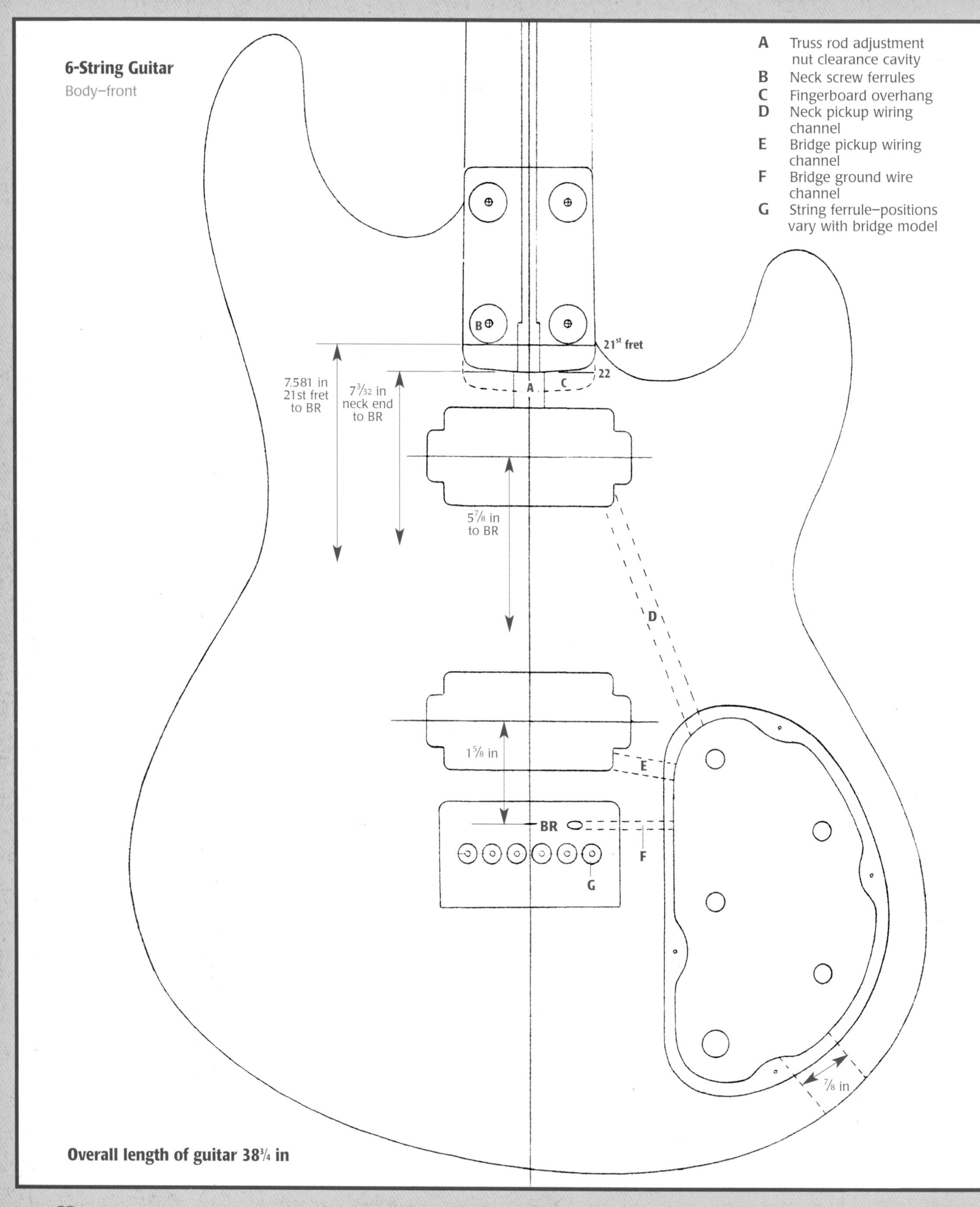
6-String Guitar
Body–front
A Truss rod adjustment nut clearance cavity
B Neck screw ferrules
C Fingerboard overhang
D Neck pickup wiring channel
E Bridge pickup wiring channel
F Bridge ground wire channel
G String ferrule–positions vary with bridge model
21st fret
22
7.581 in 21st fret to BR
7 3/32 in neck end to BR
5 7/8 in to BR
1 5/8 in
BR
7/8 in
Overall length of guitar 38 3/4 in

6-String Guitar

Body–side

A Truss rod
B Truss rod adjustment nut
C Truss rod adjustment nut clearance cavity
D Pickup cavities
E Neck screw ferrule holes
F Neck pickup wiring channel
G Bridge ground wire channel
H String ferrule holes

E
E
A
B
C
D
7/8 in
1 1/8 in
F
D
G
BR
H

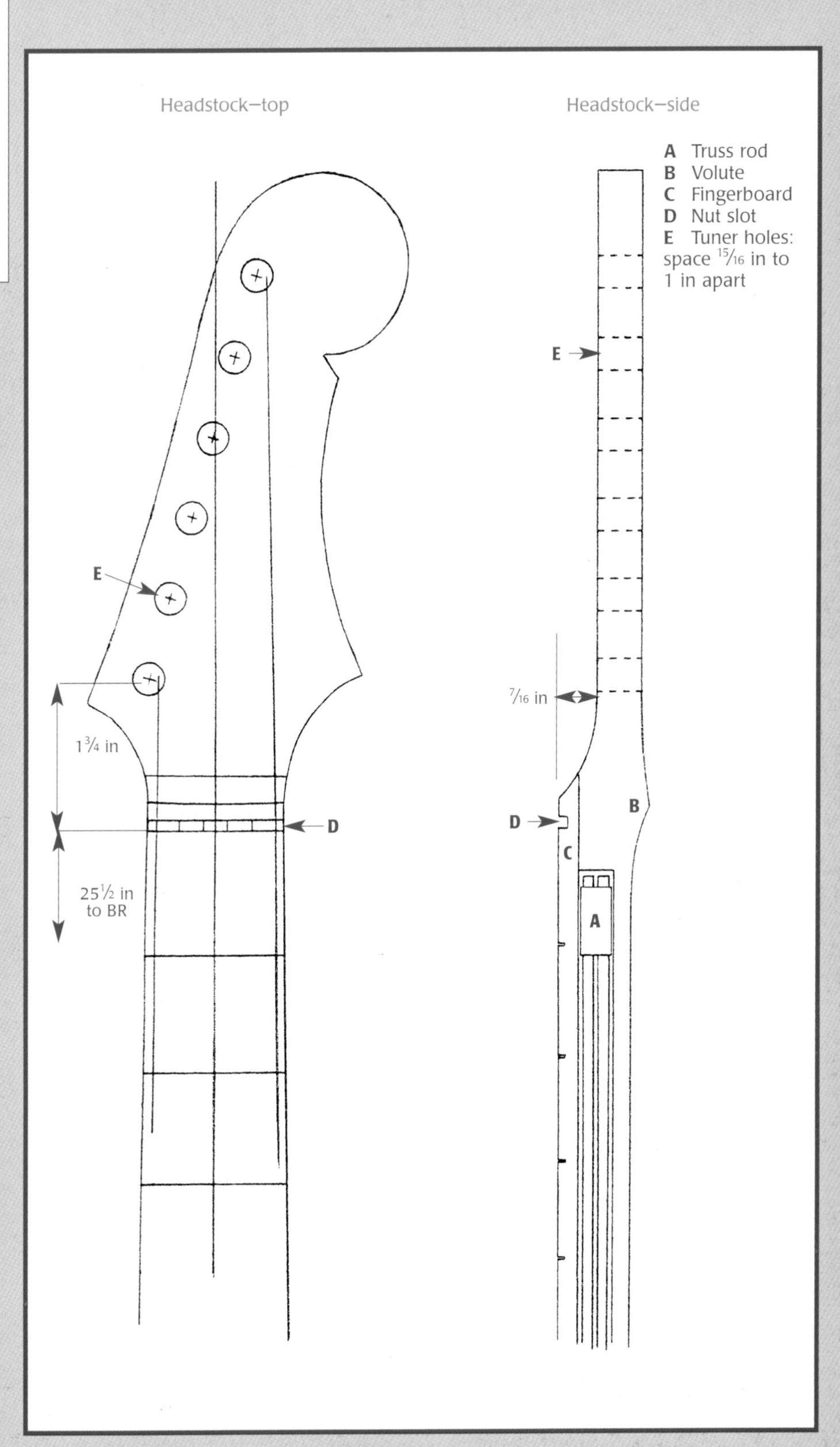

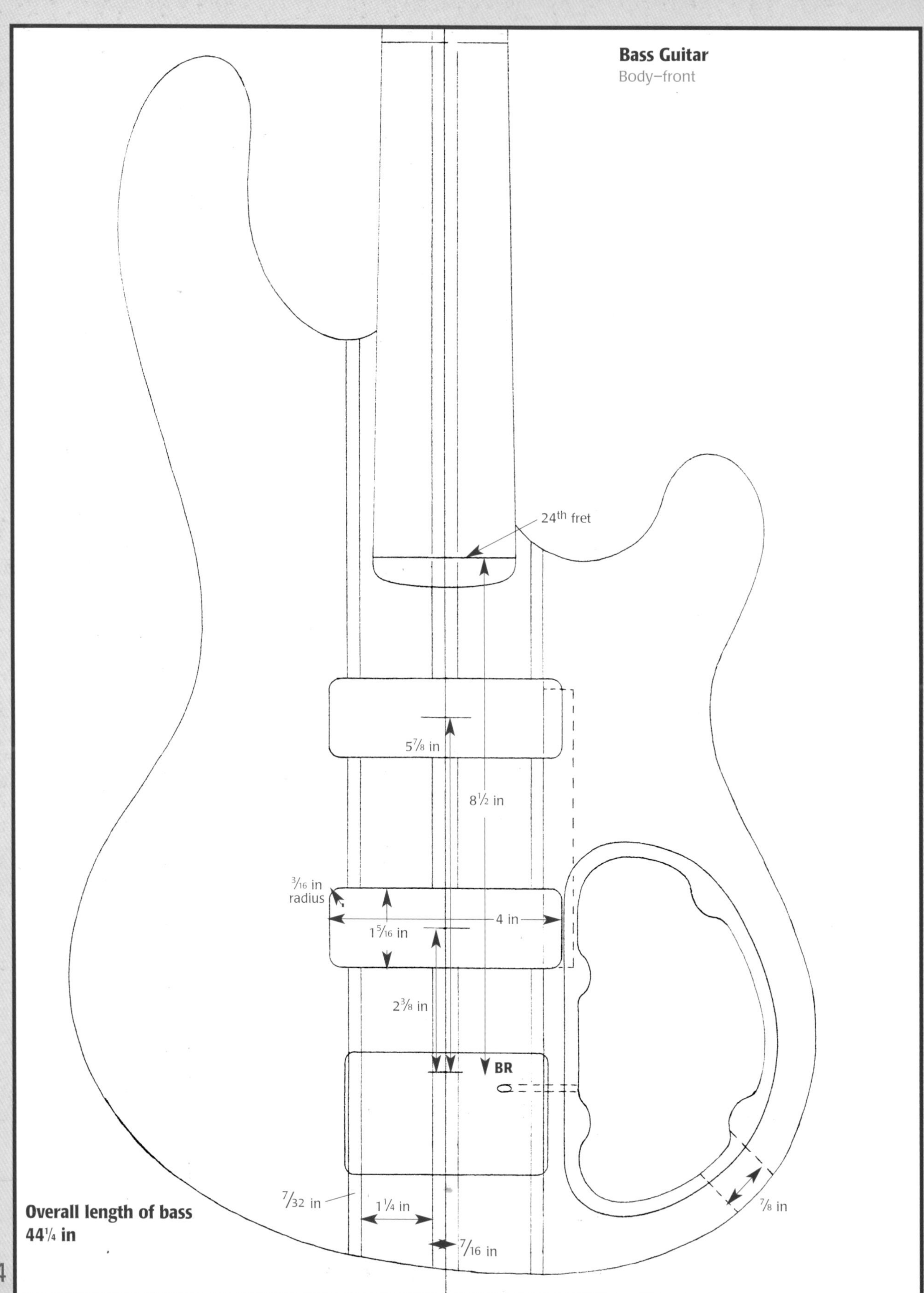
Bass Guitar
Body–front
24th fret
5⅞ in
8½ in
3⁄16 in
radius
4 in
1 5⁄16 in
2⅜ in
BR
7/32 in
1¼ in
7/16 in
⅞ in
Overall length of bass
44¼ in

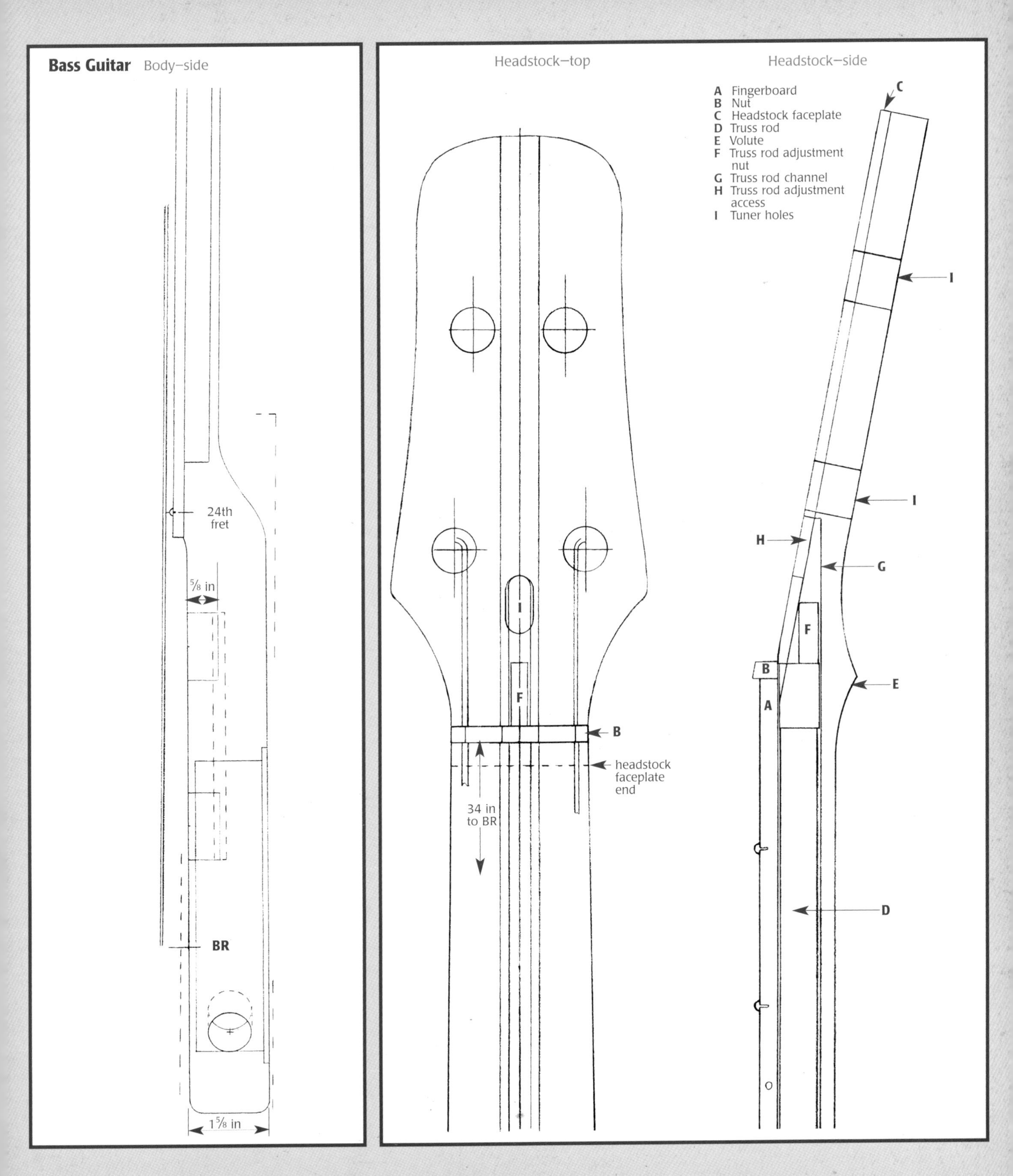
Bass Guitar Body–side
24th fret
⅝ in
BR
1⅝ in
Headstock–top
I
F
B
headstock faceplate end
34 in to BR
Headstock–side
A Fingerboard
B Nut
C Headstock faceplate
D Truss rod
E Volute
F Truss rod adjustment nut
G Truss rod channel
H Truss rod adjustment access
I Tuner holes
C
I
I
H
G
F
B
E
A
D

Playing the Electric Guitar and Bass

Appendix

Thomas Randall

The electric guitar and electric bass are two of the most important and prominent instruments in music today. While the tuning and range of these electric instruments are the same as their acoustic cousins, the styles and techniques used in playing them are often quite different. This section offers some of the basic and most popular electric guitar and bass playing techniques and provides a foundation that can be used with other guitar study methods currently available in book or video form.

GETTING STARTED

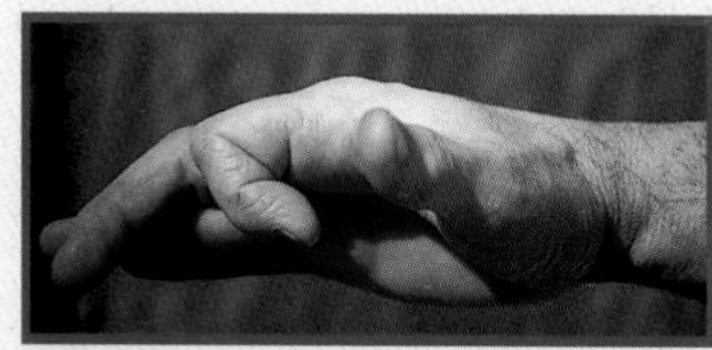

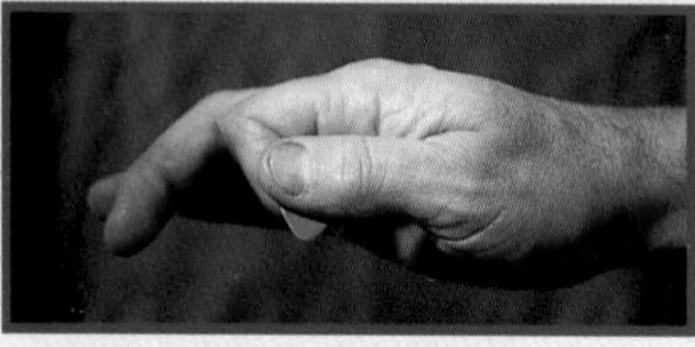

Most electric guitar and some electric bass players use a plectrum, or pick, to strike the strings. A comfortable, secure right hand grip and relaxed position will help the beginner to become familiar with the pick until it eventually becomes almost part of the hand. The index finger of the picking hand should be curled (not clenched) so that the thumb can be placed roughly parallel to the tip of the index finger. Place the pick between the thumb and index finger, with the point of the pick at a right angle to the thumb (*see* photograph). Keep the hand relaxed, and use approximately 1/4 in of the pick as the striking surface (slightly more for bass).

Pick control is crucial. Begin with a downstroke immediately followed by an upstroke on the low E string. Move through the six strings (four strings for the bass), playing a downstroke and an upstroke on each. Keep a steady beat and allow each stroke to ring out with equal volume and clarity. This down-up style of picking is the core technique of most electric guitar styles.

BASIC CHORDS, SCALES, AND TECHNIQUES

Chord positions on the fretboard are many and varied. The standard format for learning these positions is the chord box, a graphic representation of the fingerboard that indicates the location of the fingers for a given chord.

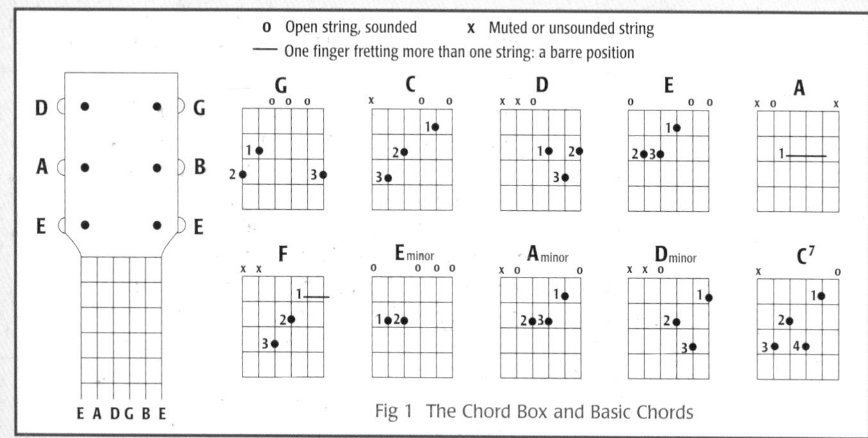

Fig 1 The Chord Box and Basic Chords

This box is assumed to represent the first three or four frets of the guitar, unless a fret number is given alongside the box. (Fig 1) illustrates the use of the chord box and gives many of the basic chord shapes that every guitarist must memorize. The fingers of the left hand are numbered 1 to 4, beginning with the index finger. The fingers of the left hand should remain rounded so that the tip of each finger comes straight down on the desired note. Most of the chords for all electric guitar playing are variations on or extensions of these chords.

Often it is necessary for one finger of the left hand to press down two or more strings (a barre or bar position) with the flat pad of the finger rather than the tip (Fig 1, F and A chords). A controlled, firm grip produces the desired notes and clarity. Beginning players often tend to clench down too hard on the fingerboard instead of relaxing the fingers and focusing on accurate placement. This is only the first of many left hand techniques that require a light touch backed by strength and control.

Chords and melodies are built from scales. The first scales to learn use many open (unfretted) strings. (Fig 2) presents the C Major scale, first in a chord box and then in tablature. To read the scale in the chord box, first play the note that appears in the farthest left position (the 3rd fret of the A string). This is C, the first note of the C scale. Next, play the notes indicated on the next string to the right, starting with the open note, D, and then E and F at the 2nd and 3rd frets. Continue with the next open string, G, and the A at the 2nd fret. Conclude with the open string B and the C at the first fret. When played correctly, you will hear the familiar sound of the major scale (do, re, mi, fa, so, la, ti, do). Practice this (and all) scales ascending and descending, using alternating down and up strokes of the pick. Always place your fingertips just behind the fret that is sounding the note.

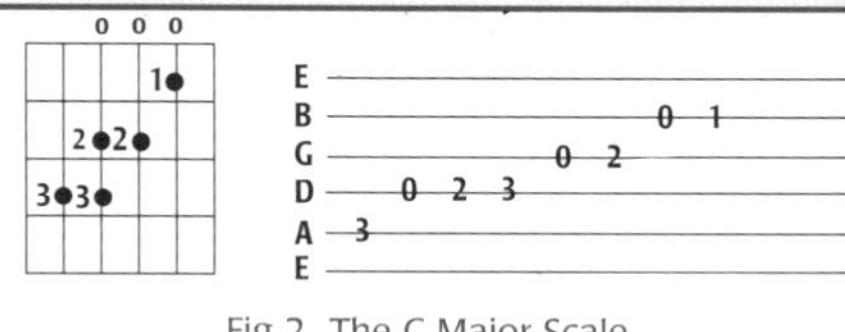

Fig 2 The C Major Scale

Tablature is also a graphic depiction of the fingerboard, showing the six (or four) strings and indicating which fret of which string will produce the desired note. Read from left to right, tablature also indicates motion through time, something the chord box is not designed to do. The numbers on the lines do not indicate which finger to use, only which fret and string to play. Fingerings may be indicated above or below the note. The tablature for the C Major scale starts with the 3rd fret of the A string, indicated by a small 3 on the 2nd line, and proceeds up the scale. Read through it and compare what you hear with the scale you produced from the chord box: they should sound the same. The G Major scale is shown in (Fig 3), once again in a chord box and in tablature.

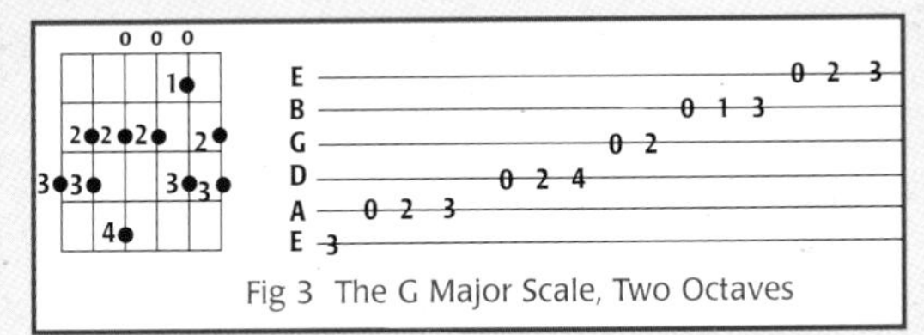

Fig 3 The G Major Scale, Two Octaves

Every musician will benefit from learning to read music from the standard staff. As a practical matter, most guitarists who play popular styles on the electric guitar rarely need this skill unless they are involved in studio, composition, or theatrical performance situations. At the very least, you will need to know the names of the notes at many locations on the fingerboard. The language of music can be learned without knowing how to read the staff, but learning to read music is recommended as it opens many doors and facilitates the study of music theory.

PLAYING RHYTHM GUITAR

Playing rhythm chords on the electric guitar requires the use of **barre chords** up and down the entire fingerboard. Much can be done with just a few positions; this section focuses on two groups or families of chords, E and A. These chords are essentially the same shapes as the E (major and minor) and A (major and minor) chords given in Fig 1. Through the use of a shifting barre position, every major or minor chord can be found using these shapes.

Barre Chords and Embellishments, Progressions

For a G# major chord

Suppose you are learning a song that calls for a G# major chord. You know from the G scale (Fig 3) that the 3rd fret of the low E string is the note G, and you know from your general study of music that a sharp (#) indicates raising a pitch by one fret (or half-step). The lowest G# note, therefore, can be found at the 4th fret of the low E string. Because the bass note of the chord is on the E string, you match it to an E major shape, with the first finger barring the 4th fret (Fig 4). The barre itself should lie flat across all of the strings, directly behind the 4th fret. This is a G# major chord. A G# minor chord can be constructed at the same location, using an E minor shape above the barre at the 4th fret. Use firm, even pressure and do not clench your hand.

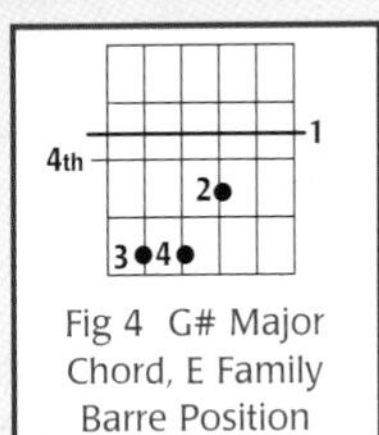

Fig 4 G# Major Chord, E Family Barre Position

For a C minor chord

Suppose, next, that you are asked to play a C minor chord. You know from the C scale (Fig 2) that the 3rd fret of the A string sounds a low C note. Because you are building a chord from a root on the A string, you will choose an A family (A minor) chord shape. With the first finger creating a barre at the 3rd fret, the other fingers form the A minor chord shape above the barre (Fig 5). This is a C minor chord.

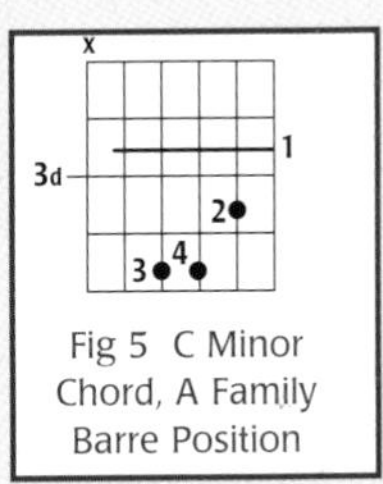

Fig 5 C Minor Chord, A Family Barre Position

For A major family barre chords

The ring finger actually barres three strings, while the index finger provides a bass note or root note, which names the chord. *See* (Fig 6), the C major barre chord, for an example of this family. It is helpful to memorize the names of the notes on the two lowest strings, as they provide locations for all of the chords. Using this system, you can find any major or minor chord you need.

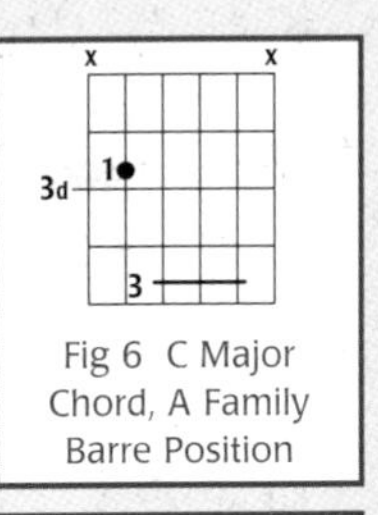

Fig 6 C Major Chord, A Family Barre Position

In many guitar styles it is not necessary to play all of the notes of a barre chord; instead, focus on the higher or lower notes. In many rock styles only the three low strings are played, usually with amplifier distortion to thicken the sound (Fig 7). In many other styles, like soft rock, reggae, and pop music, the higher strings are emphasized (Fig 8). The notes of the chord may be sounded together (as in a reggae "chop" or "skank" guitar part) or they may be articulated one at a time (an arpeggio).

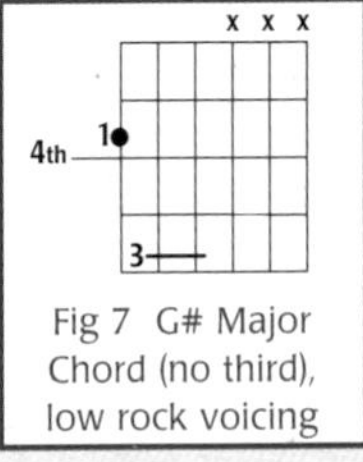

Fig 7 G# Major Chord (no third), low rock voicing

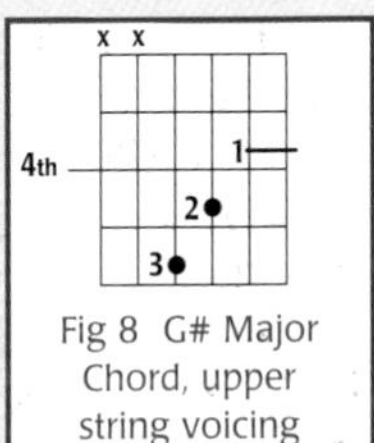

Fig 8 G# Major Chord, upper string voicing

For barre chord variation

One of the most useful variations of the barre chord is the shuffle rhythm, a versatile rock/blues accompaniment pattern. The following example corresponds to a B flat (b) barre chord location, using the E shape above a 6th fret barre. Place your left hand first finger at the 6th fret of the low E string, the note B^b (a flat is the opposite of a sharp, and indicates that a pitch should be lowered by one fret). Place the ring finger of the left hand on the A string, 8th fret. Strike these two strings twice with the pick. Stretch the 4th finger of the left hand to the tenth fret of the A string while holding the first finger on the low B^b. Strike these two notes twice, then lift the 4th finger to prepare for the next two pick strokes. (Fig 9) shows this shuffle move in chord boxes, and it can be moved anywhere on the neck as long as your root note is on the E, A, or D string.

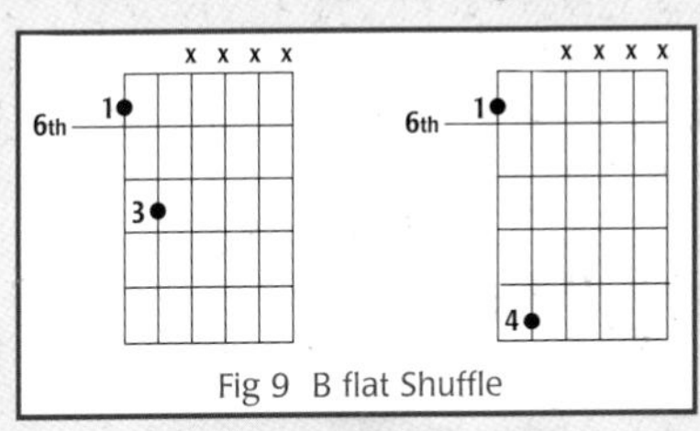

Fig 9 B flat Shuffle

There are many other ways in which a basic chord position can be adjusted or altered, creating melodic motion in the chord progression. Many well known songs from the blues and rock repertoire include sliding chord clusters in the rhythm guitar part (*Stormy Monday,* T-Bone Walker/The Allman Brothers; *Memphis, Tennesee,*Chuck Berry/Johnny Rivers; *Messing with the Kid,* Junior Wells/The Blues Brothers). Another means of creating melodic motion is by adding and removing extra notes against the chord, heard, for example, in *Pinball Wizard* by The Who and in *Sugar Magnolia* by The Grateful Dead. *See* Fig 10, p 68, for examples of each of these approaches. Many of the most effective and interesting

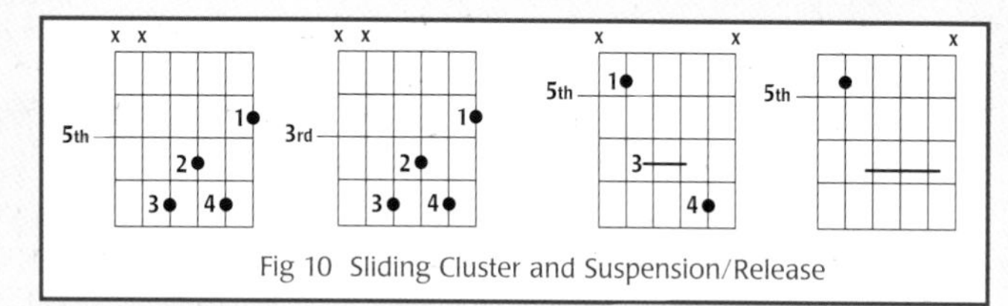

Fig 10 Sliding Cluster and Suspension/Release

rhythm guitar parts in popular music incorporate these or other modifications of the standard chords. Often this rhythm guitar part becomes the signature sound of the song itself.

Songs are built from sets of chords, often built primarily from one major scale or key. A chord progression or series of chords may be novel or stock, such as the C major-A minor-F major-G major formula which was popular in the 1950s.

If we number the steps of the scale (C major), we can place chords in a key by number. This technique allows for the transfer of information from one key to another. If C=1, D=2, E=3, etc., the stock progression given above becomes a 1-6-4-5 (or I-vi-IV-V) progression. A variation, the I-vi-ii-V, is played C major–A minor–D minor–G major. In any key, the I, IV, and V chords are major, while the ii, iii, and vi chords are minor (lower case Roman numerals).

These basic tools lend themselves to much variation often by switching major and minor chords. Try the 2nd progression with an A major or D major chord instead of the minor for an example of this kind of substitution. Alternately, a chord may be borrowed from another key entirely, creating more unexpected harmonic motion. Try substituting an A flat major chord for the F major chord in the first (I-vi-IV-V) progression and listen for the different texture. Broadly speaking, jazz chord progressions switch keys or borrow across keys much more often than do other popular music structures.

Controlling sound and sustain of the electric guitar while playing chords or melodies is often a question of allowing certain strings to ring out while muting or damping others. To play a light, percussive chord, the chording (left) hand controls the muting by releasing the pressure from the strings immediately after the chord is sounded. Do not lift the fingers from the strings, just release the pressure and the notes will quickly die off. This sets up a squeeze-strum-squeeze-strum pattern between the two hands, and produces a crisp, accurate rhythm. The right hand can also serve as a mute by resting on the strings as they are picked. The heel and palm of the picking hand dampens all the strings, a style of muting used extensively by rock guitarists. The pick plays mostly down strokes.

MELODY, LEAD, AND RIFFS

Aside from rhythm playing and chording, electric guitarists are often expected to play melodies, improvise *leads*, and fill in with short melodic passages called *riffs*, *licks*, or *breaks*. These runs of single notes require mobility on the fingerboard and coordination between the hands, with precise picking and fingering. With one fingering excercise and a few more scales, a number of these requirements can be developed quickly.

Building Mobility and Technique

First, try the fingering exercise frequently called the spider, as it resembles a spider crawling up the guitar neck. Place your left hand on the neck, about halfway up. Spread your fingers slightly and cover four frets with four fingers. This is a basic rest position. Curl the fingers so that all four fingertips are resting on the low E string, each in its own fret. Press the first finger down and strike the string with a downstroke. Press the next finger down and strike an upstroke. Press the ring finger down, strike a down stroke, and finish with the fourth finger and an upstroke. Move to the A string and advance one fret up the neck, repeating the picking pattern. Shift next to the D string, up one fret, and again play the four note pattern. Continue across all six strings in this manner. Remember to always use alternating down/up strokes with the pick, creating a smooth flow of notes. This exercise and a descending variation are shown in a chord box and in tablature in Fig 11. To expand your use of the fingerboard, devise variations of your own.

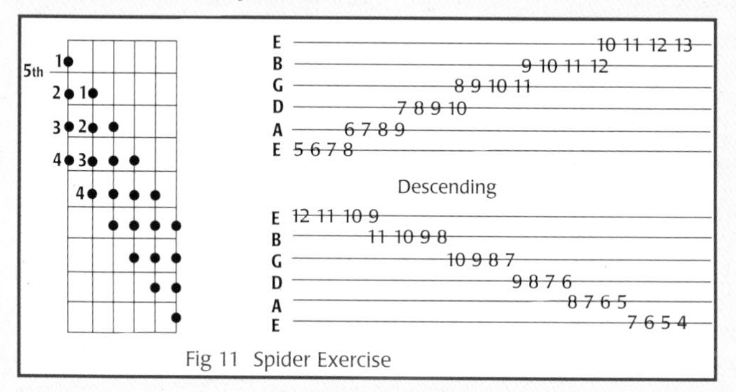

Fig 11 Spider Exercise

For a universal major scale

Earlier, we looked at two open position scales. Fig 12 gives a set of fingerings for a universal major scale which can be used anywhere on the neck. The starting note names the scale, much as the low E string provides the naming note for all E family barre chords. This scale starts with the 2nd finger of the left hand, and the example given is an A major scale,

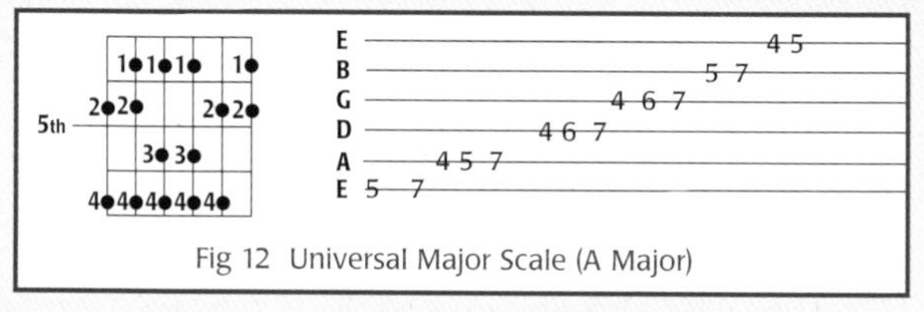

Fig 12 Universal Major Scale (A Major)

starting on the 5th fret of the low E string. Play the scale ascending and descending, with steady down-up-down-up pick strokes. You will recognize the familiar do-re-mi-fa-so-la-ti-do pattern. Don't worry about speed yet; it will develop naturally when the hands are better coordinated.

Pentatonic (5-tone) scales are important for blues and rock

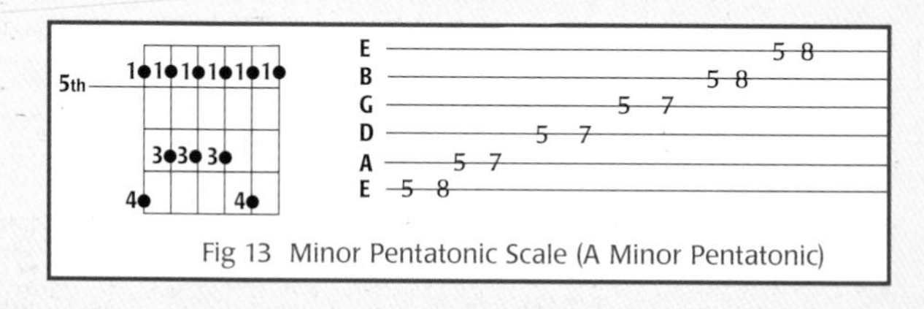

Fig 13 Minor Pentatonic Scale (A Minor Pentatonic)

lead guitar lines. The minor pentatonic scale, Fig 13, is used ffor blues melody and lends itself easily to elaboration and embellishment. The position given is for the A minor pentatonic scale, but you can create any minor pentatonic scale by using the low E string (in the same way that you use it for the universal major scale) to provide a naming note and starting place. Place your first finger on any note on the low E string and reproduce the fingerings from Fig 13. The major pentatonic scale is also a useful tool for improvising or writing a melody (Fig 14). (The opening lines of *Oh Susanna* employ a pentatonic scale.) All pentatonic scales should be practiced smoothly, with a down-up-down-up pick attack.

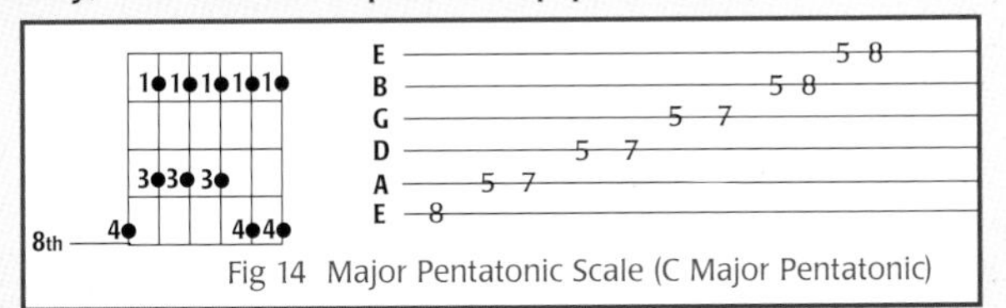

Fig 14 Major Pentatonic Scale (C Major Pentatonic)

Scales are identified and grouped by analyzing their sequence of whole steps (two fret distances) and half steps (one fret distances or adjacent notes). Some players favor certain types of scales, thus creating a distinctive and personal sound. For instance, the late lead guitarist for the Grateful Dead, Jerry Garcia, used the major scale and its various modes (alternate scales built from the major scale) extensively, while Carlos Santana's sound is rooted in the minor scale. Most jazz players make use of a wide range of scales and switch from one to the other quite often to accommodate the changing harmonies within a piece. Jazz players also use unusual altered scales to create angular and surprising melodic twists.

The **electric guitar vocabulary** contains stock phrases, referred to as *licks* or *riffs*, from which many songs and improvised solos are constructed. For blues see two moves in the key of E, given in Fig 15. The first is a stock turnaround or closing phrase, and the second is the *Suzie-Q* riff, given in key of A, in Fig 16, and is clearly within the A pentatonic minor scale set, shown in Fig 13, p 68. A good riff can be moved to a new key by shifting it up the fingerboard until it matches the key of the song being played.

More advanced techniques

As your playing improves, you may want to incorporate some different and more advanced left and right hand techniques. Certain styles of playing are virtually defined by the technique used by the right hand. For example, Chet Atkins is known for a fingerpicking style which does not make use of a standard plectrum. Instead, he uses a thumb pick while the fingers of the right hand pick the treble strings independently of the thumb. This style is strongly associated with The Nashville Sound and country music in general. Many players use some of the fingers of the right hand while holding a pick in the usual way; this gives them many options for rolling patterns which resemble Chet Atkins' style picking while retaining the speed and clarity provided by the plectrum.

Lead guitar playing makes use of many left hand tricks and techniques, such as bending the strings. When bending a note, the pitch is smoothly raised from one note to another, typically a whole step above the initial pitch. To play a basic bend, place the ring finger of the left hand on the B string at the tenth fret. This is the note A. Place the first and second fingers lightly on the same string; with all three fingers, push the string across the fingerboard until the note matches the sound of the B string fretted at the twelfth fret. Many bends are used in blues, rock, and country guitar playing and can be combined with stationary notes on other strings.

Other equally important left hand techniques are the hammer-on and its cousin, the pull-off. For both of these, a single pick stroke produces two or more melody notes. To play the hammer-on, place the index finger of the left hand anywhere on the fingerboard and pick that string. Before the note has a chance to die out, slap the ring finger of the left hand down on the fingerboard two frets above the first note you played, sounding a new, higher note. The pull-off is just the reverse of the hammer-on. Begin with the index and ring fingers of the left hand both pressing down the same string, two frets apart. Strike the string with the pick and immediately lift the ring finger. The sounded note will drop a whole step to the note fingered by the index finger. A fast flutter sound can be achieved by repeatedly hammering and pulling off in one location. Some advanced rock styles incorporate right hand hammer-on and pull-off techniques, where the picking hand crosses over to the fingerboard to execute the hammering or tapping. These techniques are widely used and allow a player to perform fast lines without picking every note.

PLAYING THE BASS GUITAR

Since its introduction in the 1950s, the electric

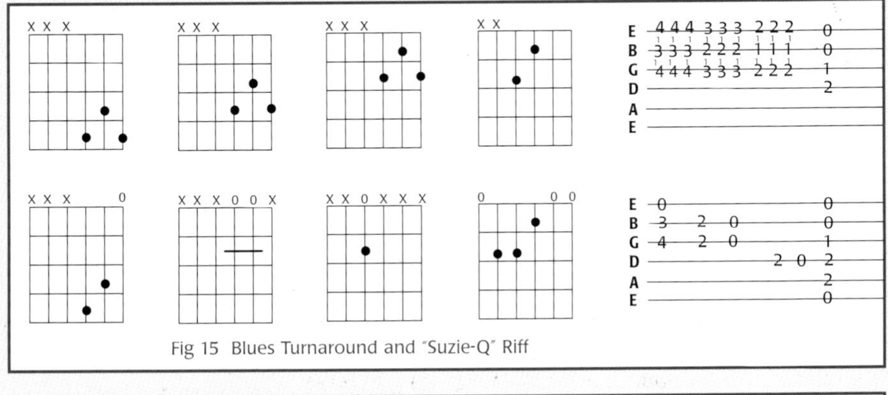
Fig 15 Blues Turnaround and "Suzie-Q" Riff

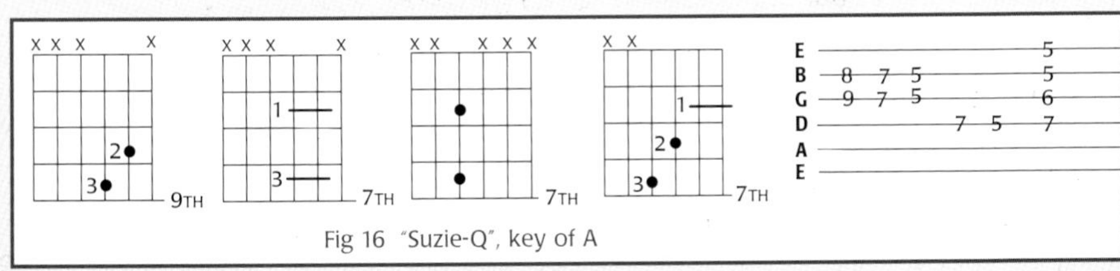

Fig 16 "Suzie-Q", key of A

bass (electric bass guitar) has replaced the acoustic (upright) bass as the lowest instrument in most popular music ensembles. Although its tuning and role in an ensemble are the same as its larger predecessor, the electric bass' ease of amplification and overall playability made it an instant success when the original Fender models were offered to the public in the early 1950s. Bass players adapted quickly to the techniques used on the electric instrument and guitar players easily switched over to bass. The sheer length of the bass neck, however, demands that players shift their left hand positions quite often, as only a few notes are available in any one location.

There are many **right hand techniques** for the electric bass. Many prominent rock players use a pick, such as Paul McCartney, Phil Lesh (Grateful Dead), and Carol Kaye (one of the most recorded studio musicians of the 1960s and 1970s). The pick produces a punchy, bright, clear tone with a lot of definition of the pitch and rhythm. Many players, such as James Jamerson of Motown Records, Donald "Duck" Dunn of Stax Records, John Entwhistle of The Who, and Chuck Rainey (another influential studio musician), developed a "two finger" approach. Using mostly (or exclusively) the first two fingers of the right hand, this style results in a thicker tone than the pick and has less attack. Starting in the 1970s, a new set of advanced techniques became popular through the rise of funk and other related forms of music. These techniques involve a variety of right hand slaps, thumb and finger "pops" (very aggressive plucking), and the snapping sound of the strings bouncing off of the frets. I recommend the standard two finger approach for the beginner.

Scale Studies for Bass

Most of the scale study in this chapter applies to the bass guitar and the tablature and chord boxes can easily be read on the bass. However, most instructional methods present material in the bass clef. For several reasons, reading music on the bass is generally easier than reading music on the guitar. First, the bass part usually proceeds one note at a time, without crowding in a lot of fast notes or chord clusters. Second, bass parts tend to be somewhat repetitive both melodically and rhythmically, so once you have read the first few phrases the rest is easy. Third, bass parts by their very nature are supporting other, more complex lines, and tend to be written rather sparsely and simply.

To begin a bass scale study, start with Fig 2 (the C major scale) and review the corresponding section at the beginning of this chapter. The first six notes of the scale will be easy to locate on the bass, because the low four strings of the guitar are tuned to the same notes as the bass, albeit in a higher register. Finish the scale by playing the B on the 4th fret of the G string and the C at the 5th fret. Similarly (Fig 3), the G major scale, is easy to transfer to the bass. Play the scale as written; when you reach the open G string, stop and begin the descent. Of even greater use will be the universal major scale (Fig 12). This set of fingerings can be shifted anywhere on the neck to produce any desired major scale. For the bass, play only the notes indicated for the lowest three strings of the guitar. These fingerings can be shifted across to an A string root and still produce a major scale. Practice all of these scales ascending and descending, keeping a steady 1-2-1-2 picking pattern in the right hand.

Bass players generally "map out" chords. There are many ways to do this and they are often specific to a certain style. The following examples are played against a C chord, using the notes of the C major scale (C, D, E, F, G, A, B, C). Because the language of music uses numbers as well as letters, think of the note E as the 3rd note of the scale, the G as the 5th, etc. In this manner, patterns are transferred to new keys, retaining the numeric information even when the letter names of the notes (in a different key) have changed.

Example **1** Use only first note of scale (root or tonic) and 5th (C and G). Play 1st beat on the C at the 3rd fret of the A string. Play 2nd beat on the G at 5th fret of D string. For contrast, substitute a low G at the 3rd fret of the low E string. Repeat the pattern, alternating C and G, for a simple country or folk bass line for a C chord, the root and 5th. You can apply this pattern to any chord root and its fifth.

Example **2** Use the root, 3rd, and 5th (C, E, G). Locate these on C major scale (universal scale fingerings or C scale Fig 2). With a steady beat and 1-2-1-2 picking, play the pattern C, E, G, E, C, E, G, E, an arpeggio for the C major chord. Slightly modified, this pattern is used in Latin American and Caribbean music. Break up the rhythm by using syncopation, uneven beats and rhythms. Try patterns in other keys by playing them in various locations on the neck.

A propulsive bass line that complements and supports the chords of a song is created by various combinations of scales, arpeggios, and connecting notes. In blues and rock styles, the major scale may be less emphasized than the pentatonic minor and major scales (Fig 13 and 14). When transferring these scales to the bass, remember that the scale has only five notes, and the sixth note concludes the scale by duplicating the first note in the next higher register. A simple pattern built from the A minor pentatonic might use only the A (7th fret of the D string), the E (7th fret of the A string), and the G (5th fret of the D string) to support an A chord. A repeating sequence such as A-A-E-G-A will help you create your own patterns or locate those played by others.

Bass lines propel the music from one chord to the next. Suppose you have been supporting a C chord with one of the simple figures outlined above and you know that in four beats the chord will change to F major. You could lead up to the F note by playing one beat on C, one beat on D, one beat on D sharp (first fret of the D string) and one beat on E. These four notes fill the four beats and lead clearly up to the F, where you would begin your next figure. Acquiring these basic moves and vocabulary will help you ask the right questions. Keep playing. Keep learning. Ask other players for their help.

Electronics

One of the best things about building your own electric guitar or bass is the ability to custom design the electronics. This allows you to determine not only the kinds of sounds the guitar will make, but how they are accessed and how many different tones it will have. You may put the volume knob wherever you'd like, choose the way you switch between sounds, and generally make an instrument that fits the way you make music. If the thought of "designing electronics" seems intimidating, you'll be happy to know that these kinds of circuits are among the easiest and most intuitive to work on. Electric instruments work on a few basic electronic principles. After these are understood, you'll be amazed at what you can do with your guitar's sound.

The "electric" parts of your new instrument give it its voice. They transform the motion of the vibrating strings into the electrical signal that leaves the output jack. In doing so, the electronics add a degree of "color" of their own, shaping the raw sound of strings and wood in subtle or powerful ways. This is important on an electric guitar or bass because these instruments are designed very differently than their acoustic cousins. Acoustic stringed instruments rely on a hollow box to transform the strings' vibrations into air movement and to shape the resulting sound by emphasizing some frequencies over others. Electric instruments do the opposite: their solid bodies are designed to avoid interacting with the air so that they can be amplified to a much louder level before they produce feedback. The result is a body which interacts with the strings very differently, reflecting back much of the strings' energy to produce more sustained notes with a broader, flatter frequency range. The less-colored tone is harmonically rich, with a more extended high and low end than an acoustic instrument, but this flatness tends to make it less musical. It is, however, an excellent place to start.

PICKUPS

Pickups do the job of changing the vibrations of the strings into electricity. As a string moves back and forth, the pickup produces an electrical current in a pair of wires, which reverses direction each time the string does. When this current is amplified and fed into a speaker, the speaker's cone moves in and out as a copy of the vibrating string, reproducing its sound. Much of what gives a pickup its sonic personality is the way it responds to different frequencies of the strings' vibrations. Some frequencies will cause the pickup to produce a stronger current than others, emphasizing those frequencies in the sound we hear. This is similar to what happens in an acoustic guitar's body, and is an important part of the instrument's tone.

Choosing a pickup for your new guitar or bass is a very important consideration. Fortunately, today's market is full of excellent choices. Several standardized pickup shapes have evolved which are produced by many different manufacturers. Once you've chosen an overall pickup type (Stratocaster style single coil, humbucker, jazz bass, etc.) you can still choose from many different-sounding models. People have tinkered with pickups since the first electric instruments appeared, and over the decades have come up with countless variations, each with unique voices and capabilities. At the same time, the almost universal appeal of the electric guitar and bass has brought about an enormous amount of tonal exploration on the part of players, creating a huge vocabulary of tones. Finding the sounds that work for you can be a lifelong process, but the resources available to today's builder make it a very enjoyable and rewarding one.

Most of the pickups used today are magnetic pickups. These were used on the earliest production electric instruments and have not changed much since their early development, especially when compared to the rest of the electronics world. Magnetic pickups produce the tones we most closely associate with electric guitars and basses. The variety of tones that this includes speaks volumes for the versatility and adaptability of these pickups.

Magnetic pickups are actually quite simple devices. A basic one consists of a small magnet with a very long, very thin piece of wire coiled around it. When the magnet is placed near a vibrating metal string, its magnetic field couples to the string and vibrates with it around the magnet, moving back and forth through the coil of wire. This causes a small electrical current to move with it along the wire, emerging at the two ends as the signal. While this describes a very basic pickup, the most advanced ones aren't much more complicated. The complexity in pickup design comes from the ways in which these few components affect the tone of the signal they produce, through the materials they are made of, their physical configuration, and countless small details which all contribute to the sound in some way. While this could be the subject of another book, all you really need to know to get started is a familiarity with the main pickup styles and what makes them sound the way they do.

PICKUP STYLES

Single-coil Pickups

Single-coil pickups (*see* drawing, p 72) were the first kind of magnetic pickups developed, and are the simplest and easiest to manufacture. Their excellent sound, inherent in their simplicity, is not easy to reproduce with newer, more complex pickup designs. Over the years single-coils have produced many of the most sought-after tones in both guitars and basses, and their versatility and expressive power keep this radio-age design at the forefront of modern music.

Single Coil Pickup

A top plate **B** polepieces **C** coil
D bottom plate **E** output wires

There are many different models of single-coil pickups, with vastly different tones, but for the most part their sound is characterized by a clear and focused treble, a tight, well-defined bass, and a dynamic responsiveness to subtleties of picking style. Their overall tone is vocal and somewhat bright. To many guitar players they seem "thin", but this tone has some advantages that aren't always apparent on first hearing. Played by itself, a guitar with single-coils doesn't always fill out the low end like a bassier one would, but in a band or in a mix this same tone "sits" beautifully with other instruments, cutting through without the muddiness that many guitarists mistake for a powerful sound. Another consideration is that single-coils were designed when the only amplifiers available were small tube models that weren't very loud, so they sound the way they are intended to when they're played through a tube amp with the volume up to at least 4 or 5, where the tone starts to fill out. At very low settings, a tube amp will sound underdriven and thin, and often a player will audition a guitar through a powerful modern amp set at 2 or 1, resulting in an anemic tone and the choice of a thicker-sounding guitar. Try single coils through a small tube amp that you can turn up, and you'll understand what they're about.

1 Jazz Bass and Stratocaster

In a bass, single-coil pickups sound punchy and articulate, with a low end that is clear and tight but not exaggerated. As in a guitar, single coils in a bass produce tones that usually work well in a mix, standing out by not conflicting with other instruments. They also match very well with tube amplifiers, complimenting their warmth and tonal complexity.

The most common type of single-coil pickup for guitars is the one used in Fender Stratocasters (Fig 1). The popularity of this guitar since its introduction in 1954 has produced a huge market for replacement pickups. Some are designed as high-quality reproductions of the best vintage Fender models, while others offer alternative tones that may be used in the original pickup locations. The number of tonal options available for this style of pickup make it an attractive choice to build with, and many guitar companies make models which use at least one of this type of pickup. Another popular configuration is that of the Fender Telecaster, whose two pickups are shaped differently from one another, unlike the Stratocaster's three identical pickups (Fig 2). While the range of models available in Tele styles is not as great as in the Strat format, there are still many to choose from.

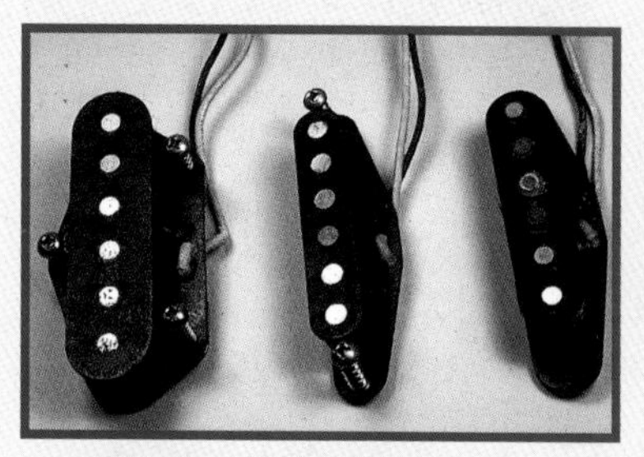

2 Telecaster Pickups: bridge (left), neck (middle), and Stratocaster pickup (right)

Another style of pickup that has seen a recent revival in popularity is the Gibson P-90, a large single-coil with a thicker, more powerful tone than the traditional Fender types. Most P-90 types currently produced are designed around the original sound of these pickups, although some variations are available, so if you choose to build with these excellent pickups, you will still have some options later, just not as many as with the more common Fender styles.

fourth switch positions, which combine two of the pickups in parallel. The same happens on a two humbucker guitar when both pickups are on together. Creative use of series and parallel combinations can broaden the range of an instrument's tone, as we will discuss below.

Another important part of pickup design is the choice of magnets. Some pickups, like vintage Fenders, use polepieces beneath each string which are individual magnets in the form of small cylinders extending between the coil windings. Other designs have one or two bar magnets on the bottom of the pickup, the magnetism being conducted to the string by non-magnetized polepieces consisting of a metal cylinder or a screw, the latter allowing each to be individually height-adjusted for a balanced volume between strings. This same design can also be made with a single wide polepiece running the full width of the strings, sometimes called a "blade." This design allows the magnet to cover the entire string area, maintaining a strong signal even when the strings are pulled to one side. They are also useful with non-standard numbers of strings, electric mandolins, etc.

The magnet's material also makes a difference. Many pickups use magnets made of alnico, an alloy using aluminum, nickel and cobalt, hence its name. This alloy has many variations, sometimes called alnico II or alnico V, each having a slightly different shape and strength of magnetic field. Another magnet used in pickups is ceramic, a less expensive material that is often identified with a somewhat brittle tone, although this only results when a pickup isn't designed well around the magnet.

The most important factor in a magnet's sound is the strength of its magnetic field, and the way that it interacts with the string. Strong magnets exert a pull on the string itself, affecting how the string vibrates. This extra pull often leads to an emphasis of the note's attack, at the expense of some sustain, but isn't necessarily a bad thing, and is part of the tone of many favored vintage pickups. In extreme cases, a magnet's pull can cause a string to produce a second frequency, or ghost note, sometimes heard as a warbly, garbled sound. This is quite audible with vintage Stratocaster pickups that are adjusted too close to the strings. They have very strong magnets, and if you play the bass strings on the upper frets you'll hear the ghost notes quite well. Some players consider this part of the charm of a vintage instrument. Many newer pickups are designed with softer magnetic fields which allow the strings to vibrate more freely, increasing sustain and harmonic accuracy.

Pickups with softer magnetic fields have another benefit which greatly increases their versatility. Because they may be adjusted close to the strings without overly affecting string movement, players may experiment with the different tones produced at various pickup heights. In general, pickups placed close to the strings will have a louder output (naturally), more treble and deep bass, and greater response to dynamics – overall a punchier sound. As the pickup is adjusted farther from the string, the tone starts to soften and become somewhat rounder and warmer. Thoughtful adjustment of each pickup in an instrument will allow for fine-tuning of the sounds of pickup combinations. If you are one of those Stratocaster players who never uses the middle pickup alone, try adjusting it to fine-tune the neck-middle and bridge-middle combinations. You may even want to angle the middle pickup to have different tones in the treble and bass strings in these combinations. It is worth spending some time exploring the possibilities, just remember to readjust pickup heights if you change the string height at the bridge, or with a truss rod adjustment.

In the years since Fender-based single-coils and Gibson-based humbuckers became the norm, many companies have emerged to make pickups to fit these models (Fig 9). In the process, the amount of sonic experimentation has been staggering, and in recent years the pickup industry has seen something of a renaissance. In the 1990s, many small manufacturers entered the marketplace, offering mostly high-quality pickups and innovative designs. A result was to drive up the level of quality throughout the industry. The internet has helped quite a bit, making more information available to players, designers, and builders. One can now choose from many types of humbuckers that fit into Strat or Jazz Bass pickup holes or single-coils to fit in humbucker holes, with tones that cover the ground between both types. Many pickups are designed as alternatives to the vintage tones, offering broader frequency response and a more accurate image of the sound of the instrument itself. These have been especially popular in basses, where they allow greater depth and articulation.

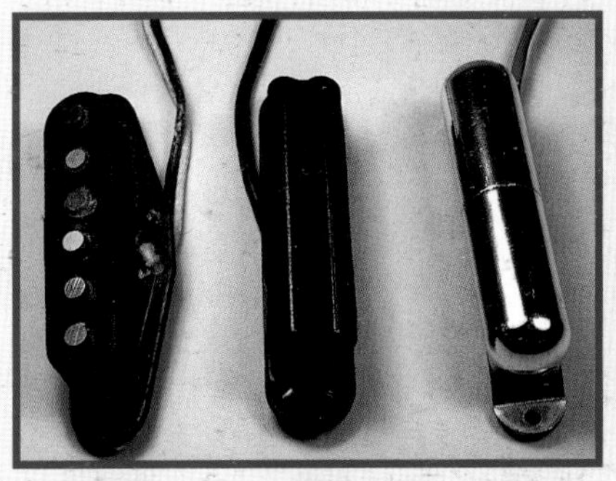

9 Pickups to fit Stratocaster type: standard Stratocaster (left), humbucker with blade polepieces (middle), lipstick tube pickup (right)

One of the holy grails of pickup design has been to make a hum-cancelling pickup that retains the tone of a single-coil. It has been very hard to do, although pickup makers have tried for quite a while. The problem is that any time you have more than one coil, an interaction occurs that removes some of the clarity, focus and air of the single-coil. Recently, several companies have released models that improve on the earlier attempts, but all of these have fallen short except one. Chris Kinman's Strat pickups are among the best available, with a tone strikingly close to the best old Fenders, yet are at least as quiet as most full-sized humbuckers. It's hard to overstate what a historical achievement this is, especially coming at a time when computers have brought so much recording power to musicians. Normal single-coils are almost useless anywhere near a computer monitor, and even today single-coil pickups remain an indispensible part of many players' sound. At the time of this writing, Mr. Kinman has released models for Telecasters, and is reportedly developing Jazz bass pickups and P-90s.

ACTIVE ELECTRONICS

Active systems utilize a small preamplifier in the instrument's circuitry, usually powered by one or more 9-volt batteries. This enables the instrument to drive long cords or chains of effects without loss of tone or excessive noise. Powerful tone-control circuits may be included on the instrument itself, and are especially useful in live situations. When individual pickups are mixed actively, each with its own preamp, they do so in a tonally neutral way, without the colorations of parallel and series connections. Active guitars and basses may be plugged directly into most mixing boards, recorders, and computer soundcards without external preamplification, producing a dry tone, uncolored by conventional amplification, which responds well to effects, equalization, and digital processing.

Active circuits have some drawbacks as well. The required batteries are inconvenient, and as they run down, the tone of the instrument may lose dynamic range and get noisy. It is expensive to make good-sounding electronics which are small, and active systems often have a somewhat grainy, brittle sound. Many of the advantages of active systems are available through other means: low-capacitance cables give passive instruments clarity and definition, and many modern amplifiers feature powerful tone-shaping circuits accessible with footswitches. Creative wiring in passive circuitry can produce tones which are often more interesting than those obtainable through the basic bass, middle, and treble knobs found on active designs, which usually duplicate controls already found on amplifiers.

If you choose to install active electronics in your instrument, they will come with instructions for the necessary wiring. It is best to purchase the system before you finalize your design so that you can allocate the space necessary for the circuit boards, battery, and controls.

PIEZO PICKUPS

These offer an interesting tonal alternative. They are usually mounted within specially made bridge saddles. These work much like small microphones, amplifying the sound you would hear with your ear against the surface of the instrument. The resulting sound is similar to an acoustic instrument, and may be blended with magnetic pickups to produce unique tones. Players often send the piezo's signal to a separate amplifier to create stereo effects, or to layer two totally different sounds.

OUR PICKUP CHOICE

For our guitar we chose Schaller humbuckers. They are very good, medium-priced pickups designed after the classic Gibson PAF tone. Like the Gibsons, they respond well when played clean or distorted, and have a versatile sound that works in any musical style. Unlike many higher-output humbuckers, their sound has detail, clarity, and dynamics. The wiring we designed for the guitar further enhances versatility with tunable single-coil tones and a convenient pickup blending system.

The pickups we chose for our bass are made by the Lane Poor Music Company of Fall River, Massachusetts. They feature a very clean, high fidelity tone with a warm but detailed sound, and are hum-cancelling. Combining the best of active and passive tones, Lane Poor pickups have a somewhat lower output than most passive types, although it is ample for everything but overdriving low-gain tube amps. The uncolored sound of these pickups means that equalization may be needed to achieve a desired tone, but there is so much tonal content, detail, and clarity that equalization and amplifier circuits respond very well, creating many sonic possibilities. They are satisfying to play, responding to subtleties of technique in a powerful, expressive way. If you like the sound of active basses but don't want to use batteries, Lane Poor pickups in a passive system are an excellent choice. We've used models HB 3.950 and SB 3.950 for bridge and neck positions, respectively.

STRING SPREAD AND PICKUP POLEPIECES

Traditionally, Fender guitar bridges are slightly wider, 2 7/32 in between the outside strings, than Gibson bridges (Tune-o-matic and others), which measure 2 1/16 in. The pickups made for these guitars have correspondingly-spaced polepieces. This means that, for instance, when using a Gibson type (humbucking) pickup with a Fender-spaced bridge, the outside strings will be slightly wide of the pickup's polepieces, and will sound quieter than the other strings.

To compensate for this, many companies make humbuckers with wider polepiece spacings, and Fender-based bridges are available which are narrower, usually somewhere in the middle of the two traditional spacings. Bridges are also available which have saddles that are adjustable for string-spacing. For our guitar, we chose a bridge and pickups which fall in the middle range. When choosing your components, be sure to take this into account, remembering that the strings get closer together as they get farther from the bridge.

PICKUP PLACEMENT

The location of a pickup in relation to the strings is an important part of how it sounds. Pickups placed near the bridge of the instrument sound very bright, while those nearer the neck are bassier. This is because of the way that a string vibrates when it is played.

A string's length and tension determine the frequency, or pitch, at which it vibrates. This pitch is called the fundamental, the frequency generated by the full length of the string. However, strings also vibrate in fractions of their length, called harmonics (below). Harmonics are multiples of the fundamental frequency, and give a string its rich, complex sound (called timbre). If you pick a string exactly at its center (the 12th fret of an open string) you will hear mostly the fundamental. The sound is bassy and round. As you pick closer to the bridge, you will hear more of the harmonics, and the sound is brighter.

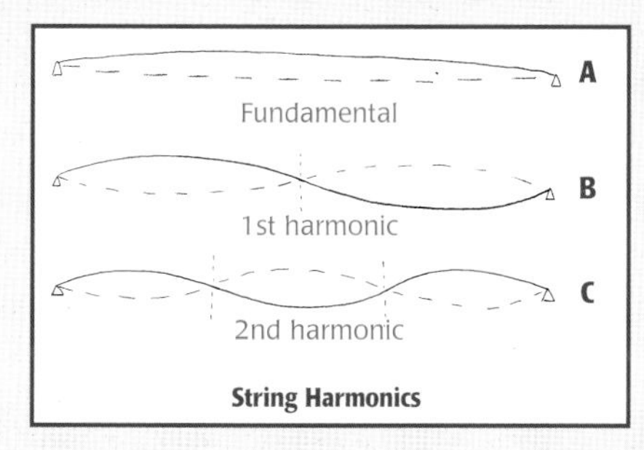

String Harmonics

A pickup senses a narrow section of the string's length, and its tone will only contain the vibrations which occur at that area of the string. Pickups near the bridge sense a large ratio of the string's harmonics, and less of the fundamental, resulting in a bright tone. Pickups nearer the neck have a strong fundamental content and are naturally bassier.

Because the string has a wider range of movement at its center than near its ends, neck pickups sense a stronger signal than bridge pickups. If two pickups of equal output are used, the neck pickup needs to be adjusted farther from the strings than the bridge pickup for the two to have equal volume. Often a pickup with a higher output is used in the bridge position to compensate for this, and many pickup models come in neck and bridge versions with compensated outputs.

When laying out your instrument, it is possible to do some fine-tuning with slight adjustments to pickup location. This is especially true of the bridge pickup, where a difference of ⅛ in will have a noticeable sonic effect. If you find that bridge pickups are unusably bright, place yours slightly farther from the bridge than normal. When measuring pickup placement on an existing instrument, be sure that the scale length matches the one you intend to use, or else compensate accordingly.

KNOBS AND SWITCHES PLACEMENT

One of the most common complaints about the Fender Stratocaster concerns the placement of its volume knob and pickup selector switch. Both are directly in the path of the picking hand, and many players accidently knock them to an unintended setting. Other players, usually those with a lighter touch, find the locations of these controls convenient for making rapid adjustments. This is especially true of players who keep their little finger on the volume knob to "swell" the note after it is picked.

In placing your components, you may duplicate those found on a familiar instrument, or design a layout which fits your own preferences. Usually, it is best to locate knobs and switches where they are accessible, but out of the way of flying picks and fingers. You might also consider the visual impact of the components on the body shape.

Once you have finalized the layout, adjust the shape of the electronics compartment accordingly. Be sure to leave room for the output jack (with plug in place). If you think you may want to modify your electronics by adding additional switches or knobs at a later date, provide space for these as well. It is wise to leave ample room around potentiometers, so that if they become loose and spin in their mounting holes, they won't contact the compartment's shielding or other components.

OTHER ELECTRONIC COMPONENTS AND WIRING

How to Solder

Soldering requires care, patience, and timing, but it is not difficult to master, and many builders find it very enjoyable. If you have never soldered before, take some time to practice by soldering together scraps of wire or old components. Better yet, get some experience on an inexpensive instrument before working on anything irreplaceable, like a vintage guitar. Fortunately, the electronic parts in an electric instrument are relatively inexpensive, and it is hard to actually ruin anything with bad soldering technique as long as you take the precautions mentioned here.

Before working inside of an electronics compartment, always mask off the surface of the instrument with cardboard or several sheets of thick paper. It is not uncommon for small blobs of hot solder to spatter or drip off of a soldering iron, and they don't get along well with wood or finishes. Similarly, avoid contacting the metal parts of a soldering iron to anything that shouldn't be burned, such as the sides of your electronics compartment. It is very easy to be focused on what you are soldering and suddenly smell burning wood.

Eye protection is very important for soldering, and the fumes from melting solder contain lead, and should be avoided.

A heat sink is a conductive material that is temporarily attached to a component to pull heat away from sensitive parts (*see* p 11, Electronics Tools). They work by being clipped to the conductor between the solder joint and the component. Heat sinks are important when soldering capacitors, resistors, or anything else you suspect could be damaged by heat. Medical hemostats are often used for this purpose, especially when the part needs to be held in place for soldering. For components which are already in place, something more lightweight is better to avoid bending anything. Copper alligator clips are an excellent choice. For better heat dissipation, a length of stripped copper wire may be soldered to the clip.

When soldering heat sensitive components which are too small to fit a heat sink, such as small switches or potentiometer lugs, solder as quickly and efficiently as possible, in several steps if necessary, to avoid building up heat in the component.

When a soldering iron is new, or has a new tip, it must be tinned with a layer of melted solder the first time it is heated up. This will keep the tip from burning and oxidizing, which would make it perform poorly. Maintain the tinning at regular intervals, and keep the tip clean by wiping frequently on a moistened sponge.

Before making solder connections, tin the surfaces to be joined with a thin layer of solder. This insures a strong bond. On small connectors with a hole in them, such as potentiometer and switch lugs, pull a thin film of solder across the hole to cover it over, then re-melt this film while gently pushing the tinned wire into place. Do not wrap wire around these lugs dry and then solder in place, or when you go to undo the connection later it will be extremely difficult, and may throw molten solder at you when the connection finally pulls free.

Connections should be made using as little actual solder as possible to achieve a solid contact. Large blobs of solder do not conduct a signal any better than a neat connection. Solder will flow toward a source of heat, making it possible to direct solder to where it is needed. Allow solder to cool at its own pace, without blowing on it, to achieve maximum strength and conductivity.

Heat-shrink tubing provides a good way to insulate any exposed connections or surfaces against contact with other parts. It comes in various diameters, 1⁄16 in being best for most instrument wiring purposes. To use it, slip an appropriate length over a wire before it is soldered in place. Solder the connection, then move the tubing over the connection and heat it briefly with a flame. The tubing will shrink around the connection, and be fixed in place.

Passive Electric Guitar & Bass Wiring

The following section describes the basics of passive electric guitar and bass wiring, as well as some options for use in designing your own instrument's electronics. It is easy to be inspired by all of the possibilities and wind up with a guitar full of controls, requiring five minutes of switching to obtain a certain sound. A better solution is to systematically explore the options in your workshop and find the sounds that work best for your music, and which suit your amplifier and other equipment. You can then find a wiring which allows you to access these sounds quickly and efficiently in a live setting, or in a recording studio where time is limited. It is usually best to pursue quality over quantity in selecting sounds. Often having too many choices proves to be more distracting than productive. Additionally, the fewer wires and switches your pickups' signal passes through, the clearer its tone, so be judicious with modifications which require additional components.

Schematics for common guitar and bass circuits are readily available in the instructions which come with pickups and pickup switches, through on-line resources, and in books that focus on music electronics. They are well worth studying to learn how the basics presented here are applied in different instruments. We will describe some of the more interesting tonal options, and show how we applied them to the wirings used in our two instruments.

Hot and ground The two electrical conductors that carry the signal from a pickup are divided into "hot" and "ground". Hot and ground refer to the two sides of an electrical circuit. The hot signal runs through the pickup-selector switch and the volume and tone controls, eventually reaching the part of the output jack which connects to the "tip" of the male connector on the cord running to the amp (*see* drawing at right). The ground is connected to the instrument's shielding, and to the part of the output jack which connects to the sleeve of the cord's connector. If the hot and ground connect with each other, the signal is shorted and cancels itself out. Pickup-selector switches work by selecting which pickup's hot signal reaches the hot side of the output jack. Volume and tone controls work by variably sending the hot signal to ground, weakening the strength of the signal.

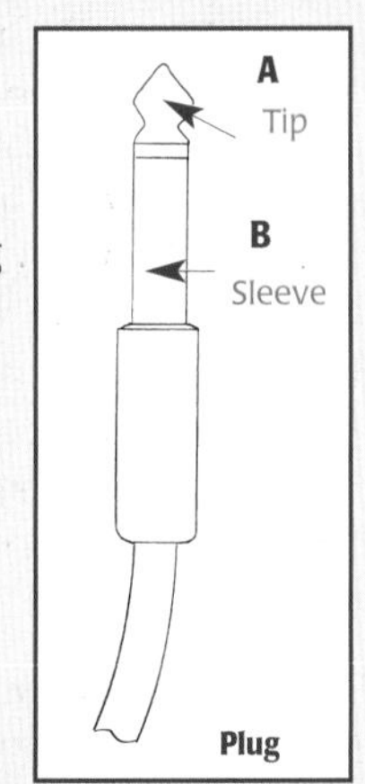

For purposes of clarity, we will refer to the hot connector of the output jack as the output. (Fig 10, p 79)

10 Electronics components
Top, L to R Three-position switch, 3-pickup SG style
Standard Stratocaster 5-position switch
Specialty 5-position
Rotary switch
Bottom, L to R Potentiometer
Potentiometer with DPDT push-pull switch
Blend potentiometer
Output jack

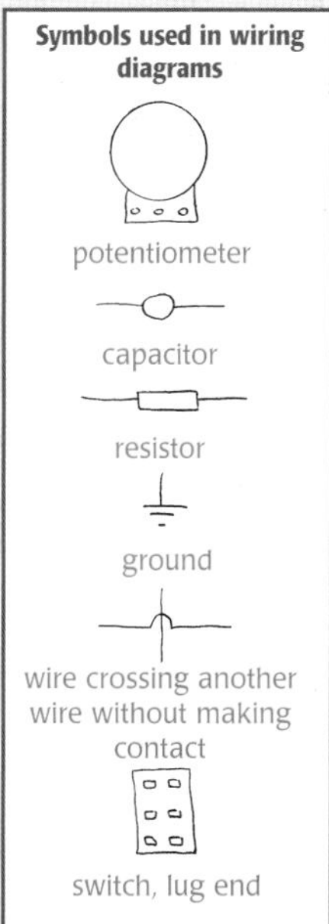

Potentiometers, or pots, are the parts inside the electronics compartment that attach to the knobs, and are used to make the volume and tone controls. A potentiometer (below) contains a semi-circular length of a material, called the "track", which is resistive to the flow of electricity. A wiring connector is placed at either end of this track, appearing as the two outside lugs on the pot's housing. The middle lug connects to a wiper, an arm fixed to the shaft that rides along the resistive track. When the wiper is at one end of the resistive track, it makes a full electrical connection to the lug at that end. As the shaft is turned, the wiper moves along the track, putting increasing resistance between itself and the first lug. Meanwhile, resistance between the wiper and the lug at the other end of the track decreases, reaching zero when the wiper makes contact with it.

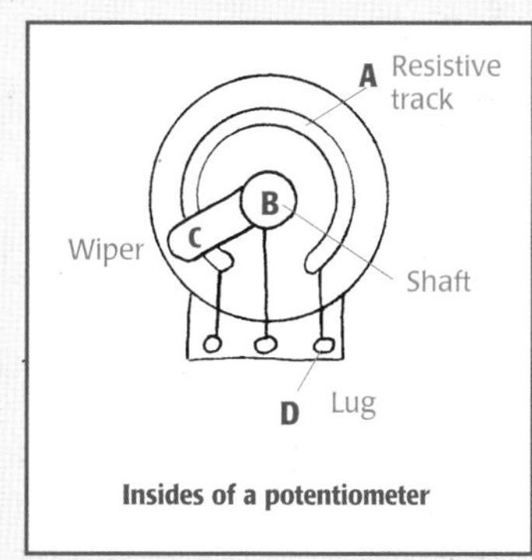

Insides of a potentiometer

Value A potentiometer's value refers to the amount of resistance between the ends of its track. Resistance is expressed in ohms, (symbolized by the greek letter Omega). Pots used in electric guitars and basses are in the range of thousands of ohms, or kilohms, abbreviated K. The two most common values used are 250K and 500K. 250K pots give the instrument a slightly darker sound, and are most often used with single-coil pickups. 500K pots, being brighter, are best suited to humbuckers. The difference in sound is caused by treble frequencies leaking through the resistance to ground. 250K pots allow more of this to happen, as will multiple pots in a circuit.

Taper The taper of a pot determines how its resistance changes over its range (drawing below). Their are two types used in instruments. A logarithmic or audio taper is designed to increase volume gradually in its lower range, and more quickly in its upper range. This is perceived by the ear as an even increase in volume as we are more sensitive to volume changes in quieter sounds. Audio taper pots are the most common type for use in master volume and tone controls.

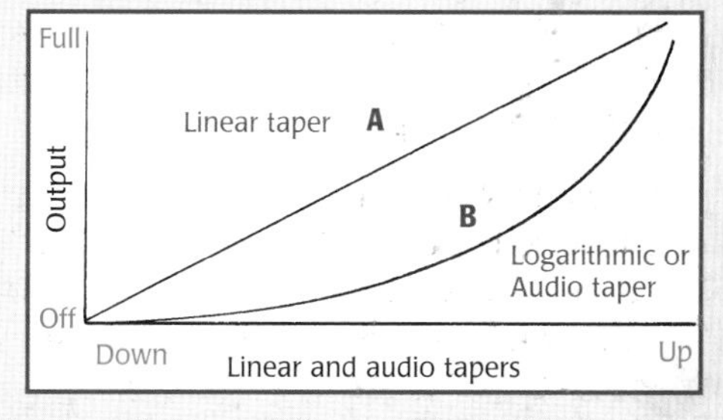

Linear and audio tapers

Linear taper pots change their resistance consistently over their range. They are the best choice when using separate volume controls for each pickup, as they provide a gradual blend between the pickups' tones.

Volume Controls A potentiometer becomes a volume control when 1) the hot signal from a pickup is connected to the lug on one end of the track, 2) the ground is connected to the lug at the other end, 3) and the wiper connects to the output (drawing below). When the wiper is at the end of the track connected to the pickup's hot wire, the signal passes unimpeded to the output jack. As the shaft is turned and the wiper moves down the track, resistance is increased between the pickup's hot and the output, and the volume drops. Simultaneously, resistance is decreased between the output and ground, contributing to the decrease in volume.

A volume control wired as in the drawing at right will turn down the volume of the entire instrument when it sends the output to ground, even if there are separate volume controls for each pickup. If you would like to be able to turn one pickup all the way down without affecting the overall volume,

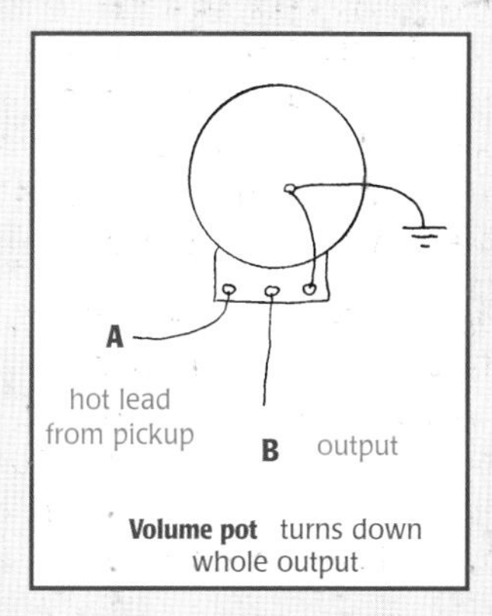

Volume pot turns down whole output

wire the pickup's hot wire to the wiper, and the output to the up end of the track (drawing at right). Pickup blend controls, discussed below, are wired in this way. The drawing immediately below shows a circuit with two separate volume pots and a tone pot. This is the circuit used in Fender jazz basses.

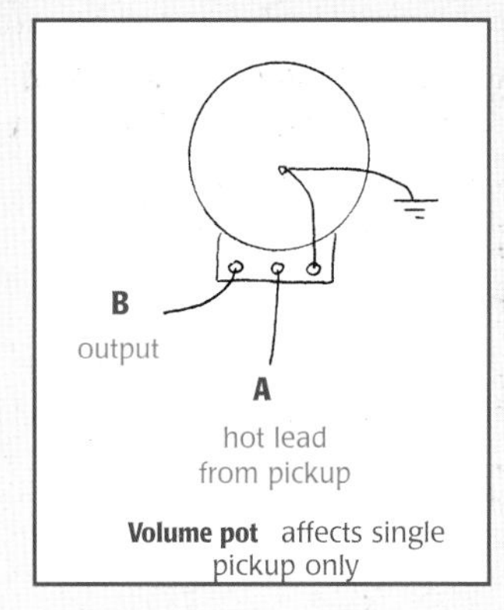

Volume pot affects single pickup only

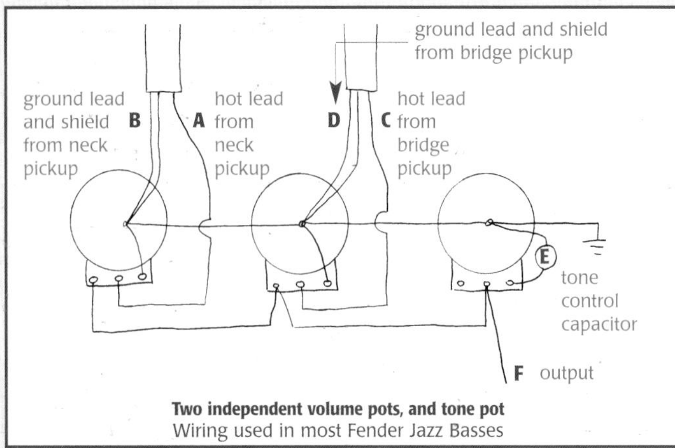

Two independent volume pots, and tone pot
Wiring used in most Fender Jazz Basses

TONE CONTROLS AND CAPACITORS

Capacitors allow treble frequencies to pass through them (Fig 11), but block bass frequencies (drawing below). A tone control is made by connecting the hot signal to one side of a capacitor, and the other to the wiper of a pot (drawing at right). One end of the pot's track is then connected to ground. As the wiper is turned toward the ground end of the track, the treble frequencies that pass through the capacitor are sent increasingly to ground, darkening the tone of the instrument.

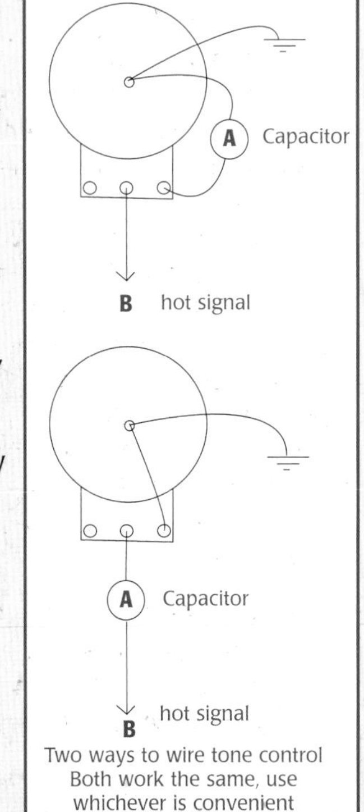

Two ways to wire tone control
Both work the same, use whichever is convenient

Capacitors come in different values, expressed in microfarads (abbreviated mfd). Capacitors used in tone controls range from roughly .05 to .01 mfd. The value you choose will determine what frequencies the tone control will attenuate. .05mfd capacitors will make a dark-sounding tone control, while a .01 mfd capacitor will ground just the highest frequencies, leaving most of the upper mids in the signal. A popular choice is a .02mfd, with a wide range of musical tones. Some experimentation will be helpful in determining which you prefer.

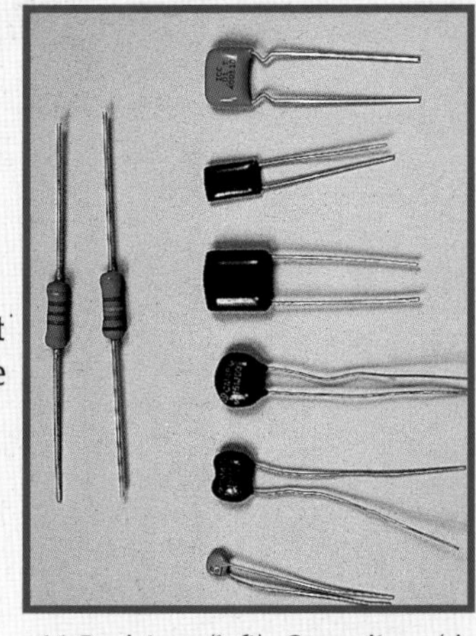
11 Resistors (left), Capacitors (right)

Separate tone controls may be made for each pickup, with capacitor values chosen for each. This is done by attaching the capacitor to the pickup's hot lead, at its connection to the selector switch (or independent volume control). However, any time that a pickup is in the circuit, its tone knob will affect all of the pickups connected to it, grounding their high frequencies as well as its own.

Capacitors may be made from different materials, resulting in different quality levels of the sound that passes through them. The least expensive kind is called "ceramic disk." They pass treble signals that sound somewhat brittle and diffuse. However, in a tone control circuit, the signal which passes through the capacitor goes to ground, so you don't hear it, and these work as well as more expensive types. In a circuit in which you will hear the signal passing through the capacitor, use a high quality type like polyester, polypropeline, polystyrene, or silver mica. They usually cost less than a dollar each, and the sound is worth it. Avoid capacitors that are "polarized," these have legs labeled with + and −.

DUAL POTENTIOMETERS

Dual, or ganged, potentiometers, have two pots on a singe shaft, placed on top of one another. There are several variations of these, but two types are especially useful for instrument wiring.

Blend pot

A bridge pickup hot lead
B neck pickup hot lead
C output

Blend pot (drawing at right): Blend pots allow you to adjust the balance between the sounds of two pickups. They feature a detent or click, at the centerpoint of the shaft's travel, at which both pots are at their full volume. Turning the shaft to one side attenuates one pickup; turned to the other side attenuates the other pickup. Some brands of blend pot have the bridge pickup pot on top, others have the reverse, so consult the instructions or test with a multimeter before wiring.

Dual concentric pot: These have two pots activated separately by two stacked knobs on a single shaft (Fig 12). They are useful for putting two knobs in a single place, such as volume and tone, separate tone knobs, etc.

12 Stacked knobs

PICKUP SELECTOR SWITCHES

In instruments with more than one pickup, switches are usually used to determine which pickup is heard. These come in a wide selection of styles, from simple ones that switch between two pickups (neck pickup, both in parallel, bridge pickup) to highly complex models with many options for creative wiring. They all work differently, but you can usually determine their function by examining the way their mechanisms make different contacts in the various switch positions, and they generally come with instructions. Some switches have enclosed housings around the connections, in which case either read the instructions or use your multimeter to determine the sequence of connections.

For our guitar we chose a 3-position switch patterned after the ones used in the 3-pickup Gibson SG and Les Paul models. It allows the custom wiring we used, as will be described below.

MINI SWITCHES

Mini switches are useful for all kinds of wiring options. They may be used to switch between different capacitors for a tone control, to switch off one coil in a humbucker, or for any number of purposes. A basic one has three lugs: in one switch position, the center lug connects the lug on one side; in the other position the center lug connects to the lug on the other side. This is called a single pole, double throw, or SPDT switch (*see* drawing below). Often, two, or even four, sets of lugs are put on a single switch to allow multiple functions. These are called double pole, double throw (DPDT) and four pole, double throw (4PDT) switches, respectively.

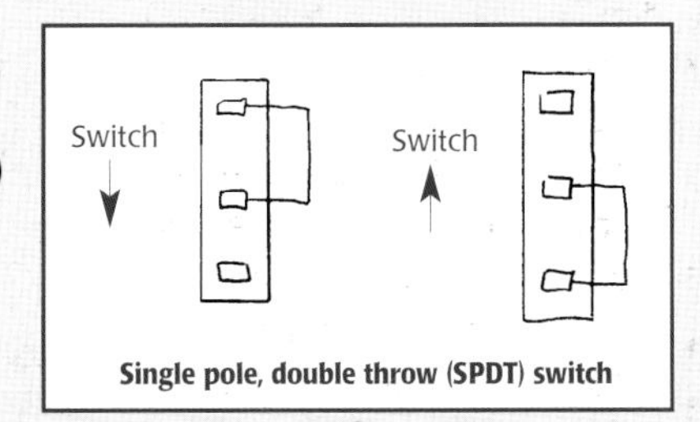

Single pole, double throw (SPDT) switch

These switches also come in three-position versions. On-off-on types have a center position in which no connection is made. On-on-on types have a center position in which both connections are made. DPDT on-on-on switches have a special arrangement for this (*see* drawing below).

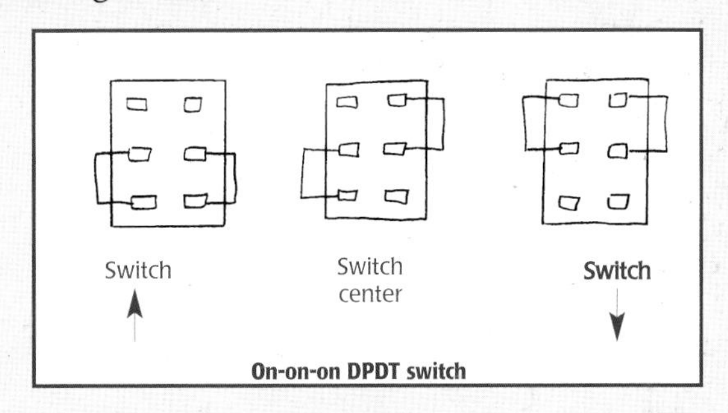

On-on-on DPDT switch

If you would like to wire extra switches into your instrument, but don't want to drill any more holes in it, consider switch pots. These feature a DPDT switch in a housing on the back of the pot, activated by pulling and pushing on the knob (they are also known as push-pull pots, *see* Fig 10, 79).

OUT-OF-PHASE WIRING

When two pickups are wired out of phase, it means that the hot and ground leads are reversed on one pickup (drawing at right). This causes the signals from each pickup to move in opposite directions, canceling out whatever is common to both signals. What is left is a thin, trebly tone that has an interesting, somewhat vocal quality. If the pickups are wired to separate volume knobs, or to a blend pot, varying degrees of this sound may be dialed in. Another way to get an interesting, half-out-of-phase sound is to insert a capacitor in the phase switch, so that the signal of the pickup whose leads are reversed will pass through the capacitor, cutting off its bass frequencies. The resulting blend will have the bass of one pickup, and the phased treble of the two pickups together. The value of the capacitor (use .1 to .02mfd) will determine the frequency at which the phased tone begins. Use a high-quality capacitor for this wiring, as you will hear the signal which passes through it.

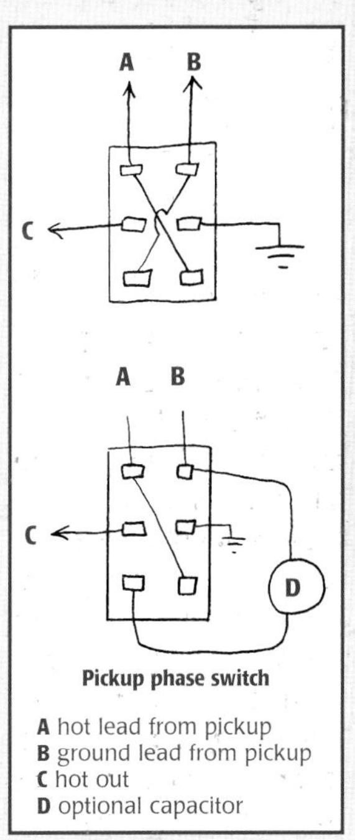

Pickup phase switch

A hot lead from pickup
B ground lead from pickup
C hot out
D optional capacitor

HUMBUCKER WIRING OPTIONS

Humbucking pickups, which you will recall contain two separate coils, usually come with four leads, plus a shield (Fig 13, p 82). These consist of two wires for each coil, and the shield is wired to ground. Humbuckers are normally wired with the two coils in series, creating their characteristically thick sound. To achieve this sound, two of the four leads are twisted and soldered together, then covered with heat-shrink tubing or tape to keep them from accidently contacting the shielding or other parts of the electronics. The remaining two leads are soldered to hot (or to a switch, volume pot, blend pot, etc.) and ground. It is important that the correct leads be chosen for each connection, so they are color-coded. Unfortunately, each pickup manufacturer has their own color scheme, so consult the instructions that come with your pickup.

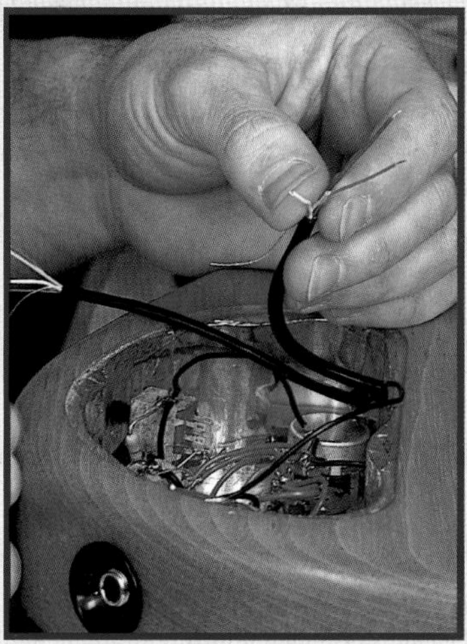

13 Leads from a humbucker, with 4 wires and shield (bare wire)

The two coils in a humbucker also provide some interesting sonic options:

Coil tap One of the easiest of these options is to turn off one of the two coils, sometimes called a coil tap. This involves sending the two connected leads to ground, usually by soldering them to a SPDT switch's center lug, and wiring one of the other lugs to ground (drawing at right). In one switch position, the humbucker will sound normal, in the other it will have a single-coil tone. This happens because, when the switch is engaged, one of the humbucker's coils has its leads wired to hot and ground, as is normal, and the other coil's leads are both going to ground.

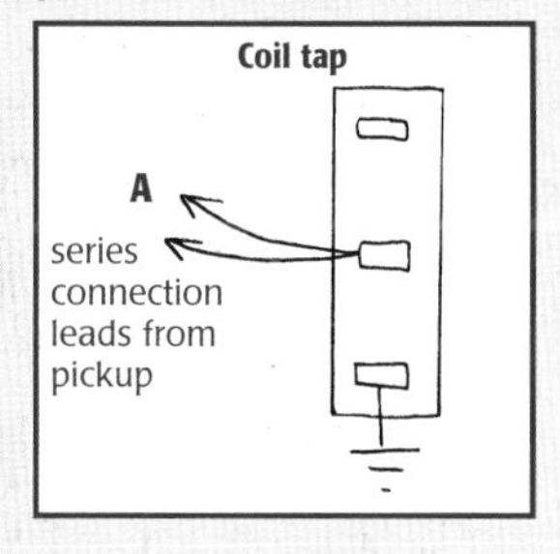

Capacitor tap The coils of a humbucker are optimized to sound good when the pickup is in its normal, series mode. As a result, the coil tapped sound can be somewhat thin, compared to the sound of a Stratocaster pickup, for instance. One way to get a much more useable single-coil tone out of a humbucker is to use a capacitor for the ground wire of the tap switch (drawing at right). As in a tone control, the capacitor sends only the high frequencies to ground, and the resulting sound has the treble of a single coil, but the bass of a humbucker.

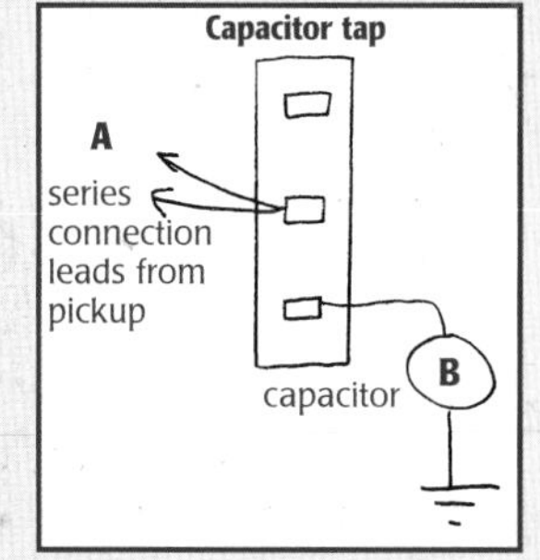

Tuned capacitor tap In the capacitor tap described above, the bass boost provided by the capacitor-tapped coil is often too much for a good single-coil sound. However, the amount of this bass boost may be fine-tuned by inserting a resistor in parallel with the capacitor, sending some of the coil's signal to ground (at right). Values for this resistor range from about 2K (bass boost almost completely attenuated) to about 100K (bass boost nearly full). To determine the best value for this resistor, first wire the capacitor tap circuit as described above. Then use test-leads to temporarily insert a potentiometer (250k is best but a 500k pot will work fine) in parallel with the capacitor, where the resistor will go. Plug in the guitar or bass, and adjust the potentiometer until the desired amount of bass-boost is reached. Unclip the test leads and measure the potentiometer's resistance on your multimeter, being careful not to move the pot's shaft. Replace the potentiometer with a resistor of the value on the meter, and you have achieved your sound. You could just as well wire the potentiometer permanently in place and have a variable bass boost for your single-coil sound. In practice, however, most players find one optimal tone and stick to it. With the variable version it can be difficult to quickly dial up the right amount of boost. One option is to permanently mount the potentiometer inside the electronics compartment, in the form of a screwdriver-adjustable trim pot. A 100K audio-taper pot will provide a smooth range of control.

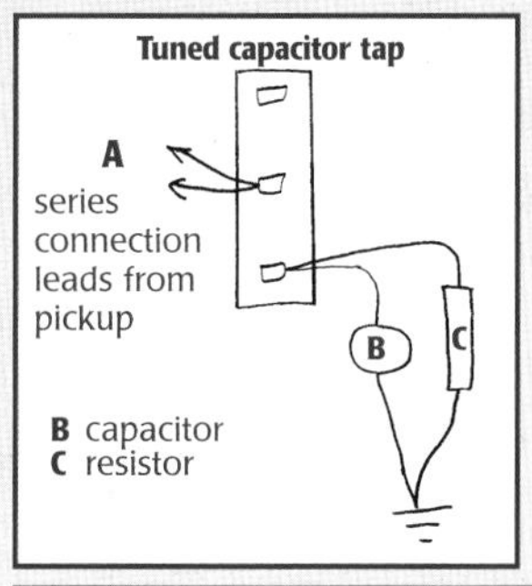

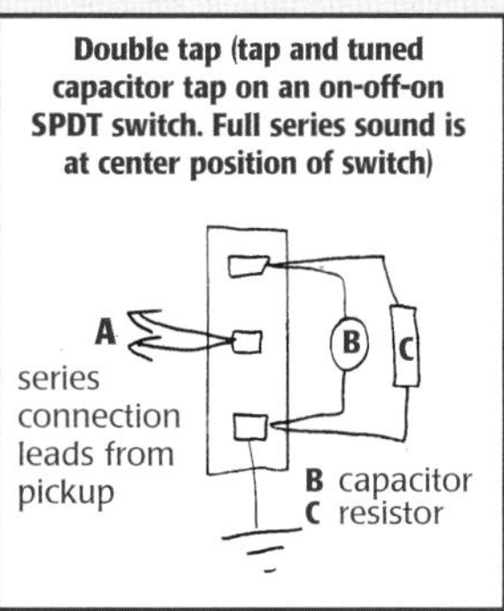

Tuned tap Dispensing with the capacitor and using only a resistor in the tap circuit will create a sound between a humbucker and a single-coil. Unlike the capacitor tap, the tapped coil will affect the entire frequency range, attenuating the treble of the other coil as it does in the full-series humbucker setting, only less.

A single on-off-on SPDT switch may be used to access two different tap sounds (see drawing above).

Series-parallel switch When one coil of a humbucker is switched off, as above, the pickup loses its hum-canceling quality. An alternative is to switch the coils from series to parallel (at right). This produces a tone that is similar to the tapped sound, but lower in output and thinner. It also lacks the tone-shaping options of capacitor tapping, but provides a usable option when hum is to be avoided at all costs. Series-parallel switches may be used together with coil taps, as long as you can manage all of the switches.

Series parallel switch

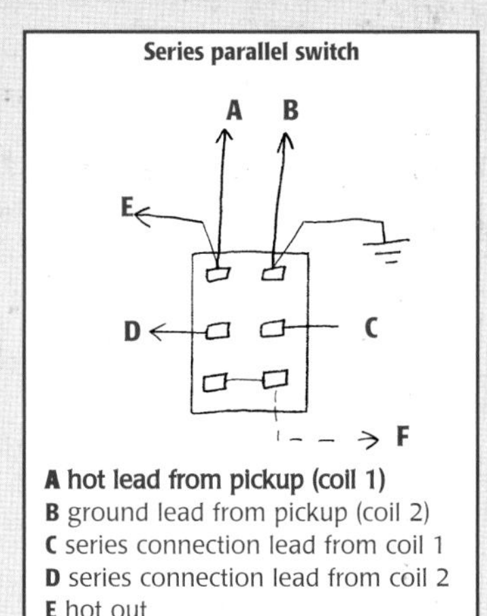

A hot lead from pickup (coil 1)
B ground lead from pickup (coil 2)
C series connection lead from coil 1
D series connection lead from coil 2
E hot out
F to optional tap switch

OTHER WIRING OPTIONS

Two Pickups Series/Parallel

A 4PDT switch is useful whenever several functions need to be activated from a single switch. One example at right is to direct the outputs of two pickups between the main selector switch/blend knob and a series connection. This allows for quick switching between the main pickup selector switch and a preset series sound. The tone-shaping options described in the tuned capacitor tap section above may also be used to modify the series sound in this switch.

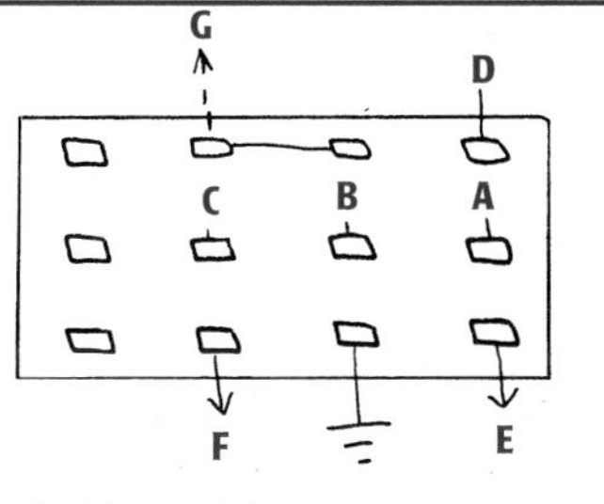

A Pickup 1 hot
B Pickup 1 ground lead
C Pickup 2 hot lead (pickup 2 ground lead to gound)
D hot out for series sound
E pickup 1 parallel hot out (to switch or blend pot)
F pickup 2 parallel hot out (to switch or blend pot)
G optional capacitor/resistor to ground

Eliminating Treble Loss in a Volume Knob

One problem that often keeps players from using the volume control on their instrument is a loss of treble as the knob is turned down. This is caused mostly by capacitance in the cable that runs to the amplifier. One solution is to buy an expensive low-capacitance cable. However, it is better not to have your tone dependent on a cable, as these have a way of being misplaced.

A better solution is to wire a small capacitor and resistor across the hot and output legs of the volume pot(s) (at right). This bleeds a small amount of treble past the pot's resistance, effectively making the sound brighter as the volume knob is turned down, balancing out the loss from the cable. Additionally, this circuit allows for a degree of tone-shaping, as you may elect to deliberately tune your volume control to make the tone brighter or darker as the volume is decreased. Using the volume knob to adjust overdrive in a tube amp, for instance, you may find that a brighter sound with the knob set lower works well with less-distorted tones.

Treble bypass for volume pot

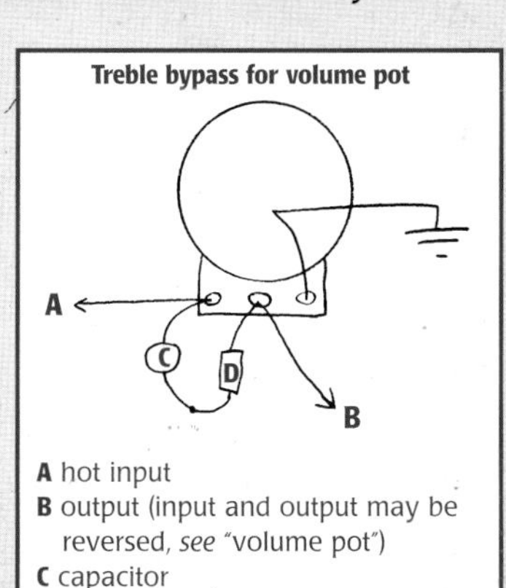

A hot input
B output (input and output may be reversed, *see* "volume pot")
C capacitor
D resistor

The capacitors that work best for this are in the range of 120-220pf (picofarads) for guitar, or 60-150pf for bass. As with the tone controls, the capacitor's value determines the frequency at which the treble bypass begins. Experimentation allows fine-tuning the effect. Begin with a capacitor in the middle of the range. These values are available in silver mica capacitors, as well as some of the other high-quality types, and their use insures that the sound will remain clear and detailed as the volume knob is turned down. The resistor is wired in series with the capacitor to attenuate the amount of treble passing through it. A 100K resistor is a good place to start. To find the resistor value that best suits your tone, use a potentiometer temporarily clipped in place of the resistor, as described above in the tuned capacitor tap section, p 82.

AVOIDING ELECTRIC SHOCK

Playing an electric instrument presents some potential for electric shock. This can occur when the grounding in your amplifier is inconsistent with the grounding in a PA system, or in other bandmates' amplifiers. When your hands are touching your instrument's strings (or any other part connected to ground), and you come into contact with an oppositely-grounded microphone, for instance, a "ground loop" is created, and a sizeable shock can pass through your body. Ground-loop potential can also occur if your amplifier is improperly wired, if you use a 3-prong to 2-prong plug-adapter, or if the electrical outlets you are plugged into are wired incorrectly. Any time two pieces of equipment have an opposite ground, a potential for shock exists.

To help avoid this, purchase an inexpensive outlet tester at an electrical retailer, home center, or hardware store. It has a three-prong plug on a small housing, and a series of lights which indicate when an outlet is ungrounded, or has its leads reversed. Test all of the outlets in your practice space, when you go to a friend's house to jam, and in any live venue. If you have occasion to play an event where a generator supplies the power, check that the generator is properly grounded to a grounding stake or water pipe before plugging anything in.

As a further precaution, you can wire a simple safety device into your guitar which will reduce any shock that may occur, at least through contact with your strings. We first encountered this in Adrian Legg's book, Customizing Your

Electric Guitar (an excellent resource, by the way). Wire a 220K resistor and a .001 mfd capacitor (rated for 500 volts), in parallel, between the electronics ground and the ground wire to the bridge (below). Cover the leads with heat-shrink tubing to avoid unintentional contact with other components.

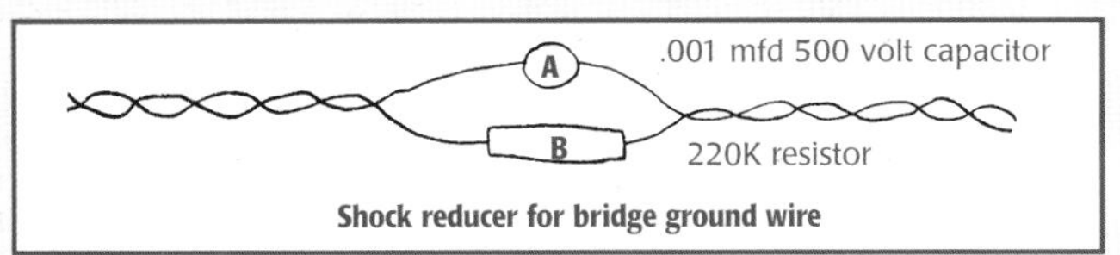

Shock reducer for bridge ground wire

This system will limit any shock to roughly 40 volts, which would be unpleasant, but probably not lethal. Be aware that the other parts of the guitar which attach to the ground, like the output jack, metal knobs, etc. will still be connected directly to ground, and may cause a shock if you are touching them when your lips contact that oppositely-grounded mic.

If you are ever in doubt about a grounding situation, DO NOT test it by holding your strings in one hand and touching the mic, or friend's strings, etc., with the other hand. Electrical currents which travel from one hand to the other pass directly through the heart, and may be fatal. A better solution is to connect a voltmeter between your strings and the suspected piece of equipment. Test on both AC and DC settings. Any voltage present on the meter represents a dangerous situation.

GROUND AND SHIELDING

To complete the grounding of all components in the electronics compartment, run a wire from the ground (sleeve) lug of the output jack to the backs of all of the potentiometers and to ground connectors on any switches that have them. Backs of potentiometers are the most common place for making ground connections in the wiring, from pickup leads, switches, etc.

The shielding in your instrument protects the electronics from hum and buzz. Good shielding completely surrounds all of the hot circuitry with ground, canceling out any electromagnetic interference. Shielding may be made from adhesive-backed copper foil (Fig 14), or by painting the entire interior of the electronics compartment with a special conductive paint, available through instrument builders retailers and some electronics suppliers.

14 Copper shielding tape in electronics cavity

If you choose to use conductive paint, first solder a length of wire to a metal washer, then screw the washer into the wood of the electronics compartment. Paint over the washer, screw and solder joint as you shield the compartment, and solder the wire to ground. This will insure a good connection between ground and the shielding paint. Extend the paint to the recess for the compartment door, and paint the back of the door as well. Several coats may be necessary for complete shielding.

To use copper foil, cover the sides and bottom of the compartment with the foil, overlapping the pieces by ⅛ in to ¼ in. On the sides, leave small tabs to reach onto the compartment door recess where the screws are placed, so that foil surrounds the screw hole, insuring good contact with the back surface of the door. Once the tape is in place, trim around the wiring component and output jack holes with a knife. They may be located by looking for the indentations left in the shielding after it was pressed into place. Line the back of the door with tape. Place small solder joints at all connections between copper sheets. Solder a length of wire to one of these joints, and attach it to ground.

WIRINGS IN OUR GUITAR AND BASS

Guitar Wirings

The wiring we chose for our guitar, (Fig 15-21) features a wide range of humbucking and single-coil tones, yet it is easy to use and provides quick access to sounds. It uses a combination of a three-position pickup switch (for neck pickup, both pickups, and bridge pickup selections) as found on many two-humbucker guitars, and a blend knob for balancing the sounds of the two pickups. The blend knob is only active when the switch is in the middle position, allowing the player to dial in a sound on the blend knob, but still have instant access to either pickup alone. Both pickups have independent tone controls, each with a push-pull switch to activate tuned capacitor taps for their pickups. A master volume completes the controls.

Our tone controls use a .047mfd capacitor for the neck pickup, and a .01mfd for the bridge. This choice allows a darker tone on the neck pickup, suitable for jazz, and a roll-off of only the highest frequencies on the bridge pickup, a sound that works well with high-gain distortion.

For our tuned capacitor taps, we've used a .047mfd in the neck, attenuated almost fully with a 5k resistor. This sound has a slight bass-boost at a low frequency, giving it just a little extra depth over the sound of the full tap. Our bridge pickup's tap uses a .022mfd capacitor for a boost that extends up into the midrange, attenuated with a 33k resistor, which gives it a noticeably fuller sound than the single-coil alone.

The blend pot in this wiring is somewhat unusual since the down ends of each pot's track are not sent to ground. This is because the pickup selector switch sends a pickup's signal to the blend pot even when that pickup is selected alone on the switch. If the blend pot's tracks were grounded, it would still affect the sound when the switch was not in the middle position. Because of this, the blend pot only attenuates each pickup with the resistance in its track, so it does not quite blend fully to either pickup alone, although it is very hard to tell in the sound. This has two benefits. The blend pot adjusts the balance a little more gradually, giving it a finer range of control, especially around the center click. Also, by not having another pair of grounded potentiometers in the circuit,

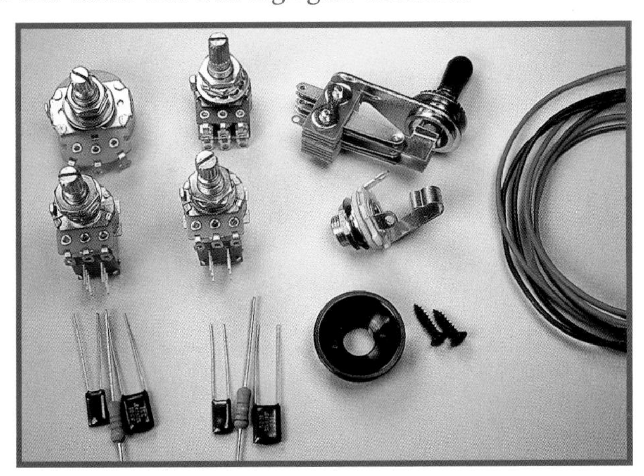

15 Electronic components for guitar

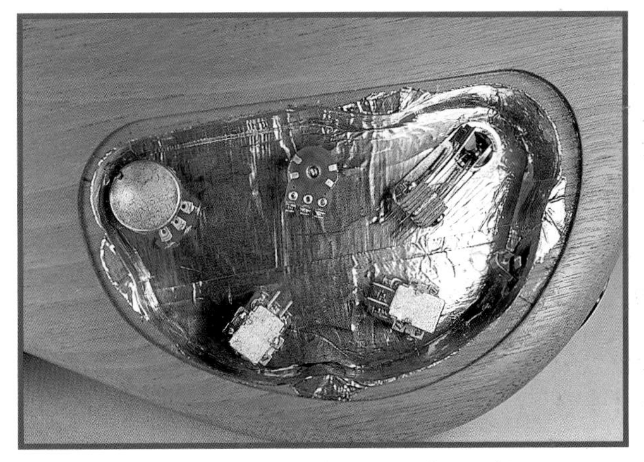

17 Components mounted in electronics cavity

16 Installing the output jack plate

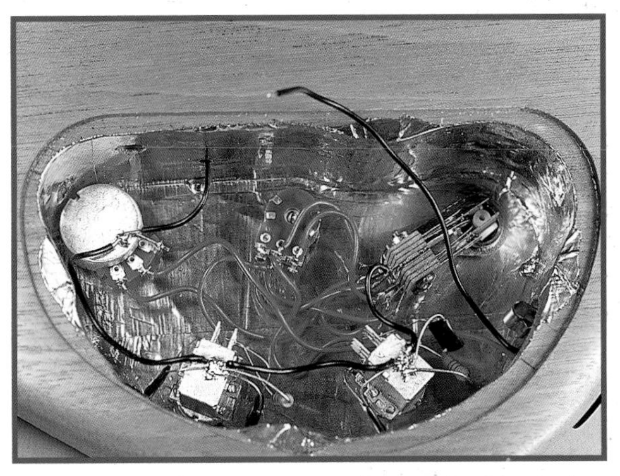

18 Hot circuitry and tap capacitors and resistors wired in place, ground wires on pots, bridge

bleeding treble to ground, the overall tone of the guitar is clearer and more open.

Bass Wirings

The bass uses a much simpler wiring (Fig 22), utilizing a pickup blend control, master volume, and separate tone controls for each pickup. If you would like to use the pickup selector switch from the guitar's wiring, you may wire it as in that circuit. A phase switch (p 81) could also be used on one of the pickups, giving a somewhat acoustic-like sound when the blend control is set slightly off-center. The two pickups series/parallel switch (p 81) is also a good option for the bass, to access a thicker, louder sound without disturbing the setting on the pickup blend control. We opted for a simpler wiring, as the Lane Poor pickups work very well with our amplifiers, and allow a for great deal of sonic variety through playing technique.

The values of our tone control capacitors are a .047mfd for a deep cut at the neck, which gives a good fingerstyle tone when rolled off slightly, and a .022mfd at the bridge, which leaves the midrange full and punchy even when most of the high treble is rolled off.

20 Completed electronics and shielded cavity door

21 Testing wiring

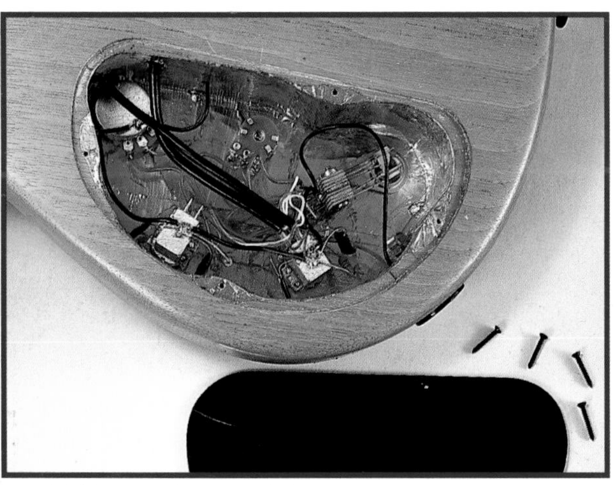

19 Pickup leads connected

22 Electronic components for bass

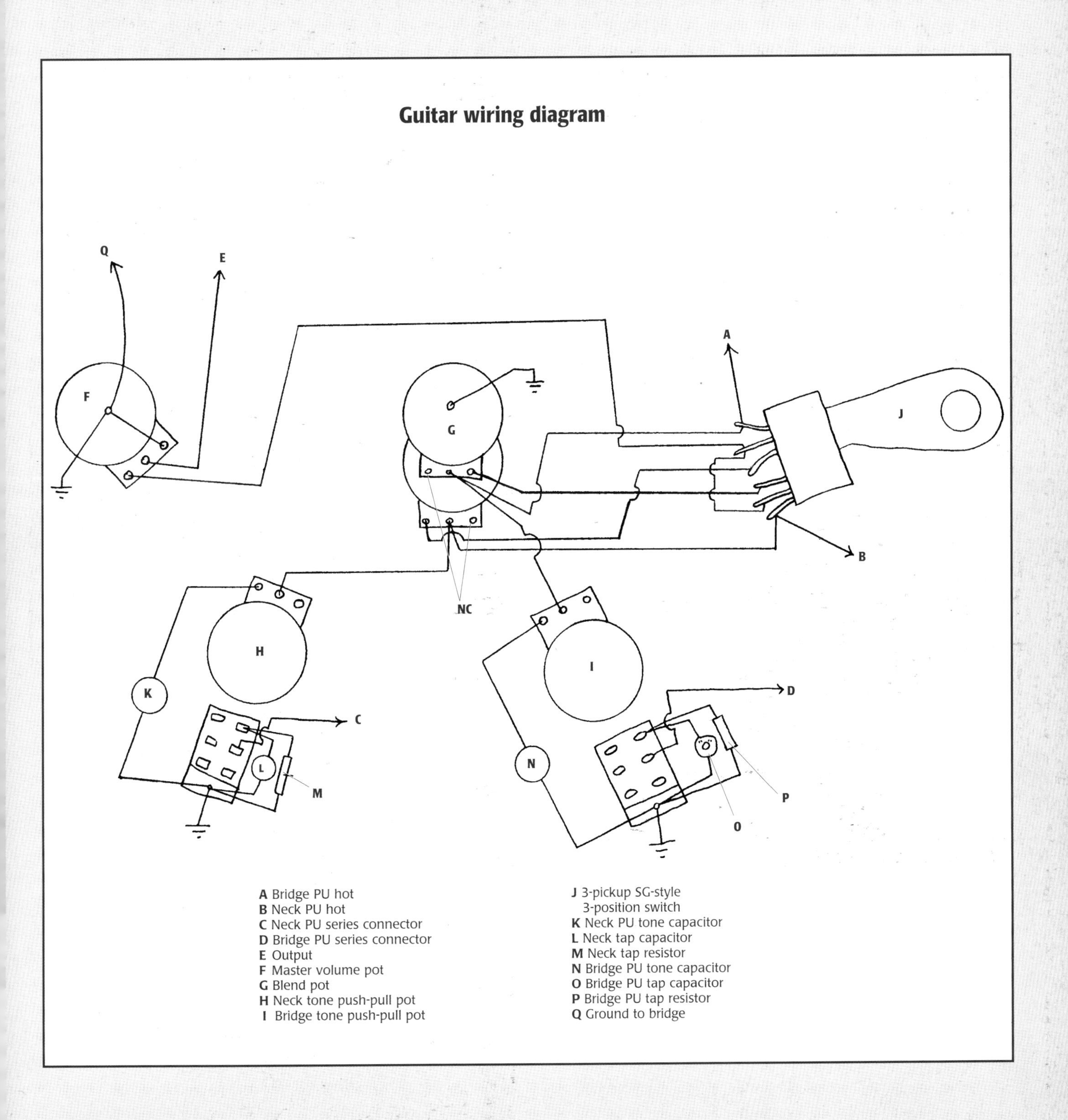
Guitar wiring diagram
Q
E
F
G
A
J
B
NC
H
I
K
C
L
M
D
N
P
O
A Bridge PU hot
B Neck PU hot
C Neck PU series connector
D Bridge PU series connector
E Output
F Master volume pot
G Blend pot
H Neck tone push-pull pot
I Bridge tone push-pull pot
J 3-pickup SG-style 3-position switch
K Neck PU tone capacitor
L Neck tap capacitor
M Neck tap resistor
N Bridge PU tone capacitor
O Bridge PU tap capacitor
P Bridge PU tap resistor
Q Ground to bridge

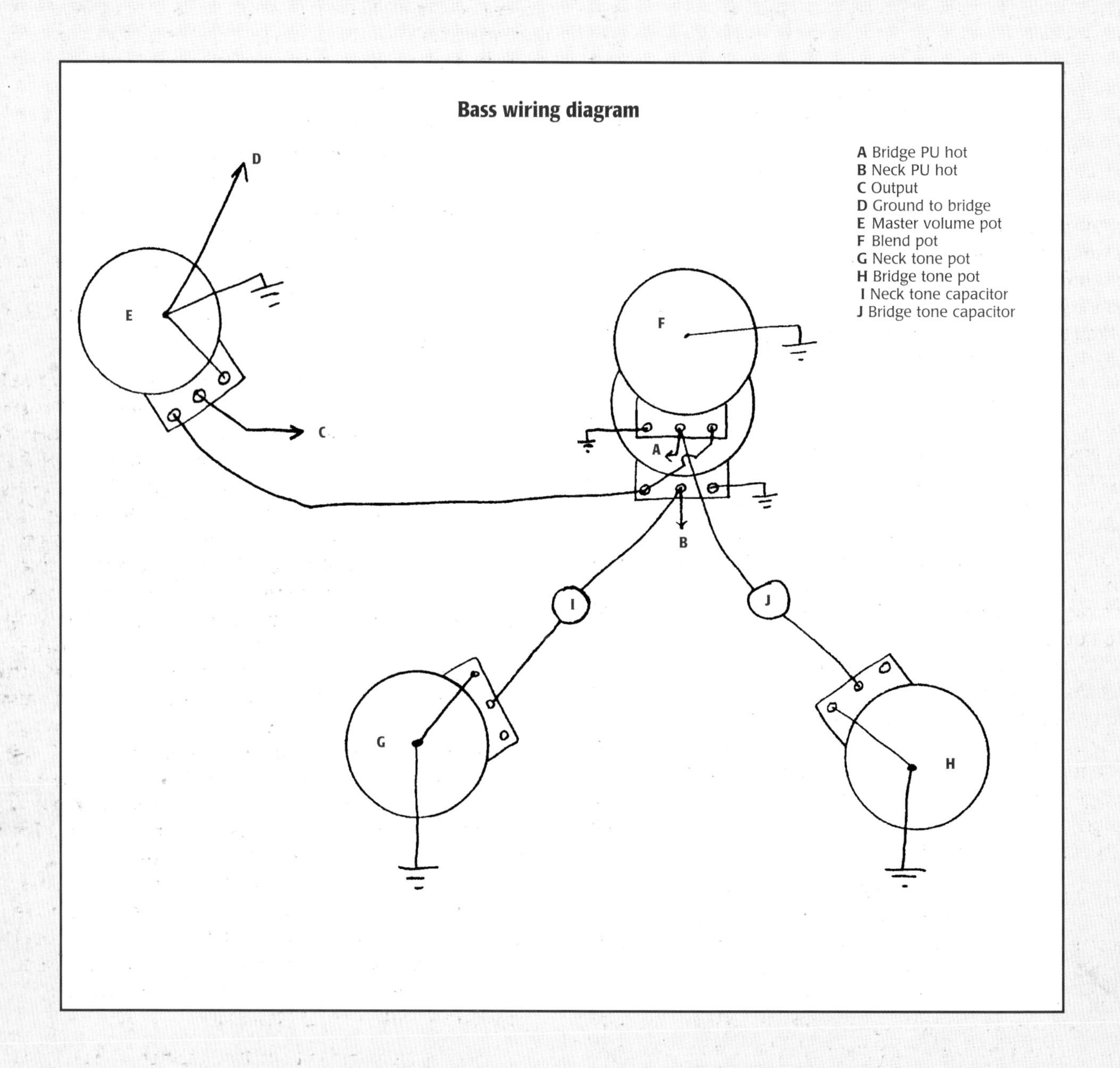
Bass wiring diagram
A Bridge PU hot
B Neck PU hot
C Output
D Ground to bridge
E Master volume pot
F Blend pot
G Neck tone pot
H Bridge tone pot
I Neck tone capacitor
J Bridge tone capacitor
D
E
C
F
A
B
I
J
G
H

Wood and Tone

Appendix

One of the most common myths about electric guitars is that their sound comes entirely from the electronics, and that the wood they are made of doesn't affect the tone. Many people are surprised to learn that electric guitars are made of wood at all, assuming that anything that modern must be made of plastic. In fact, the material that an electric guitar is made from, usually wood, is an integral part of its sound. It is, after all, the only thing that the strings are attached to, and the way it behaves has everything to do with how the strings vibrate, and hence what the electronics sense. Just how much of the tone comes from the wood depends a lot on how the instrument is used. A guitar or bass with clean-sounding pickups played through a hi-fi amplifier will retain more of the sound that you hear when the instrument is unplugged. Through a fuzzbox, wah pedal and flanger, the wood is more of a link in a long chain, but like any link its part is critical.

In choosing woods for your instrument, you should, as always, trust your ears, playing as many different instruments as possible, both amplified and unplugged. We have spent countless hours playing guitars and basses with our ears bent over the body, and pressed against it, to hear each instrument's acoustic signature. While you can learn a great deal from reading about the tonal effects of different woods, sound is a difficult thing to describe, and the complex interactions between the different parts of the instrument of do not lend themselves well to systematic description. A better way to approach an understanding of this complex subject is to hear it for yourself, spending time in a music store and with friends' instruments, unplugged in as quiet a space as possible. If you find a store with a large selection of one model of instrument, compare the tones of different weights of the same type of body wood, maple and rosewood fingerboards on otherwise similar instruments, and anything else that you can isolate this way.

Listen for features of the note's attack: is it peaky or compressed, twangy or more consistent with the sound of the sustaining tone? Attack is what the ear uses most to identify a sound, and is often overlooked in the obsession with sustain. Note how an instrument responds to playing dynamics: does the tone change significantly as you play the notes harder? Do you want it to, or would you rather have a more consistent tone between loud and soft playing? When listening to the sustain, discern weather the full range of harmonics carries into the sustained tone, or if the sound tends to ring more on the fundamental. Lastly, play all over the fingerboard, and listen for how these characteristics change from note to note. Some instruments are more tonally consistent across their range, and others have large variations. Neither is necessarily better, it really depends on what you want. Sometimes an instrument with a lively, dynamic tone will have a few "dead spots", specific notes which don't ring as well as the next, while a neutral, unexciting instrument with less resonance will sound consistently bland on every note.

Wood affects tone differently depending on where it is in an instrument. The body is the largest piece by volume, and its most important quality is its resonance. Guitar bodies, like marimba keys, vibrate at frequencies which, in turn, influence how the string sounds, from attack through sustain. While a solid body reinforces a broad range of frequencies, it has a complex set of resonances which give the tone a great deal of its character.

Solid bodies can be made light or heavy, as solid as possible or with hollowed-out "tone chambers," and the result will be audible through whatever electronics are used. The shape of a body influences its tone as well. Two bodies made of the same board and carved to the same weight will sound very different if one is large and thin and the other compact but thick. The first will ring at a lower note, with a deeper, more airy resonance, while the second will have a higher resonance and a sharper, more solid tone. Many of these variations produce the sonic results that you would expect: hollowing-out cavities in a solid body produces a tone that could best be described as "hollower," with a pronounced attack and more complex resonance, but at the expense of some of the sustain of an all-solid body. One aspect of tone that may seem couterintuitive is the relationship between weight and sustain. It is widely believed that a heavier body will ring longer, absorbing less of the string's energy, but this is not always true. Many times we've encountered a lightweight instrument that sustains beautifully, sometimes even better than a heavier body of the same wood. Sustain, like most things, comes from good construction, a solid connection between strings and body, and an ability of the instrument's parts to interact well. This is more complicated than simply adding weight, but it means you can get substantial sustain from a comfortable, lighter-weight instrument.

The neck plays a different role than the body, being structural as well as resonant. In addition to holding the tension of the strings, it forms a bridge between the two ends of the vibrating strings. A neck that is too flexible will absorb energy from the strings, robbing them of tone and sustain, so neck wood is chosen for strength and stiffness as well as resonance. Stiffer necks tend to favor both treble and bass response, giving more of both, and will improve both dynamics and sustain. However, necks that are too stiff may sound harsh and glaring to some. The stiffness of a given neck wood may be altered by the orientation of its grain: vertical grain (quarter sawn) makes a stiffer neck than horizontal grain (flat sawn). Builders will use this to increase stiffness in softer wood, like mahogany, or moderate the stiffness of hard, rock maple necks. Another way to make a stiffer neck is, of course, to carve it thicker. Chunky necks almost always sound better than thinner ones. If you have small hands and absolutely have to have a thinner neck, Choose a stiff wood like rock maple, and a vertical grain orientation.

Often necks are made of more than one piece of wood laminated together. This can make a stronger neck which is less likely to warp or twist with humidity changes. It also lets you blend the qualities of different woods, both visually and sonically. In a neck-through body instrument the neck wood also becomes a significant part of the body, depending on the width of the center piece, and should be selected accordingly. Because stability is so important in the neck, be wary of choosing highly figured woods. Woods with flames or birdseyes make very beautiful necks, but are far less stable than the clear, straight-grained woods you usually find in the best-sounding instruments. Necks made of birdseye or tiger maple can sometimes feel lumpy under the thumb, as the wood responds inconsistently to humidity changes. With maple, the best figure is most commonly found in the softer varieties of the wood, which aren't the best for necks.

One way to design a stiffer neck, regardless of the wood used, is to inlay structural beams of carbon fiber on either side of the truss rod. Carbon fiber, or graphite, has a very high strength to weight ratio, and will noticeably increase the stiffness of a thinner neck. Carbon-fiber reinforced necks, or necks made entirely of graphite, tend to have the sonic qualities of stiffer necks listed above, with increased impact and longer sustain, but can be somewhat "ringy" to those used to the sounds of traditional neck woods.

Fingerboards have a large effect on an instrument's tone, in relation to their small volume of wood. This is because the fret and fingerboard act as a second bridge on the other end of the strings, and affect the tone in much the same way as the bridge material (see Design Considerations and Preparation, p 13). Harder, heavier woods will emphasize high end and produce a stronger attack, while softer fingerboards will give a warmer, more midrangey sound. Fingerboards are available in alternative materials such as phenolic (which is made of sheets of parchment and resin) or woods treated with resins to stabilize them, and these have an aggressive, dynamic sound due to their extreme hardness.

Below is a list of some common woods used in the various parts of electric instruments. These descriptions are, of necessity, somewhat general, and many wood species have large variations in density which will affect their sound. Generally, denser pieces will sound sharper and more percussive, lighter pieces will be airier and more resonant.

BODY WOODS

Mahogany has a warm, midrange-rich tone heard in many of the classic Gibson electrics. It is very dynamic, with excellent sustain even in lighter pieces. Mahogany has several sub-species, such as the Sapele we used for the body-wings of our bass, each with slightly different sonic qualities which are best discerned by tapping on individual pieces, whenever possible. Our piece of Sapele had a tap-tone which revealed a ringy, bright quality which translated into the tone of our bass, producing a quick, articulate attack with rich harmonics. The mahogany we used in our guitar body is on the lightweight end of the wood's range, and has a highly resonant, percussive tone with a characteristically detailed midrange, slightly rounded treble and warm, mellow bass.

Maple Harder maple makes for a dense, heavy body that is well-suited to smaller body shapes. It has a broad range of tonal qualities, with a combination of detailed treble, midrange warmth and solid bass. As a body wood, hard maple has a dynamic, slightly aggressive quality which can be heard in the all-maple Rickenbacker basses used by Paul McCartney, and by Chris Squire on the Yes recordings of the 1970s. Softer varieties of maple sound predictably more airy, sometimes with a diminishing sustain in the higher frets, but maintain the combination of warmth and aggressiveness.

Ash Ash is available in a very wide range of densities. Heavier types, sometimes called northern ash, have a bright, focused, percussive tone similar to hard maple, but with slightly less of the aggressive growl. Many 1970s-era Fenders are made of dense ash, and basses of this type are favored by many slap-style players. Light ash, sometimes called swamp ash, is favored for its warmth, airiness and dynamic response, and is the body wood responsible for many of the most desirable vintage Fender guitars and basses.

Alder Used on Fender guitars finished in solid colors, Alder is a lighter-weight wood with a balanced tonal spectrum and an excellent response to dynamics. Like swamp ash, it is found in some of the most prized early Fenders, and is an important part of the percussive, twangy sound they are known for.

Poplar A light wood, poplar sounds similar to alder, but with some of the aggressive, growly midrange of hard maple. Poplar was used in many of the early Music Man Stingray basses, and is partly responsible for that instrument's powerful tone.

Basswood This is light wood with some interesting tonal qualities. Basswood features very good sustain, which usually extends to the higher regions of the fretboard. It has a slightly compressed response to dynamics, which sets it apart from some of the other lighter woods. Basswood is resonant, slightly midrangey, and makes a good match with humbucking pickups in a guitar to produce smooth lead tones with consistency across the instrument's range.

Walnut Walnut has a decidedly dark tone in most instruments, with an uninspiring dynamic response if used for an entire body. It can work well as body wings in a neck-through-body instrument when combined with a bright, dynamic neck wood like maple.

Cherry Most cherry available today is moderately light-weight and has a unique tone for solid-body instruments, less dynamic than most woods but with complex overtones and an articulate attack. Combined with a piezo pickup or a high-fidelity type of magnetic pickup, it produces a passable faux-acoustic tone.

NECK WOODS

Maple A hard, straight-grained piece of maple is one of the best choices for neck wood. It is stable, rigid, and makes for a percussive tone with excellent sustain. Maple is the wood used in all of the classic Fender necks, and most of the other higher-quality electrics produced over the years. Select a heavy piece that has a tight grain and a sharp, almost metallic ring with as little "airiness" as possible.

Mahogany Mahogany can make an excellent neck wood, especially when it will be used for a fairly thick neck. It is not as stiff as maple, and we like to use it with a vertical grain orientation to help maximize its tone. Mahogany's richness is apparent when it is used as a neck wood, contributing warmth and a slightly subdued attack, in comparison to maple.

Wenge A wood favored by some builders of modern basses, wenge is dense and stiff, with a strong attack, good sustain and complex harmonic content somewhat similar to carbon-fiber necks, but "woodier." Wenge is extremely hard on tools, which will need frequent sharpening.

Exotic Woods Tropical hardwoods like the ziricote we used for laminates in our bass provide interesting visual possibilities. Sonically, they are not always quite as dynamic as traditional woods. However, The denser varieties will add a good structural element to a multi-laminate neck, when extra stiffness is desired, although we prefer to combine them with maple to insure stability. Woods which make a good choice for this purpose include bubinga, cocobolo, purple-heart, African blackwood, zebrawood, and almost any other dense exotic with a good tap-tone. Be aware that many of these woods contain toxic oils, and their dust should not be breathed. These oils can also interfere with many glues, and pieces should be test-glued to insure they will not produce weak joints. Many builders who use these woods prefer to use epoxies which are specially formulated for tropical hardwoods.

FINGERBOARDS

Ebony We chose ebony for our guitar fingerboard. It is a dense, hard wood, providing clear treble, powerful attack and good sustain. Many varieties of ebony are available, some jet black and others with gray or light brown streaks.

Rosewood Rosewood fingerboards have a warmer tone with more midrange than ebony or maple. Brazillian rosewood was the wood of choice for fingerboards in many early Fenders and Gibsons, but this almost magical wood is now highly regulated (and with good reason) due to its increasing rarity in the wild. Several other varieties are currently available, the best-known being Indian rosewood. We used a rosewood fingerboard on our bass to compliment the brightness of the other woods.

Maple: Maple makes a bright, dynamic fingerboard wood not unlike ebony, but slightly warmer. Fenders with maple fingerboards are known for having a brighter, snappier sound than their rosewood counterparts.

Exotic Woods The denser exotic woods mentioned in the neck wood section make good choices for fingerboards as well. Their colorful appearance is very attractive to many builders. Many of these woods are related to rosewood, and have similar tonal qualities, although some are denser, making them sound closer to ebony. Avoid varieties with large pores, as these will accumulate dirt and grime.

Finishing Options

Many new finishing products and improvements on old standbys have been developed in recent years. The introduction of non-toxic, environmentally-friendly, water-based products, for example, have made the finishing process safer and more efficient.

In addition to the shellac and varnish approach, discussed on p 50, some alternative finishes may be desirable. Every product has its own properties and procedures. Some research, sharing ideas with knowledgeable people, and experience are your best guides. Below are some common finishing materials briefly explained.

Lacquer

Nitrocellulose lacquer is favored by many electric guitar makers because it dries to a warm color and provides a hard finish necessary for a good-sounding instrument. Professionals usually spray lacquer onto instruments with a compressed or airless spray gun in a well-ventilated, explosion-proof booth. However, buying spraying equipment and setting up an appropriate environment is expensive, and learning how to use it effectively is time consuming. Moreover, as a volatile organic compound (VOC), lacquer is carcinogenic and bad for the environment. Nonetheless, lacquer has been a preferred finish for guitars made during the past several decades.

If you insist on lacquer, it comes in convenient aresol cans for smaller projects like your guitar. Though relatively expensive and ecologically indefensible in this form, it is the least wasteful method to use and the quickest finish for a short-term project.

Alternatively, consider using one of the newer water-based lacquers. Safer, healthier, and easier to clean up without polluting, these products are steadily improving.

Several thin coats of lacquer produce a finish that is impervious to almost everything. The exact number of coats depends on your technique and the look and sound you're striving for. Often builders prefer a thinner finish to avoid dampening the tone of the instrument. Many thinner coats are better than fewer thick coats. Shellac, sanding sealer, or vinyl sealer is recommended for a sealing coat although thinned lacquer itself may be used as a sealing coat. Commercial lacquer thinner or acetone are the diluents and clean-up for lacquer. Several brands of stains can be suspended in the lacquer for coloring and highlighting the wood. Several thin coats with a light sanding (as described on p 49) in between give the best results.

Oil

A simple way to finish your instrument is with an oil designed specifically for use with wood. This finish is often preferred by fine woodworkers because it seals, conditions, and protects all at once. Though requiring intermittent maintenance, it is easier to refurbish and repair than most any other finish. Unlike varnish and lacquer, oils penetrate the wood rather than building on its surface. Danish, Swedish, tung, boiled linseed, and gun stock oils are some of the common oils available on the market today.

Most of these oils are waterproof and dry to a hard finish, a property which is desirable for stringed instruments. Oils are easy to apply and with a bit of polishing yield a lustrous finish. Since different oils have different application requirements, be sure to follow exactly the directions on the container and talk to a knowledgeable person about the different brands and techniques.

Tung oil is a good all purpose oil to begin with and one used by many guitar makers. "Watco" oil is also a popular brand. Boiled linseed oil is a traditional finish but has a slow drying time and requires more work than some of the more contemporary kinds. Two to four coats of oil are usually sufficient for a good finish on your instrument depending on the hardness of the wood and the manufacturer's suggestions.

French Polishing

French polishing is an age-old technique of applying finish by rubbing or "padding" very thin coats of a finishing compound (most often shellac, but also varnish or lacquer) onto wood. The finish is temporarily kept from drying too fast by "suspending" it with a little non-drying oil (mineral oil or walnut oil) on a golfball-size padding cloth, a wad of cotton called a "fad". Working one small area at a time, the finish is slowly built up through the repeated application of coats. Finally, any oil residue is "spirited off" with a quick wipe of a cloth with a little alcohol on it.

As you may sense, French polishing requires practice to be able to apply coats quickly and evenly without the padding cloth sticking or leaving a textured surface. Though we suggest simpler finishing methods for the novice, consult books on finishing for more information on this age-old and interesting technique.

Poly Finishes

Modern chemistry has provided us with new finishing products from which to choose. Varnishes using polyesters, polyvinyls, polyurethanes, acrylics, and other synthetic compounds are available at most home center stores. Though not the first choice of instrument makers, these products provide a highly protective, serviceable finish.

There are interesting, potentially useful products coming out regularly. Gel finishes, water-based finishes, epoxy finishes, new formulations for padding and spraying, and various "cross-breeding" of old and new finishes are now easy to find.

The challenge is to find the right finish for a particular application. Specialty suppliers that deal in guitar and instrument making equipment are probably your best bet in gathering information on this complex subject. And talk with experienced woodworkers. Invariably, they will be more than willing to share their favorite methods and techniques.

Tool Sharpening

Appendix

The tools you use to make your instrument must be sharp. Dull tools are a source of danger and frustration. With practise and patience you should be able to sharpen your tools so they can shave. You could always identify a woodworker in the old days by a bald patch on his arm from testing the sharpness of his tools. Only then are they ready for working the wood.

Traditionally, sharpening was always done by hand on whet stones using oil or water as a lubricant. The process began with roughing out a uniform edge on a new or damaged tool with the use of a grinding stone or other very coarse stone. From this point, each stage used a progressively harder smoother stone to get a fine edge. Honing was usually done "freehand", allowing experience and feel to guide the blade to produce just the right bevel on the cutting edge. Stones still give a superior cutting edge and the invention of honing guides has made it much easier to get a uniform bevel and shaving edge.

Stones come in a variety of sizes and shapes depending on the size and shape of the blade being sharpened. Curved chisels, for instance, use conical or cylindrical stones. Some stones are available in combinations, a different grade on each side. A sequence of stones are choreographed in the following fashion. A grinding stone is usually necessary to sharpen tools that have been badly damaged or abused or to prepare new blades that are unsharpened. A course carborundum stone is often used for blades that have minor chips or are very dull. Traditional oil stones like the India stone, which comes in a medium and fine grit, is an intermediary honing stone used to prepare the blade for a fine stone. A Washita stone is a good basic stone for medium to fine honing as is the soft Arkansas stone. A hard Arkansas stone is usually used to produce a fine shaving edge on the tool and the leather strop to remove the metal burr or wire and put a final polish on the blade. All stones are used with a medium to light grade honing oil. Basically, most sharpening jobs require two stones—medium and fine. Newer types of diamond whetstones, ceramic sharpening stones, and Japanese water stones are also now available.

Sandpaper and emery cloth glued to a perfectly flat surface have also been used effectively for sharpening. A light touch on a power sander may be used for the initial grinding stages followed by progressively finer grades of sandpaper and finally a fine emery cloth. It is possible to produce a shaving edge by this method. Sandpaper and emery cloth also have the advantage of being relatively inexpensive and easy to find.

SHARPENING PROCEDURE

1 The blade may need to be ground on a grinding wheel, belt sander, or coarse stone depending on its condition. Do not leave the blade on a power grinder long enough for it to overheat and change color because it will lose its temper and quickly dull again. If there is much power grinding to be done, cool the blade in water often as you grind.The underside of the blade should be flat across its entire width. Lay the blade flat or at a slightly increased angle on it back and grind away until you achieve a flat surface across its width.

2 Now hone the blade at a slightly increased angle (½ degree to 1 degree) on a medium stone (India, Washita, or soft Arkansas) until an even polished bevel has been achieved across the blade. A honing guide will help you hold a consistent angle and aid in controlling the pressure.

3 On a fine stone like a hard Arkansas, hone the blade to a high polish either at the same angle or slightly increased by ½ degree. Take time to do this carefully.

4 To remove the hair edge or burr that usually develops from honing, pull the blade along a leather strop quickly applying pressure evenly across the blade. This will produce a final polished shaving edge.

Bass Guitar

Electric Guitar

Index